Walzer and War

"One mark of a classic work is its persistent power to reward engagement with fresh insight. *Walzer and War* shows that Michael Walzer's *Just and Unjust Wars* has just such power to generate important new lines of thought about the ethics of war. Walzer revived 'just war' thinking; now this book revives him."
—Nigel Biggar, *Regius Professor of Moral and Pastoral Theology at the University of Oxford, and author of* In Defence of War

"There couldn't be a better time to honor and reaffirm the importance of Michael Walzer's groundbreaking and magisterial *Just and Unjust Wars*. These essays by leading scholars elucidate Walzer's original insight, that war must be fought justly and that just war theory is not a niche discipline in either history, law, or philosophy. Walzer needs to be read and reread, critically, but never ever abandoned. This is a most fitting companion for keeping *Just and Unjust Wars* relevant and alive."

—Nancy Sherman, *University Professor, Georgetown University and author of* Afterwar

"This is an excellent collection of interesting essays rethinking and reevaluating Walzer's highly influential work. Especially illuminating are the discussions of Walzer's assumptions, and the authors make admirable progress in understanding and confronting the moral dilemmas of going to war and conducting it."

—Virginia Held, *Distinguished Professor Emerita, The Graduate Center, City University of New York, and author of* How Terrorism Is Wrong: Morality and Political Violence

Graham Parsons · Mark A. Wilson
Editors

Walzer and War

Reading *Just and Unjust Wars* Today

Editors
Graham Parsons
Department of English
and Philosophy
United States Military Academy
West Point, NY, USA

Mark A. Wilson
Ethics Program
Villanova University
Villanova, PA, USA

ISBN 978-3-030-41659-1   ISBN 978-3-030-41657-7   (eBook)
https://doi.org/10.1007/978-3-030-41657-7

This Palgrave Macmillan imprint is published by the registered company Springer Nature
Switzerland AG
The registered company address is: Gewerbestrasse 11, 6330 Cham, Switzerland

For our students

ACKNOWLEDGEMENTS

This volume grew out of a unique collaboration between our two institutions—West Point and Villanova University. For five consecutive years, between 2013 and 2018, we organized a joint conference on the ethics of war and peace. First drafts of the essays collected in this volume were presented at the 2017 conference which celebrated the 40th anniversary of the publication of *Just and Unjust Wars* by bringing this distinguished group of scholars together to reflect on it. This book could not have been possible without the help of those who made this conference a reality. The editors would like to thank Joe Mazzocchi, Gary Bridges, Terron Johnson, Caroline Pagan, Kris Fox, Scott Parsons, Josh Carlisle, Harry Jones, Mark Doorley, and Peggy Elder, as well as the Department of English and Philosophy at West Point and the Ethics Program at Villanova.

Our friend and former colleague, LTC (Ret.) Mike Saxon, deserves special credit for conceiving of the topic of this volume and giving rise to the fruitful collaboration between us that produced it. We miss working with him.

Anca Pusca, Balaji Varadharaju, Katelyn Zingg, and the team at Palgrave have been extremely professional and supportive of us throughout.

Work on this project benefited from funding by the European Research Council via a fellowship with the Individualisation of War Project at the European University Institute in Florence, Italy during 2018–2019. We are grateful for this funding and for support from Jennifer Welsh and David Rodin at the Individualisation of War Project.

As any editor knows, the quality of the work that ends up in print depends entirely on the quality of the authors behind it. We have been especially blessed to get to work with such a gifted group of authors. While it has been humbling, their brilliance has made our job relatively easy.

Finally, we are deeply grateful to Michael Walzer. Michael's contributions to our fields of study and to our own thinking have been enormous. We have been honored to get to work with him on this project. Despite his professional success, he has been astonishingly warm and open to engaging with the other contributors to this book. It would seem that they don't make scholars like him anymore.

CONTENTS

Notes on Contributors

Lisa Sowle Cahill is the J. Donald Monan, S.J., Professor of Theology at Boston College. She received her M.A. and Ph.D. degrees from the University of Chicago Divinity School. Lisa Cahill is a past president of the Catholic Theological Society of America (1992–1993), and the Society of Christian Ethics (1997–1998), and is a fellow of the American Academy of Arts and Sciences. Her works include *Global Justice, Christology and Christian Ethics* (Cambridge University Press, 2013), *Theological Bioethics: Justice, Participation, and Change* (Georgetown University Press, 2005), *Bioethics and the Common Good* (Marquette University Press, 2004), *Family: A Christian Social Perspective* (Fortress, 2000), *Sex, Gender, and Christian Ethics* (Cambridge University Press, 1996); *A Theology and Praxis of Gender Equality* (Bangalore: Dharmaram Publications, in press); and *"Love Your Enemies": Discipleship, Pacifism, and Just War Theory* (Augsburg Fortress, 1994). A revised version, *"Blessed Are the Peacemakers": Just War Theory, Pacifism, and Peacebuilding*, was published in 2019. She has served as theological advisor to the Catholic Peacebuilding Network, and participated in a Rome conference in 2016 (sponsored by the Pontifical Council for Justice and Peace and Pax Christi International) to advance nonviolence and just peace as priorities of Catholic social teaching. She is the author of several scholarly articles and chapters on war, peace, and peacebuilding.

James M. Dubik is Senior Fellow at the Institute for the Study of War and the Institute of Land Warfare, a member of the Council on Foreign Relations, the National Security Advisory Council, the U.S. Global Leadership Coalition, the U.S. Army Ranger Hall of Fame, a distinguished member of the U.S. Army 75th Ranger Regiment, and formerly Professor, Georgetown University's Center for Strategic Studies. He received his Ph.D. in philosophy from Johns Hopkins University and his Master of Arts and Science from the U.S. Army Command and General Staff College. He is the author of *Just War Reconsidered: Strategy, Ethics, and Theory*, a contributor to *Army* magazine, and a co-author with General Gordon Sullivan of *Envisioning Future Warfare*. His forthcoming book is entitled *Waging War and Using Force*.

Judith Lichtenberg is a Professor of Philosophy at Georgetown University. Previously she taught at the University of Maryland, where she held a joint appointment in the Department of Philosophy and the Institute for Philosophy and Public Policy. Among her papers on war are "War, Innocence, and the Doctrine of Double Effect," "How to Judge Soldiers Whose Cause Is Unjust," and "Is the War Convention a Convention?" She also writes about international and domestic justice, moral psychology, nationalism, and higher education. Her book *Distant Strangers: Ethics, Psychology, and Global Poverty* was published by Cambridge University Press in 2014. With Robert Fullinwider, she co-authored *Leveling the Playing Field: Justice, Politics, and College Admissions* (2004); she is the editor of *Democracy and the Mass Media* (1990).

David Luban is University Professor at Georgetown University Law Center and currently holds the Distinguished Chair in Ethics at the Stockdale Center for Ethical Leadership, United States Naval Academy. His books include *Lawyers and Justice: An Ethical Study* (1988), *Legal Modernism* (1994), *Legal Ethics and Human Dignity* (2007), and most recently *Torture, Power, and Law* (Cambridge University Press, 2014). Luban is a member of the American Academy of Arts and Sciences, and has been a Guggenheim Fellow, a Woodrow Wilson Fellow, and a Fellow at the Institute for Advanced Studies (Jerusalem). He is on the editorial boards of *Ethics & International Affairs* and *Legal Ethics*, and is a founding editor of the weblog *Just Security*. He has held visiting chairs at the Fordham, Harvard, Stanford, and Yale Law Schools, and also visited at Dartmouth College, the University of Melbourne, and the Interdisciplinary Center (Israel). His research centers on just war theory, national security, international criminal law, legal ethics, and legal theory. His particular interest is moral responsibility in organizational settings, where agency and knowledge are fragmented, and loyalties to colleagues and the organization may conflict with duties to others. At the moment, he is writing a book on the legal and moral philosophy of Hannah Arendt.

Margaret Moore is Professor in the Political Studies department at Queen's University, Canada where she teaches political philosophy. She is the author of *A Political Theory of Territory* (Oxford University Press), which won the 2017 Canadian Philosophical Association Best Book prize, was short-listed for the CB Macpherson Best Book award by the Canadian Political Science Association (2016) and received Honourable Mention for the International Studies Ethics Best Book award. She has published two earlier books, both with Oxford University Press: *Foundations of Liberalism* and *Ethics of Nationalism*, as well as edited or co-edited three volumes and a special journal issue. Her current work is on the norms of the international system, such as sovereignty, human rights, boundary drawing, and territorial claims. She currently holds a SSHRCC Insight grant on corrective justice and land and has been awarded the 2018 Olof Palme Professorship at the University of Stockholm.

Graham Parsons is Associate Professor in the Department of English and Philosophy at West Point and was a fellow of the Individualisation of War Project at the European University Institute in 2018–2019. He completed his Ph.D. in philosophy from The Graduate Center, City University of New York in 2012. He has published several articles on the philosophy of war and peace and the obligations of soldiers in journals such as *Social Theory and Practice*, *Philosophia*, and *Journal of Military Ethics*. He is currently working on a series of articles examining the role gender has played in the development of just war theory. He teaches a variety of philosophy courses at West Point, including the ethics course required for all cadets. He also regularly lectures in the Bard Prison Initiative and is the head coach of West Point's Ethics Bowl team.

Sally J. Scholz is Department Chair and Professor of Philosophy at Villanova University. Her research is in social and political philosophy and feminist theory. Among her publications include the books *On de Beauvoir* (Wadsworth 2000), *On Rousseau* (Wadsworth 2001), and *Political Solidarity* (Penn State Press 2008). She co-edited *Peacemaking: Lessons* *from the Past, Vision for the Future* (with Judith Pressler); *The Contradictions of Freedom: Philosophical Essays on Simone de Beauvoir's "Les Mandarins"* (with Shannon Mussett); and *Philosophical Perspectives on Democracy in the 21st Century* (with Ann Cudd). She has published articles on solidarity, oppression, and just war theory among other topics. Scholz has served as chair of the American Philosophical Association Committee on Lectures, Publications, and Research (2011–2014), chair of the APA Committee on the Status and Future of the Profession (2015–2018), and President of the North American Society for Social Philosophy (2015–2019).

Henry Shue studied political theory at Princeton with Michael Walzer and is now Senior Research Fellow at the Centre for International Studies, University of Oxford. A selection of his articles from 1978 to 2015 appeared in *Fighting Hurt: Rule and Exception in Torture and War* (2016). He edited and contributed to *Nuclear Deterrence and Moral Restraint* (1989) and co-edited and contributed to *Preemption* (2007), *Just and Unjust Warriors* (2008), and *The American Way of Bombing* (2014). Aside from work on violence, he has written *Basic Rights: Subsistence, Affluence, and U.S. Foreign Policy* (1980; 2nd ed., 1996); *Climate Justice: Vulnerability and Protection* (2014); and a continuing series of articles on climate change.

Jeremy Waldron is a University Professor at New York University School of Law. He was previously University Professor in the School of Law at Columbia University. He was born and educated in New Zealand, where he studied for degrees in philosophy and in law at the University of Otago. He was admitted as a Barrister and Solicitor of the Supreme Court of New Zealand in 1978. He studied at Oxford for his doctorate in legal philosophy, and taught at Oxford University as a Fellow of Lincoln College from 1980 to 1982. From 1982 to 1987, he taught political theory at the University of Edinburgh, and from 1987 to 1995, he was a Professor of Law in the Jurisprudence and Social Policy Program in the School of Law at the University of California, Berkeley. He was briefly at Princeton, as Laurance S. Rockefeller University Professor of Politics, before moving to New York in 1997. Professor Waldron has written and published extensively in jurisprudence and political theory. He is the author of *Torture, Terror, and Trade-offs: Philosophy for the White House* (Oxford University Press, 2010) as well as *The Right to Private Property; Liberal Rights; Law and Disagreement; The Dignity of Legislation; God, Locke, and Equality;*

The Harm in Hate Speech; and, most recently, *One Another's Equals: The Basis of Human Equality*. Professor Waldron is a member of the British Academy, the American Academy of Arts and Sciences, and, in 2011, he received the Phillips Prize from the American Philosophical Society for lifetime achievement in jurisprudence.

Michael Walzer is Professor Emeritus of Social Science at the Institute for Advanced Study, in Princeton, New Jersey. As a professor, author, editor, and lecturer, he has addressed a wide variety of topics in political theory and moral philosophy: political obligation, just and unjust war, nationalism and ethnicity, economic justice, and the welfare state. His books (among them *Just and Unjust Wars, Spheres of Justice, The Company of Critics, Thick and Thin: Moral Argument at Home and Abroad, On Toleration*, and *Politics and Passion*) and essays have played a part in the revival of practical, issue-focused ethics and in the development of a pluralist approach to political and moral life. His *Just and Unjust Wars* has achieved a canonical status in the area of military ethics. At West Point, it has been required reading for most of the last 40 years. Walzer is a former contributing editor for *The New Republic*; he retired in 2014 as co-editor of *Dissent*, which is now in its 65th year. His articles and interviews appear frequently in the world's foremost newspapers and journals. He is currently working on the fourth volume of *The Jewish Political Tradition*, a comprehensive collaborative project.

Jennifer M. Welsh is the Canada 150 Chair in Global Governance and Security at McGill University and a Senior Research Fellow of Somerville College, University of Oxford. She was previously Professor and Chair in International Relations at the European University Institute and a Professor in International Relations at the University of Oxford, where she was a co-founder of the Oxford Institute for Ethics, Law and Armed Conflict. In 2013, she was appointed by the UN Secretary-General to serve as his Special Adviser on the Responsibility to Protect, a position she held until March 2016. Professor Welsh is the author, co-author, and editor of several books and articles on humanitarian intervention, the evolution of the notion of the "responsibility to protect" in international society, the UN Security Council, and Canadian foreign policy. Her most recent book is *The Return of History: Conflict, Migration and Geopolitics in the 21st century* (2016). From 2014 to 2019, she directed a European Research Council project entitled "The Individualisation of War: Reconfiguring the Ethics, Law and Politics of Armed Conflict."

Mark A. Wilson is a Teaching Professor of Ethics and previously Chair of the Returning Soldiers Project at Villanova University. He received his Ph.D. in religious studies from Indiana University, where he received a Charlotte W. Newcombe Dissertation Fellowship. His teaching and research integrate Christian ethics with moral psychology, philosophy, and issues in applied ethics. He has written on Michael Walzer, Jeff McMahan, and topics surrounding moral injury, and he is currently completing a manuscript entitled *Moral Trauma, Grief, and the Recovery of Responsibility.* He is on the editorial board of *The Journal for Peace and Justice Studies,* and, with Lt. Col. Michael Saxon (Ret), he is the co-founder of the annual Villanova-West Point Ethics of War and Peace Conference.

CHAPTER 1

Introduction

Graham Parsons and Mark A. Wilson

WHY WALZER, STILL

It is indisputable that *Just and Unjust Wars* has impacted the world to an extent rarely achieved by a single-volume, philosophical monograph. Its publication in 1977 is routinely described as a pivotal moment in the study of international relations and the conduct of war. During the 1950s and 1960s the influence of just war theory—the view that war ought to be guided by moral principles—had reached its nadir. The policy-making establishment in the United States generally rejected foundational moral commitments and instead embraced realism and the primacy of brute national interest. By and large, just war thinking remained alive only in theology programs and debates in Catholic social thought. While other works share responsibility for the reversal of fortunes of realism and just war theory during the last decades of the twentieth century, *Just*

G. Parsons (✉)
Department of English and Philosophy, United States Military Academy, West Point, NY, USA
e-mail: graham.parsons@westpoint.edu

M. A. Wilson
Ethics Program, Villanova University, Villanova, PA, USA
e-mail: mark.wilson@villanova.edu

© The Author(s) 2020
G. Parsons and M. A. Wilson (eds.), *Walzer and War*,
https://doi.org/10.1007/978-3-030-41657-7_1

and Unjust Wars deserves the lion's share of the credit. Almost single-handedly, Michael Walzer resuscitated just war theory and produced a widespread disavowal of realism in academia and policy-making circles. As David Luban testifies in the first chapter of this volume, "[In 1977], the need was urgent to set aside the emotions and anger that were tearing the country apart and reflect on Vietnam from a broader, more dispassionate, more philosophical, moral point of view. But before Walzer, I think few of us had any idea how to start." Through Walzer's singular influence, just war theory became the dominant framework for discussions of war within military, academic, and public arenas, as well as in international law. Any student, teacher, or researcher engaged in issues such as the ethics and law of war, terrorism, international relations, political sovereignty, humanitarian intervention, or insurgency is an inheritor of the discussions begun by *Just and Unjust Wars*.

And yet, in some fields there is great skepticism about the value or relevance of the book today. Particularly in philosophy, many scholars acknowledge the impact of the book and are grateful for the defeat of realism yet view the book mainly as the representative of a misguided, even poor, approach to the ethics of war. As a colleague said to one of us in an attempt to dismiss the importance of engaging with the book today, "Walzer's been refuted." Over the last twenty-five years or so, a school of thought has emerged that has built itself around a rejection of a central tenet of Walzer's theory—the moral equality of combatants—and some of its associated commitments. Known as "revisionist" just war theorists, these scholars have tried to develop a systematic ethics of war that is purged of a Walzerian attachment to the moral equality of combatants.[1] In this way, there is an anti-Walzerian spirit built into the identity of this movement; *Just and Unjust Wars* is precisely what they are committed to "revising." It is in light of such views that a defense of the present volume seems necessary.

We admit that *Just and Unjust Wars* has flaws. One of us even thinks the theory it expounds is fundamentally incoherent.[2] Moreover, we acknowledge that the revisionist attack on the moral equality of combatants is powerful and has produced valuable reassessments of just war theory. Nevertheless, we think reengaging with *Just and Unjust Wars* remains highly valuable, indeed, urgently necessary.

First, as a methodological matter, revisiting canonical philosophical texts is a central feature of good scholarship. Too many scholars view such activity as merely the job of niche thinkers who study the history of philosophy or ideas. Their view seems to be that conversations can quickly evolve so as to make some works irrelevant and, therefore, there is little danger in ignoring them. Our view, however, is that works that are currently not central to conversations are often still highly relevant and that there is in fact great danger in allowing partisans of on-going debates to decide who is worthy of attention. Often, the sense that a work is no longer relevant is an illusion that is easily revealed by open-minded engagement with it. But, more fundamentally, we fear that the hard rejection of works such as Walzer's is symptomatic of a tendency among scholars to approach works merely in search of a reason to ignore them. It is disturbingly common for scholars to read a work simply in search of a flaw significant enough to justify rejecting it entirely. As one of our mentors once described it, these readers are merely looking to find "where to put the knife."[3] This approach not only undermines potentially valuable dialogue between scholars and prevents the discovery of important insights, but it also leads to a radical ahistoricism that fails to appreciate the true complexity and robustness of the connections between thinkers and movements. No work is flawless, even the most important examples of human thought. One can accept that *Just and Unjust Wars* is imperfect and yet still find it immensely valuable.

Second, regardless of any methodological disputes, we think that it is simply untrue that *Just and Unjust Wars* does not have much to offer today. On the contrary, the book remains deeply edifying to contemporary readers and scholars. This is so for several reasons.

1. *Just and Unjust Wars* surveys an astonishingly wide variety of topics and debates. It is so much more than a defense of the moral equality of combatants. Indeed, it is hard to think of another book published since 1977 that contains and defends an innovative theoretical framework for evaluating the resort to and the conduct of war while engaging with such a range of types of wars, moral problems peculiar to war, and rich discussions of real-world cases. Whether or not one rejects some portion of Walzer's account, the book attains a level of comprehensiveness that remains extraordinary even after all these years. This is supported by the fact that the essays contained below tackle such a wide variety of topics.
2. Walzer's style rewards reconsideration more than most philosophical works. There is a certain irony here. The very features of the book

that so frustrate analytic philosophers are simultaneously the features that help make it worth revisiting. Walzer is willing to openly express uncertainty, to be vague, to make generalized claims about history and human nature, even to be contradictory. Such authenticity, imprecision, boldness, and openness to paradox is a major reason that some contemporary philosophers are so ready to dismiss him. However, it is this way of approaching his subject that makes the book unusually lasting. While it can be frustrating to try to pin him down, Walzer's work is nevertheless extremely rich. There is always something new to discover in it. It invites readers to engage in the conversation and to continue the inquiry. The novel readings of him offered in the chapters below confirm that the book is still an invaluable resource for new insights.

3. Walzer's method in *Just and Unjust Wars* deserves reconsideration in light of the methods adopted by some of his harshest critics. Walzer's book aims to provide practical guidance for political and military leaders as well as combatants caught up in the messy real-world of domestic politics, international diplomacy, bureaucratic constraints, military regimentation, and combat. The book seeks true practical wisdom. As Walzer describes the research he undertook for *Just and Unjust Wars* in the Postscript to the Fifth Edition:

> the greater part by far of my reading was not in theory at all but in military history, both academic and popular, and then in the memoir literature produced by soldiers of different ranks (preferably the lower ranks: junior officers and foot soldiers, who make the toughest moral decisions on the battlefield); and then in wartime journalism and commentary (especially about Vietnam, the immediate occasion of my own writing). Finally I read many of the novels and poems that deal with the experience of fighting and with the company of soldiers. The nontheoretical genres, and the books and articles they include, seemed to me the critically necessary material for my project.... I wanted the moral arguments of my own book to ring true to their authors—and to the men and women about whom they were writing.[4]

In the main, Walzer's critics in the revisionist school don't share this immediate practical focus. Instead, they seek to map out the abstract, universal moral rules of intergroup conflict, or what some call the "deep morality" of war. To be sure, these critics believe that there is, or can be, important practical import to insights about ultimate moral principles. However, this practical import is often of secondary concern to them. Indeed, in some of the major revisionist studies it can be hard to tell what, if any, changes to the practice of war and war-making they are calling for. Rather than talking to real-world decision-makers, these studies seem to be talking to those in the abstract, logical space inhabited by (some) philosophers. For those of us who have worried that these studies have lost their bearings,[5] there is good reason to return to *Just and Unjust Wars*. While we might disagree with the content of his advice at times, we can appreciate the advantages of his practical focus and learn from it.

4. Last, in recent years new threats have emerged to justice-based approaches to war and international affairs, whether Walzerian or revisionist, which should give common cause to everyone concerned with making international affairs more ethical. Whatever differences exist between Walzer and the revisionists, or between Walzer and the peacebuilders,[6] these seem to be insignificant when compared to the differences between them and the xenophobic, race-based nationalists that are resurgent around the world today. All those who look at war through an ethical lens ought to join forces to resist this common enemy. Even if we find fault in *Just and Unjust Wars*, we ought still to be proud allies of its call to humanize war and international politics.

Contributions

Each of the essays in this volume makes a singular contribution to the discourse on the ethics of war, highlighting the most lasting and salient impacts of *Just and Unjust Wars*. Honoring Walzer's methodological complexity, the contributors reflect an interdisciplinary approach, drawing from fields of just war theory, international law, cultural criticism, and military leadership. Some of the contributors have been engaged in the critical appraisal of the book for decades. Others are scholars looking at the work through new lenses. Still others are veterans of war and policy-making who bring the benefit of practical experience to the discussion. This is not merely a celebration of Walzer (though there is much to celebrate), but a collection of essays that to varying degrees reconsider, repurpose, and confront *Just and Unjust Wars* with the aim of advancing contemporary scholarship.

The essays are divided into two parts. Part I, "A Good War," examines issues surrounding Walzer's treatment of the *jus ad bellum*, the portion of just war theory concerned with how to justify entering war and how to frame debates thereon. Part II, "A Good Fight," focuses on the conduct of war and the means through which wars are fought, understood traditionally as the *jus in bello*.

The opening essay by David Luban, "Prefaces and Postscripts," situates *Just and Unjust Wars* within the context of its composition in the 1970s amid the Vietnam war protests. As Walzer notes in the Preface to the First Edition, "I did not begin by thinking about war in general, but about particular wars, above all the American intervention in Vietnam. Nor did I begin as a philosopher, but as a political activist and a partisan."[7] Part of Luban's aim is to recognize that reading *Just and Unjust Wars* today demands attention to its historical situatedness, though not because the concepts are antiquated—they are, as Luban notes, timeless—but rather because Walzer's methodology is deeply committed to the concrete experiences of war. As Luban notes, Walzer's suspicion of philosophical abstraction is driven by a desire to "ring true" to the men and women who participate in war; consequently, Walzer rejects the sort of hypothetical "toy cases" offered by contemporary revisionists and instead employs a narrative, historically located style of casuistry, one that is highlighted by the topical discussions in the Prefaces to the second through fifth editions.

Luban (following Walzer) is not concerned with reading *Just and Unjust Wars* in a vacuum. He is, rather, intent to explore the tensions that Walzer's method creates, specifically regarding how human rights, understood individually or collectively, ground Walzer's thinking. Luban invites us to wonder why Walzer says relatively little about human rights, particularly in light of the explosion of human rights discourse in the '70s, and what this might mean within our current climate, where the very concept of human rights seems under assault by populist and authoritarian nationalism.

In a similar vein, Margaret Moore's "Territory, Self-Determination, and Defensive Rights" presses foundational questions about the relationship between individual and collective rights, but is concerned specifically with how these rights buttress claims for political sovereignty, territorial integrity, and by extension defensive war. In sympathy with (but distinct from) Walzer's claim in *Just and Unjust Wars* that "the land follows the people,"[8] Moore advances a theory of collective self-determination as the most compelling basis on which to rest claims for defensive rights. Moore finds fault with many contemporary accounts that seek to ground defensive war as either an extension of individual human rights of self-defense or within considerations of justice. Moore argues that those committed to the former view are forced, among other things, to deny that invasions of territory *per se* (e.g., bloodless invasions) justify defensive engagement, as no individual rights have been compromised. On the other hand, a view predicated on conceptions of justice—whereby a state's entitlement to defense derives from its promotion of justice vis-à-vis its citizens—runs afoul of our basic intuitions that even unjust states have some basic rights to territorial defense. To think otherwise would imply that just states, say the United States in the aftermath of the Second World War, could legitimately assume the territory of an unjust state, such as Germany. A justice account also struggles to explain how to afford territorial rights to unjust states or states whose territories were acquired through colonialism or genocide.

Moore's alternative is to see defensive rights to territory as attached not to individuals or to states (just or unjust) but rather to the rights of peoples to collective self-determination. Understood in this way, defense of territory is logically independent of the state. As Moore notes, her theory of collective self-determination has potentially profound implications for, among other things, how we might justify humanitarian interventions and civil wars, which is to say, the types of wars that have proliferated in the last forty years.

"Rethinking Humanitarian Intervention," by Jennifer Welsh, combines a richly historicized examination of *Just and Unjust Wars* with a consideration of developments in international relations on the topic of humanitarian interventions. Contrary to popular belief, Welsh argues, the priority given to national sovereignty, and therefore nonintervention, is of relatively recent vintage: it originates in the work of modern theorists such as Emer de Vattel and culminates in the UN Charter. As Welsh describes it, the evolution of Walzer's thinking on the topic of humanitarian intervention might be seen to reflect an inversion of history. In the First Edition of *Just and Unjust Wars*, Walzer offers a rather restrictive set of exceptions to respect for sovereignty, and then gradually—but only partially—loosens these restrictions through his subsequent amendments in the Prefaces to the Third through the Fifth Editions.

Most noteworthy for Welsh is the fact that Walzer only partially revises his approach to intervention. While he acknowledges the pressing and expanding concerns for atrocity crimes and the need for capable bodies to respond, he also consistently measures this need against concerns about sufficiency, understood in terms of motivation, political legitimacy, and utility. Coupling an analysis of Walzer with the "Responsibility to Protect" articulated by the 2005 United Nations World Summit Outcome, Welsh observes that Walzer's "principled pragmaticism" offers an important heuristic for examining questions of intervention in the post-Cold War era. While the instances of potentially justified intervention multiply over time, so too do the concerns about mixed motivations and whether multilateralism really mitigates such concerns. Welsh foregrounds Walzer's work as part of an exigent need to balance sins of commission and omission, interventionism and isolationism, as we reckon with conceptions of a shared responsibility to serve refugees and victims of brutality.

Sally Scholz's "War, Collective Responsibility, and Contemporary Challenges to Democracy" shifts the discussion from broader considerations of what "just war" means to normative questions about how individual citizens are to participate in debates prior to, during, or after wars. Scholz suggests that notions of citizen-action and collective responsibility are only implicit in *Just and Unjust Wars*, despite the origins of the work within Walzer's own activism. With an extended analysis of notions of collective responsibility, she asks how we should understand a citizen's moral obligation and potential culpability as they pertain to wars waged by one's state. Can citizens of the United States, for instance, be held morally accountable for any unjust war pursued under the auspices of their interests? How does the relationship between policy elites and common citizens complicate this analysis?

Using Walzer's discussion of J. Glenn Gray's claim that moral responsibility for war should be proportionate to the degree of freedom in democracy, Scholz defends a moral obligation for both policy elites and individual citizens to "collectivize intentionally," to work toward informed, deliberate, and sustained debates about the justification for wars. Moreover, Scholz argues that the failures of democratic citizens to collectivize intentionally, even while complicated by increasingly manicured media sources and the rise of a narrow nationalism, may make them morally liable.

Lisa Cahill's essay, "Peacebuilding and Counterinsurgency" concludes Part I by examining questions of moral dilemma, tragedy, and the intersection of just war theory and pacifism. As Luban observes in the first chapter, Walzer is "orthodox" only by his current legacy, not by reference to his engagement with the prominent figures in just war theory.

The voices of Augustine, Aquinas, and other pre-modern authors are quite muted in *Just and Unjust Wars*. From this vantage, Cahill notes that Walzer's sense of the moral dilemmas of war is, in important ways, more acute and demanding than his historical precursors.

Cahill's more substantive and ambitious claim is that there is little daylight between just war theory and pacifism within contemporary discussions of counter-insurgency and peacebuilding. Reminiscent of the dialogues between Reinhold Niebuhr and Martin Luther King Jr., Cahill argues that the ethics of war and pacifism are not different in kind, but rather informed by the same commitment to peace. If accepted, this claim means, minimally, that the sort of ambivalence found in Walzer on the tragedy of war positions his view much closer to pacifism than realism. Maximally, it means that the guiding principles of current strategies of counter-insurgency might in fact be better fulfilled through nonviolent means. Simply put, Cahill bids us to question the tradition of just war thinking, and Walzer's place in it, at least regarding the extent that war can ever be fully and simply justified.

In Part II, the focus of the volume shifts from considerations about when and how to conceive of justified reasons for wars and their ends, to the means by which wars are fought. Drawing on his extensive experience, not least as Commanding General of the Multinational Security Transition Command in Iraq, Lieutenant General (Retired) James Dubik foregrounds what might be considered the practical failures of the orthodox approach to the ethics of war. In "Fighting Versus Waging War," Dubik probes the disconnect between the obligations of individual combatants in war, especially common soldiers, and the military leadership in war who are charged with devising strategy and holistic mission goals.

Dubik introduces a distinction between fighting a war—on the part of regular service members—and the strategic decisions involved in waging war—on the part of senior civil and military leaders. The elision between fighting and waging wars, which Dubik takes to be part and parcel of the orthodox and Walzerian views, has resulted in a failure to articulate explicit ethical guidelines for responsible leadership at the strategic levels. In *Just and Unjust Wars*, Walzer acknowledges that senior military leadership (e.g., generals) might have different responsibilities than rank-and-file soldiers, but his discussion of this is brief and seems to Dubik to at least partially collapse the difference. The results of this are, according to Dubik, potentially devastating. The failures of the US wars in Afghanistan and Iraq, where debates about particular actions in war were divorced from strategic goals, testify to the need to distinguish fighting war and waging war. Dubik offers a novel set of principles designed to structure discourse in light of a more differentiated understanding of *jus in bello* that respects the divide between strategy and tactics.

In "Reflections on 'Supreme Emergency,'" Jeremy Waldon explores one of the most contentious of Walzer's claims. Walzer acknowledges that the prohibition against intentionally targeting noncombatants is meant to be absolute. And yet, in *Just and Unjust Wars*, Walzer famously (or infamously) defends the indiscriminate bombings of German cities by the British in the Second World War from 1939–1942. Under these extreme circumstances, Walzer claims, Churchill, and the British people faced the "ultimate threat to everything decent...an ideology and a practice of domination so murderous, so degrading...that the consequences of its final victory were literally beyond calculation, immeasurably awful."[9] In the presence of a catastrophic and imminent threat to an entire community, Walzer argues, the principle of noncombatant immunity may be suspended. But suspended for whom and in what sense?

Waldron provides a nuanced exploration of the possible ways to understand supreme emergencies, detailing a range of arguments for viewing it as a legal doctrine, a moral analysis, a communitarian political proposition, or a discourse on the role morality of politicians. While observing that there are reasons to embrace each of these interpretations, Waldron concludes that none of them is satisfactory. The supreme emergency is best understood, Waldron avers, not as a doctrine for the conduct of war but as a meditation on the possible limits of regulating war.

Through the lens of the Law of Armed Conflict and *jus in bello*, Henry Shue's "Keeping Exceptions Exceptional in War," explores the concept of moral exceptions within war and the role of rules in setting boundaries for justified action. There is a temptation, Shue notes, for philosophers (particularly revisionists) to seek increasingly subtle and theoretically precise rules that have built-in exceptions. Shue considers, by example, the rule to never target noncombatants. Theoretically, we should be inclined to favor a more complex rule, for instance, never target noncombatants unless they are morally liable for the conduct of an unjust war. While the adoption of the complex rule is desirable in principle, Shue argues that it is unsustainable and morally perilous in practice.

Faithful to Walzer's "principled pragmaticism," as Welsh describes it, Shue posits that the rules of combat must be crafted with sensitivity to the psychological and epistemological constraints experienced by actual combatants. Exceptionless rules are, to oversimplify Shue's point, feasible rules, even though they may prove inferior in purely notional accounts. Combatants in war act in extraordinary circumstances and attempts to idealize the rules of war fail to appreciate the limitations of human conduct *in extremis.*

In "Autonomy, Obedience, and Manifest Illegality," Judith Lichtenberg examines the exceedingly complicated and tenuous relationship between a combatant's obligation to obey orders and the obligation to heed the dictates of one's conscience and potentially the laws of war. On the one hand, Lichtenberg observes, combatants are required to subordinate their wills to superior commands. On the other hand, they are bound by duty and law to refuse illegal orders. This tension raises fundamental questions about the nature of moral responsibility for those who fight wars.

Through an examination of Walzer's discussion of the My Lai massacre, Lichtenberg defends his "particularist" approach to this tension, one that balances the idea that soldiers are never merely cogs in a military machine—they never relinquish their autonomy altogether—with the Cimmerian reality that in combat freedom and responsibility are mitigated by ignorance and duress. Any judgment of specific crimes of war, then, must attend to the particularities of circumstance and weigh the prospects of autonomy against the diminished capacities for free action.

In the final essay, "Walzer's Soldiers: Gender and the Rights Of Combatants," Graham Parsons problematizes one of the core assumptions of both international law and Walzer's understanding of the *jus in bello*— the idea that all combatants are prima facie legitimate targets and that no fundamental moral harm or tragedy occurs when they are killed in battle. As discussed by Waldron, Shue, and Lichtenberg in this volume, the principle of discrimination prohibits the targeting of noncombatants. Conversely, the principle gives a broad license to kill combatants.

On Parsons's reading, this sanguine treatment of killing combatants reflects a deep-seated and deeply troubling paradigm where soldiers are males, males are naturally servants of the state's wars, and servants are disposable with minimal grievance or grieving. Parsons's provocative claim is that the very concept of discrimination, a bedrock feature of *jus in bello*, is structured by gendered norms of masculinity that solemnize self-sacrifice as a preeminent virtue. This masculinized vision of the warrior class, where honor entails a readiness to die in combat, has roots in the foundations of the just war tradition and continues to be reflected by Walzer's theory. A properly ungendered account, Parsons suggests, would require us to dramatically reimagine the principle of discrimination and our understanding of combatants' liability to attack.

Taken together, these essays testify powerfully to the importance of *Just and Unjust Wars*, elucidate and augment Walzer's profound insights, and advance his conviction that personal, public, and policy debates on the ethics of war must continually balance a philosophical commitment to principle and logical coherence with a humanistic understanding of ambiguity that may even border on paradox. Walzer and the contributors to this volume remind us of Philip Marlowe's wisdom: be wary of the "austere simplicity of fiction" and more mindful of the "tangled woof of fact."[10] *Just and Unjust Wars* can be "refuted" only when we think it presents an answer rather than a call to question.

NOTES

1. Some representative examples of this movement are Jeff McMahan, *Killing in War* (New York: Oxford University Press, 2009); Cecile Fabre, *Cosmopolitan War* (Oxford: Oxford University Press, 2012); Helen Frowe, *Defensive Killing* (New York: Oxford University Press, 2014); Kai Draper, *War and Individual Rights: The Foundations of Just War Theory* (New York: Oxford University Press, 2016); and Adil Haque, *Law and Morality at War* (New York: Oxford University Press, 2017).
2. Graham Parsons, "The Incoherence of Walzer's Just War Theory," *Social Theory and Practice* 38, no. 4 (October 2012): 663–88.
3. Credit for this line (and much more) belongs to the late Kant scholar, Arnulf Zweig.
4. *Just and Unjust Wars*, 5th ed. (New York: Basic Books, 2015), 336.
5. Some who have explicitly argued that directly action-guiding norms for war must depart from the principles of abstract moral theory include, Allen Buchanan, "A Richer *Jus Ad Bellum*," in *The Oxford Handbook of Ethics of War*, eds. Helen Frowe and Seth Lazar (New York: Oxford University Press, 2018), 167–84; David Luban, "Just War Theory and the Law of War as Nonidentical Twins," *Ethics and International Affairs* 31, no. 4 (2017): 433–40; Henry Shue, "Keeping Exceptions Exceptional in War: Could any Revisionist Theory Guide Action?" Chapter 9 below; and Jeremy Waldron, "Civilians, Terrorism, and Deadly Serious Conventions," in *Torture, Terror, and Trade-Offs: Philosophy for the White House* (New York: Oxford University Press, 2010), 80–110.

6. For a discussion of the peacebuilding movement, see Chapter 6, Lisa Cahill's "Peacebuilding and Counterinsurgency: Alternatives to the Moral Dilemma of War."
7. *Just and Unjust Wars*, xxiii.
8. Ibid., 55.
9. Ibid., 252.
10. Raymond Chandler, *The Big Sleep* (New York: Vintage Paperbacks, 1950), 157.

REFERENCES

Buchanan, Allen. "A Richer *Jus Ad Bellum*." In *The Oxford Handbook of Ethics of War*, edited by Helen Frowe and Seth Lazar, 167–84. New York: Oxford University Press, 2018.

Chandler, Raymond. *The Big Sleep*. New York: Vintage Paperbacks, 1950.

Draper, Kai. *War and Individual Rights: The Foundations of Just War Theory*. New York: Oxford University Press, 2016.

Frowe, Helen. *Defensive Killing*. New York: Oxford University Press, 2014.

Haque, Adil. *Law and Morality at War*. New York: Oxford University Press, 2017.

Luban, David. "Just War Theory and the Law of War as Nonidentical Twins." *Ethics and International Affairs* 31, no. 4 (2017): 433–40.

McMahan, Jeff. *Killing in War*. New York: Oxford University Press, 2009.

Parsons, Graham. "The Incoherence of Walzer's Just War Theory." *Social Theory and Practice* 38, no. 4 (October 2012): 663–88.

Waldron, Jeremy. "Civilians, Terrorism, and Deadly Serious Conventions." In *Torture, Terror, and Trade-Offs: Philosophy for the White House*, 80–110. New York: Oxford University Press, 2010.

Walzer, Michael. *Just and Unjust Wars*. 5th ed. New York: Basic Books, 2015.

CHAPTER 2

Prefaces and Postscripts: Walzer's *Just and Unjust Wars* Today

David Luban

I

I must begin with a personal recollection. In 1977 I was teaching philosophy at Kent State University, my first job out of graduate school, and I visited Cambridge over winter break. In those days before Amazon and the Internet, visiting an academic center with a major bookstore was a pilgrimage of sacred status, and the Harvard Coop was my temple of choice, up there with the legendary bookstores of Hyde Park. At the Coop the first thing I saw on display was stacks of the newly-published *Just and Unjust Wars*. I was already a Walzer fan from reading *Obligations*,[1] so I made a beeline for the new book and, as the cliché goes, snapped it up and read it straight through when I got home. The next fall I taught a seminar on *Just and Unjust Wars*, and my students and I worked our way through it chapter by chapter over a full ten-week quarter.

D. Luban (✉)
Georgetown University Law Center, Washington, DC, USA

Stockdale Center for Ethical Leadership, United States Naval Academy, Annapolis, MD, USA

G. Parsons and M. A. Wilson (eds.), *Walzer and War*,
https://doi.org/10.1007/978-3-030-41657-7_2

When I leafed through *Just and Unjust Wars* in the Harvard Coop, I naturally fixed on the opening sentences of Walzer's preface:

> I did not begin by thinking about war in general, but about particular wars, above all about the American intervention in Vietnam. Nor did I begin as a philosopher, but as a political activist and a partisan.[2]

On the next page, he explained his reason for writing the book: "I promised myself that one day I would try to set out the moral argument about war in a quiet and reflective way. ... I want to defend the business of arguing, as we did and as most people do, in moral terms. Hence this book...."

This stuff was like Chapman's Homer to me—"then felt I like some watcher of the skies when a new planet swims into his ken." The need was urgent to set aside the emotions and anger that were tearing the country apart and reflect on Vietnam from a broader, more dispassionate, more philosophical, moral point of view. But before Walzer, I think few of us had any idea how to start. *Just and Unjust Wars* was my first exposure to just war theory, and to say it was my best exposure would greatly understate how powerfully it affected me. To borrow a Holmesian phrase, it hit me where I lived.

That, it turned out, was literally true, for the Vietnam War was omnipresent in Kent, Ohio throughout the late '70s when I taught there. Even seven years after May 4, 1970, the shooting cast a shadow over the campus, and that shadow was the shadow of the war, inextricably linked with the antiwar movement and the backlash against it. I knew some of the wounded students—one paralyzed for life—as well as the parents of one student, Allison Krause, who was killed. In that year of 1977, I memorably paced off the shooting with one of the National Guardsmen involved, who came back to town as an act of expiation. The Vietnam vets studying at KSU on the GI Bill were my age, and some became my friends and co-activists.

II

I've been emphasizing *Just and Unjust Wars*' Vietnam connection, but an admirable fact about the book is that it is timeless as well as timely. This places Walzer in the company of the just war theorists of the past. When Grotius wrote *The Rights of War and Peace*, he very much had in mind the war between Portugal and the Dutch East Indies Company. But his famous defense of private war is not simply a brief for the Dutch East Indies Company, although the Company happened to be Grotius's client. The arguments transcend their epoch and they matter now. So too with *Just and Unjust Wars*. To be sure, the book discusses the Vietnam War more than once, and passes severe moral judgment on its justice and conduct. Walzer has said that Israel's Six-Day War was also on his mind when he wrote the book, and his chapter on prevention vigorously defends Israel's preemptive strike against the Egyptian air force. But what's noteworthy about these case-judgments is that Walzer treats them no differently, no less evenhandedly, and at no greater length, than any of his other historical illustrations—no differently than, say, the War of the Spanish Succession or Bradley's bombing of St. Lô.

Just and Unjust Wars is now in its fifth edition, and each succeeding edition includes an "updating" preface discussing issues raised by the wars fought since the last edition. But these prefaces are like the book itself—they raise issues of abiding, not just temporary, importance, and Walzer treats them that way. Can any modern war be just?—That's the question in the preface to the 1992 edition, raised by objectors to the first Gulf War. What about humanitarian interventions?—that's his question in the 1999 edition's preface, the year of Kosovo and four years after Srebrenica. And what of the use of force-short-of-war, the *jus ad vim?*—a concept that Walzer introduced into just war theory in the preface to the 2005 edition when he considers what might have been done instead of invading Iraq. In the fifth, and most recent edition, the preface discusses the morality of asymmetrical conflicts, with the U.S. vs. Taliban and Israel vs. Hamas conflicts in view. In the fifth edition he also added a new postscript—his rejoinder to revisionist just war theory. There, he reflects on the method of moral argument when we think philosophically about war. Like the book itself, the prefaces and postscript are at once timely and timeless.

III

Within contemporary academic debates, philosophers often call Walzer's version of just war theory the "standard" or "orthodox" view, and I couldn't help noticing that in his new postscript Walzer borrows those words as well.[3] Now in one way it's undeniably orthodox: his fundamentals coincide in most respects with the international law of armed conflict. Walzer's theory of just cause is that of the U.N. Charter. The moral equality of soldiers is the law of the Geneva Conventions; so is the moral equality of "their" civilians and "ours."[4] The very architecture of the law of war separates *jus ad bellum* and *jus in bello* by placing their rules in different legal instruments.

But in the tradition of just war philosophy, there is nothing standard or orthodox about Walzer at all—something I never appreciated until, a few years ago, I finally doubled back to read the historical authors Walzer cites: Aquinas and Augustine, Vitoria and Grotius and Pufendorf.[5] Call them "the Greats" for short. Among the Greats, aggression was by no means the unique crime of war, nor was self-defense the sole just cause. Nor did the Greats unanimously accept the moral equality of combatants: for example, Vattel argued that as a moral matter it is wrong for soldiers to fight on the unjust side, although the law should treat combatants symmetrically.[6] That sounds more like McMahan than it does like Walzer.

This is not a criticism of Walzer. Just the opposite. What reading the traditional sources highlights is how deeply original *Just and Unjust Wars* is. It may have revived a forgotten tradition, but it is not merely a twentieth-century update of traditional doctrines, nor are Walzer's arguments a restatement of the Greats. If *Just and Unjust Wars* is by now the "standard" theory, and therefore the latest of the Greats, that is because Walzer made it so.

IV

One way *Just and Unjust Wars* is hardly standard is its distinctive philosophical style, the use of "historical illustrations" not merely to *illustrate* but to propel his moral argument. In his preface, Walzer describes his method as "casuistic",[7] and so it is. Some cases describe single incidents, some describe entire wars, some scrutinize discrete philosophical arguments, like Mill on non-intervention or Sidgwick on *in bello* proportionality and necessity.

Today's analytic just war theory in what I'll call the Oxford Style also makes crucial use of cases.[8] But the cases are radically different from Walzer's, and serve different purposes. Walzer insists on real cases, while the Oxford Style makes a point of using unreal or "toy" cases. This is for a reason. The point of an Oxford Style case is to pare away all morally con-founding side issues so only the principle under scrutiny is tested. When a sequence of toy cases is artfully constructed, you will find yourself pulled toward one and only one intuitively right answer for each case in the sequence, and those answers will vary as the philosopher manipulates first one variable and then another. The procedure is like a law professor's cascade of hypotheticals as she torments her first-year students to force them to explain how Case A, where you found for the plaintiff, wouldn't compel you to find for the plaintiff in Case B where justice plainly runs the other direction. The idea is to subject principles to a stress test in a controlled setting.

Walzer's cases don't work that way, and they do a different job. It matters crucially to him that his are real cases, and although he makes them brief—which is no less a form of abstraction than the Oxford Style—they are never toy cases. In the fifth edition postscript, he explains how he prepared to write *Just and Unjust Wars*, first by reading the Greats and the manuals of international law. But, he continues,

> the greater part by far of my reading was not in theory at all but in military history, both academic and popular, and then in the memoir literature produced by soldiers of different ranks (preferably the lower ranks: junior officers and foot soldiers, who make the toughest moral decisions on the battlefield); and then in wartime journalism and commentary (especially about Vietnam, the immediate occasion of my own writing). Finally I read many of the novels and poems that deal with the experience of fighting and with the company of soldiers. The nontheoretical genres, and the books and articles they include, seemed to me the critically necessary material for my project .... I wanted the moral arguments of my own book to ring true to their authors—and to the men and women about whom they were writing.[9]

It obviously bugs Walzer that analytic philosophers don't think they need that kind of reading, or at any rate that they don't write as if they need it. Oxford Style philosophers may respond that real-life cases contain too many confounders to be useful in a stress test of moral principles. You do a stress test in a doctor's office, not while the patient is playing foot-ball. But stress-testing isn't Walzer's aim, which, in the words I've just quoted, is rather to make "the moral arguments of my book ring true" to the soldiers. (Parenthetically, I can't help wondering whether memoirs by civilians trapped in a battle space, or burying their collaterally damaged children, or crowded into DP camps, don't also belong on the required reading list, to make the moral arguments ring true to those men and women as well. A reading list should include a little more *Mother Courage* and a little less Band of Brothers.)

Perhaps more important than this difference, it's crucial to the Oxford Style that the toy cases are usually set in civilian life: Anne coerces Barry to break Camille's leg, which Dipak can prevent by shooting Anne, or the like. The thought is presumably that we can see the moral essentials most clearly outside the fog of war. Doing so will enable us to think better about the wartime cases. That may be true, provided the examples are ecologically valid when transferred from civil society to the battlefield. Walzer suspects they can't be, and in the postscript to the fifth edition, he complains that the Oxford Style constructs what would be a marvelous morality of war if war were a peacetime activity—in my view one of the deepest-cutting philosophical one-liners I've ever read.[10] The distinctiveness of war must not get blurred in the fog of peace.

Apart from ringing true to soldiers, it seems to me that Walzer intends his examples to serve four other functions: first, to reassure us and himself that the issue on the table is a real one, with real urgency; second, to convey to civilian readers something of what decision-making in war must feel like; third, to verify that his prescriptions aren't too fanciful or demanding for soldiers and sailors to use in actual combat; and fourth, to give readers food for thought. On the "food for thought" point, one of the most attractive features of *Just and Unjust Wars* is that every case in it invites further reflection and conversation. Nothing ends with a "QED," and the reader is tempted to continue the conversation with "But wait a minute …." not with "well, that settles that."

One way to describe this stylistic difference is through a lovely distinction Avishai Margalit draws in *The Ethics of Memory*, between "i.e." philosophy and "e.g." philosophy—roughly, philosophy proceeding top-down from first principles and philosophy proceeding bottom-up from examples.[11] Rawls's theory of justice is paradigmatic "i.e." philosophy. "E.g." philosophy like Margalit's starts with cases, and it wends its way to its conclusions by reflecting on those cases. "E.g." philosophy never lets the cases get wholly out of sight. It takes comfort from Sidney Morgenbesser's dictum that to explain why a man slipped on a banana peel you do not need a general theory of slipping.[12]

Now in my view *Just and Unjust Wars* lies near the happy Aristotelian mean between "i.e." and "e.g.". Walzer is more systematic than, say, Jon

Elster, whose best writing is "e.g." all the way down. By contrast, Walzer's initial statement of the Legalist Paradigm has nothing of the "e.g." about it: it's a straightforward catalogue of six general propositions.

Overall, though, Walzer's method of organizing theory around real cases places him in the "e.g." camp. "I.e." just war theory first works out a general theory of the use of lethal violence in individual self-defense, then applies it to wartime. "E.g." philosophy resists such procedures and demands that just war theory start with war—or rather, with *wars*, plural, meaning actual cases. Both methods have their strengths and their risks. The chief risk of Walzer's procedure is that the cases might not generalize as far as he wants them to generalize. The chief risks of the Oxford Style are scholasticism and unreality.

V

As befits a birthday party, let me return again to the moment of birth. It is worth remembering two major events of 1977. That June, diplomats adopted the Protocols Additional to the Geneva Conventions, the first treaties to set out the *jus in bello* rules of distinction and proportionality in the form familiar today. No doubt Walzer's book was already in galleys by then, so there was no influence in either direction. Walzer was not keeping track of the Geneva negotiations, but it's remarkable how closely significant Additional Protocol rules track *Just and Unjust Wars*.

To take the most telling example, recall Walzer's distinctive version of the doctrine of double effect: he insists that it's not enough for soldiers *not to intend* to cause civilian collateral damage; they must *intend not* to do so. Additional Protocol I imposes a legally novel affirmative obligation to take all feasible precautions to avoid civilian harm[13]: this is, in essence, Walzer's concept of "intending not," cast in the form of legal rules. Now I don't much believe in *Zeitgeists*, but it's hard not to suspect that the Geneva drafters and Walzer were breathing the same intellectual and moral air. When we reread these pages today, we should remember that Walzer wrote his double effect analysis without the benefit of any hard-law rules to draw on.

There are also differences. Notably, Walzer is suspicious of *in bello* proportionality and its utilitarian assumptions, whereas Additional Protocol I embraces it. This is a crucial difference, because Walzer's mistrust of utilitarianism is central to his argument. It brings me to the second event of 1977 that matters.

During the first half of 1977, the Carter administration was formulating and publicizing its pro-human rights foreign policy—a watershed moment for the human rights movement. Following two years after the Helsinki Accords, it was a pivotal moment in American diplomacy that deeply boosted human rights movements around the world.

The relevance is obvious. Walzer's first edition preface cautions that he is not going to expound any theory of morality from the ground up. But, he continues,

> I want to suggest that the arguments we make about war are most fully understood … as efforts to recognize and respect the rights of individual and associated men and women. The morality I shall expound is in its philosophical form a doctrine of human rights.[14]

It's worth recalling that Walzer began work on *Just and Unjust Wars* the year after Rawls published *A Theory of Justice*, defending the priority of the right over the good in the teeth of the utilitarian conventional wisdom of the previous two decades of moral philosophy.[15] In 1974 Nozick published *Anarchy, State, and Utopia*, with its strongly individualistic theory of natural rights.[16] Alan Donagan's rights-based *The Theory of Morality*[17] appeared the same year as Walzer's book, and so did Dworkin's *Taking Rights Seriously*, announcing that rights are moral trump cards[18]; Charles Fried would publish *Right and Wrong*[19] the following year. For the moment, human rights had become the *lingua franca* of moral philosophy. As I recall, most of these philosophers had been meeting on a regular basis to discuss their works-in-progress, rather like the Oxford Inkling meetings where Tolkien and C.S. Lewis read rough drafts to their friends over beer and bangers at a pub. What this efflorescence of rights theories means for just war theory is worth thinking about, and I will reflect on it shortly.

Let's return to human rights as they function in *Just and Unjust Wars*. Remember that Walzer calls his book "a doctrine of human rights." But human rights actually play a smaller direct role in the argument of *Just and Unjust Wars* than this language would lead us to expect. It makes two important cameo appearances, once in the *jus ad bellum* and once in the *jus in bello*.

The former is the one that over the years I've had the most trouble with.[20] In Walzer's theory, aggression is the crime of war because it assaults the right to self-determination of political communities.[21] Now, political communities are collectives, so we are talking here about collective or group rights. Let's reread what Walzer says about human rights in his first preface: he calls them "the rights of individual *and associated* men and women." Walzer leaves space for collective rights. It's easy to overlook those words "... and associated," especially because later Walzer says that the rights of states "derive ultimately from the rights of individuals."[22] It's natural, but I think mistaken, to read *Just and Unjust Wars* as a doctrine of individual human rights.

Walzer gets from individual rights to community rights via a metaphorical social contract—a metaphor, he tells us, "for a process of association and mutuality,"[23] a common life shaped over a long period of time. He wants us to recognize that this common life matters to us as much as personal liberty and free speech matter to us. It matters enough to be included as the substance of a right. Is it, though, a collective or an individual right? I think it must be collective. If we're forced to analyze it as an individual human right, it would be the individual's right to share in the common life of her people.

But that is an awkward and misleading way to put it: it sounds like an individual right against exile or isolation or group persecution, which is not at all what Walzer is talking about. I take this as evidence that the right to a common life fits more comfortably as a group right, not an individual right.[24] It's the revisionists who are really the individual-rights theorists in today's just war theory, for it is they whose starting question is what makes an individual liable to be killed notwithstanding the right to life.

As Walzer elaborates the right to share in a common life, it generates a political right of self-determination. The latter move, I should say, doesn't follow automatically. It isn't automatic that the Kurds and Catalans and Kosovars need political self-determination to enjoy their common life, and it isn't hard to imagine scenarios where political self-determination could ruin the Catalans' common life as it exists today, turning a prosperous province into a struggling statelet.

But suppose we accept the premise that peoples have a collective right of self-determination. Walzer derives two of his major doctrines from it: first, that military aggression is the crime of war. Second, in one of the most famous parts of the book, Walzer endorses John Stuart Mill's argument against military interventions to free an oppressed people: for Mill and Walzer, self-determination requires that they be left to work out their destiny for themselves, whether it be authoritarian or democratic.

Recalling the opening words of his first preface, it now seems glaringly obvious that Walzer had Vietnam in mind. The U.S. claimed to be supporting South Vietnam's self-determination, but in reality we were propping up a puppet government. Regardless of what we—or many South Vietnamese—thought of the Communists, self-determination meant the Vietnamese should work their destiny out themselves, violently or not, as in the end they did. Whatever we think today about Vietnam's government, it's *their* government.

But there's a complication here. Walzer's model of a Burkean social contract—a common life worked out by a people over time—fits homogeneous states best, and stable, historically multi-ethnic states second best. Artificially pieced-together multi-ethnic states where tribal or clan or religious ties are stronger than ties to the whole, and where group antagonisms run just below the surface, are a less good fit. And states plagued by political, racial, or religious oppression don't fit at all. In a racist or apartheid state, the right of political self-determination benefits the common life only of the dominant group, and therefore it isn't truly a common life. Not only does it exclude the victim groups from that common life, it impedes them from fashioning a common life of their own. As I shall suggest in my conclusion, this is a grave danger today.

By no means am I suggesting that outside military intervention is the cure for the disease of oppression—"Libya" is the two-syllable refutation of that thought. But when sovereignty serves as a screen for oppression, and large parts of the nation don't enjoy its common life, Walzer's theory isn't the explanation of what's wrong with intervention. He recognized this in the first (and succeeding) editions,[25] but it isn't until the preface to his third edition, where—with Srebrenica in mind—he fully acknowledges that in states like Bosnia the value of sovereignty to the victims is small and the barrier to intervention is low.[26]

Besides its role in the theory of *jus ad bellum*, human rights also figure in the *jus in bello*—but, I think, mostly indirectly. There is a small section titled "Human Rights," built around a case study, "The Rape of the Italian Women." The example, drawn from World War II, is that the Free French fighting in Italy needed the aid of Moroccan mercenaries, who insisted on the right to rape Italian women as part of their fringe benefits. Does military exigency justify the deal?[27] Tony Pfaff has written about a parallel dilemma 60 years later, in Iraq. Should U.S. police trainers turn a blind eye to an Iraqi policeman who used torture, because firing him would turn his powerful family against us?[28]

Walzer writes that "men and women ... have a moral standing independent of and resistant to the exigencies of war. A legitimate act of war is one that does not violate the rights of the people against whom it is directed."[29] I believe this is the only place where Walzer directly invokes individual rights. And to me it's noteworthy that the context is a critique of utilitarianism, which Walzer introduced in the preceding section. Throughout the book, we see a suspicion of utilitarianism—not only here, but also in the analysis of preventive war and in his "skepticism of the proportionality rule" that he explicitly acknowledges in the fifth edition preface.[30] One philosophical function of rights-talk has been to counteract utility-talk, and that seems to me an important function rights-talk plays in *Just and Unjust Wars*.

Now, in his discussion of human rights Walzer also acknowledges in passing that rights can be "surrendered or lost" by voluntary actions.[31] One might say that the granular, detailed analysis of rights-forfeiture is one of the main occupations of the analytic just war theory industry. But Walzer doesn't really take it up, because—in my reading—the kind of legalistic and Hohfeldian intricacy of analytic just war theory is not the approach to human rights he favors. Immediately following the Rape of the Italian Women, we find Walzer's discussion of "The Status of Individuals"[32] and the famous examples of "naked soldiers"—cases where soldiers are morally revolted by the prospect of picking off an individual enemy soldier taking a bath, or pulling up his trousers, or enjoying a beautiful sunrise, or lighting a cigarette. Although Walzer doesn't call this a human rights issue, it seems like a natural continuation of the preceding section on human rights—intended as such. To me, it describes an experience of the other that underlies all genuine human rights thinking: the experience of human solidarity across lines, including battle-lines. Confronted by the individuated, helpless, and momentarily non-threatening enemy, one says simply, "*Ecce homo*," behold the man.

Gabriella Blum has coined the phrase "the individualization of war,"[33] by which she means the gradual infusion of individual-rights thinking into the laws of war—and individualization has become a major topic in contemporary writing. In his fifth edition postscript, Walzer takes care to emphasize that war is an intensely collectivizing experience.[34] It's part of his rejoinder to the revisionist penchant for thinking of killing in war as, so to speak, a mere accumulation of individual killings in war. But I find in his discussion of the naked soldier—and in his critiques of utilitarianism, and in his stated commitment to human rights—a countervailing sympathy for individualization. I would describe it as humanistic, in the sense reflected in Terence's beautiful line "I am human, and nothing human is alien to me." Warfare is not alien, but neither is the sheer humanity of the human being on the other side. To be sure, that enemy "alienates himself from me when he tries to kill me, and from our common humanity," as Walzer acknowledges. "But," he continues, "that alienation is temporary, the humanity imminent."[35] One way, then, to identify the difference between the analytic philosophy of human rights and the approach in *Just and Unjust Wars* is the difference between a kind of legalistic focus on the logic of rights and a kind of humanism, each with its own strengths and weaknesses. Human rights theory can't do without an analysis of rights and liabilities. But just war theory would be morally impoverished without the kind of humanism we find in *Just and Unjust Wars*.

VI

My remarks so far have been, so to speak, a preface to *Just and Unjust Wars*. I want to conclude with a postscript. I have been emphasizing that the year 1977 was a time of human rights ascendancy, in philosophy, in foreign policy, and in public discourse. Today, unfortunately, we are in an era of human rights retreat if not collapse. At the apogee of human rights, politicians would deny their human rights violations. Today they feel no need. In our time of authoritarian populism, leaders spit on human rights and their supporters cheer. I am not talking only about Myanmar and the Philippines and Turkey and Syria. I'm talking about Western-style democracies as well.

We see it in continental Europe's elections and the British yellow press's loathing for the European Court of Human Rights. Our own president said he would bring back waterboarding in a heartbeat, whether it works or not, because they deserve it.[36] In 2017, Israel's supreme court rolled back its landmark anti-torture decision of 1999,[37] and much of the Israeli public views its human rights organizations as enemies of the army.

In 1977, philosophers might have been inclined to see utilitarianism as the opponent of rights theorizing. Today, we must recognize that the opponent of rights is populist nationalism. One hallmark is a pugnacious commitment to state sovereignty as a shield against outside human rights pressure, something we see vividly today in Hungary and Poland. Another hallmark is, unfortunately, a powerful commitment to the rights of political communities, but one that comes coupled with an angry sense that the political community doesn't include everyone who lives in the state's territory—not the refugees, not the immigrants, not the ethnic and racial minorities. These are the alien other, not part of "our" communal life. Earlier, I remarked on how Walzer's concept of political community works best to model homogeneous nation-states like Norway, and worst to model multi-ethnic states with angry majorities.

Now none of this directly undermines the validity of Walzer's theory of *jus ad bellum*; but it does weaken the political theory on which it rests. It raises an orange flag over state sovereignty grounded in the rights of political communities, when the communities are being flagrantly gerrymandered to exclude minority residents. More damagingly, rage at the alien other places enormous stress on one of Walzer's central commitments: the moral equality of civilians, carrying the requirement that soldiers must take equivalent risks to spare "their" civilians and ours.

Ultimately, though, the humanism of *Just and Unjust Wars* plainly outshines the weakness I've identified. Unfortunately, at age forty, the humanism of *Just and Unjust Wars* finds itself under worldwide siege. As an admirer of the book and the vision behind it, I can only wish for the siege to break—and for many happy returns, and a next edition with a preface that affirms human rights in a time of peril.

NOTES

1. Cambridge: Harvard University Press, 1970.
2. *Just and Unjust Wars*, 1st ed. (New York: Basic Books, 1977), xi.
3. *Just and Unjust Wars*, 5th ed. (New York: Basic Books, 2015), 345.
4. Additional Protocol I draws no nationality distinction when it imposes obligations not to target civilians and to take all feasible steps to protect them. "Protocol Additional to the Geneva Conventions of 12 August 1949, and Relating to the Protection of Victims of International Armed Conflict (Protocol I)," United Nations, June 8, 1977, https://www.un.org/en/genocideprevention/documents/atrocity-crimes/Doc.34_AP-I-EN.pdf.
5. *Just and Unjust Wars*, 5th ed., 336.
6. Emer de Vattel, *The Law of Nations*, eds. Béla Kapossy and Richard Whatmore (Indianapolis: Liberty Fund, 2008), Bk. III, Ch. XII, §§188–192, 589–93; Bk. III, Ch. III, §39, 489.
7. *Just and Unjust Wars*, 1st ed., xvi.

8. I use the term because many of the philosophers who utilize arguments based on stylized hypothetical examples draw inspiration from some central figures in contemporary just war theory who are associated with Oxford University, either as faculty members, fellows, or students.

9. *Just and Unjust Wars*, 5th ed., 336.

10. Ibid., 338. Walzer first used this line in his "Response to McMahan's Paper," *Philosophia* 34, no. 1 (January 2006): 43.

11. Cambridge: Harvard University Press, 2004.

12. Sidney Morgenbesser, "Scientific Explanation," in *International Encyclopedia of the Social Sciences*, ed. David Sills, vol. 14 (New York: MacMillan, 1968), 122.

13. "Protocol Additional to the Geneva Conventions of 12 August 1949": art. 57(2).

14. *Just and Unjust Wars*, 1st ed., xvi–xvii.

15. Cambridge: Harvard University Press, 1971.

16. New York: Basic Books, 1974.

17. Chicago: University of Chicago Press, 1977.

18. Cambridge: Harvard University Press, 1977.

19. Cambridge: Harvard University Press, 1978.

20. See David Luban, "Just War and Human Rights," *Philosophy & Public Affairs* 9, no. 2 (1980): 160–81; Luban, "The Romance of the Nation-State," *Philosophy & Public Affairs* 9, no. 4 (1980): 392–97; and Luban, "Preventive War," *Philosophy & Public Affairs* 32, no. 3 (2004): 214–17.

21. This topic is the focus of Margaret Moore's chapter in this volume.

22. *Just and Unjust Wars*, 5th ed., 53.

23. Ibid., 54.

24. Graham Parsons thinks the tension between group and individual rights is why it is so hard to make *Just and Unjust War*'s *ad bellum* and *in bello* theories hang together. Graham Parsons, "The Incoherence of Walzer's Just War Theory," *Social Theory and Practice* 38, no. 4 (October 2012): 663–88.

25. *Just and Unjust Wars*, 5th ed., 101.

26. *Just and Unjust Wars*, 3rd ed., xiv.

27. *Just and Unjust Wars*, 5th ed., 133.

28. Tony Pfaff, *Development and Reform of the Iraqi Police Forces* (Carlisle: Army War College Press, 2008), 31–48, https://ssi.armywarcollege.edu/pubs/display.cfm?pubID=840.

29. *Just and Unjust Wars*, 5th ed., 135.

30. Ibid., xv.

31. Ibid., 135.

32. Ibid., 138.

33. See Gabriella Blum, "The Individualization of War: From War to Policing in the Regulation of Armed Conflicts," in *Law and War*, eds. Austin Sarat, Lawrence Douglas, and Martha Merrill Umphrey (Stanford University Press, 2013), 48–83.

34. *Just and Unjust Wars*, 5th ed., 340–41.

35. Ibid., 143.

36. Jenna Johnson, "Donald Trump on Waterboarding: 'If It Doesn't Work, They Deserve It Anyway'," *Washington Post*, November 23, 2015, https://www.washingtonpost.com/news/post-politics/wp/2015/11/23/donald-trump-on-waterboarding-if-it-doesnt-work-they-deserve-it-anyway/?utm_term=.344cae181ab2.

37. HCJ 5722/12 *Abu Ghosh* et al. *v. Attorney General* et al., Israel Supreme Court (2017). At the time of this writing, the decision is not available in English translation. For detailed summaries, see Elena Chachko, "'Pressure Techniques' and Oversight of Shin Bet Interrogations: Abu Gosh v. Attorney-General," *Lawfare*, December 22, 2017, https://www.lawfareblog.com/pressure-techniques-and-oversight-shin-bet-interrogations-abu-gosh-v-attorney-general; and Yuval Shany, "Back to the 'Ticking Bomb' Doctrine," *Lawfare*, December 27, 2017, https://www.lawfareblog.com/back-ticking-bomb-doctrine. A more recent case, HCJ/AH 9105/18 *Tbeish v. Attorney General*, Israel Supreme Court (2018), available in English at http://versa.cardozo.yu.edu/sites/default/files/upload/opinions/Tbeish%20v.%20Attorney%20General.pdf, is a further rollback of the 1999 decision. See Smadar Ben Natan, "Revise Your Syllabi: Israeli Supreme Court Upholds Authorization for Torture and Ill-Treatment," *Journal of International Humanitarian Legal Studies* 10, no. 1 (June 2019): 41–57.

BIBLIOGRAPHY

Ben Natan, Smadar. "Revise Your Syllabi: Israeli Supreme Court Upholds Authorization for Torture and Ill-Treatment." *Journal of International Humanitarian Legal Studies* 10, no. 1 (June 2019): 41–57.

Blum, Gabriella. "The Individualization of War: From War to Policing in the Regulation of Armed Conflicts." In *Law and War*, edited by Austin Sarat, Lawrence Douglas, and Martha Merrill Umphrey, 48–83. Stanford: Stanford University Press, 2013.

Chachko, Elena. "'Pressure Techniques' and Oversight of Shin Bet Interrogations: Abu Gosh v. Attorney-General." *Lawfare*, December 22, 2017. https://www.lawfareblog.com/pressure-techniques-and-oversight-shin-bet-interrogations-abu-gosh-v-attorney-general.

Donagan, Alan. *The Theory of Morality.* Chicago: University of Chicago Press, 1977.

Dworkin, Ronald. *Taking Rights Seriously.* Cambridge: Harvard University Press, 1977.

Fried, Charles. *Right and Wrong.* Cambridge: Harvard University Press, 1978.

Johnson, Jenna. "Donald Trump on Waterboarding: 'If It Doesn't Work, They Deserve It Anyway'." *Washington Post*, November 23, 2015. https://www.washingtonpost.com/news/post-politics/wp/2015/11/23/donald-trump-on-waterboarding-if-it-doesnt-work-they-deserve-it-anyway/?utm_term=.344cae181ab2.

Luban, David. "Just War and Human Rights." *Philosophy & Public Affairs* 9, no. 2 (1980): 161–80.

———. "The Romance of the Nation-State." *Philosophy & Public Affairs* 9, no. 4 (1980): 392–97.

———. "Preventive War." *Philosophy & Public Affairs* 32, no. 3 (2004): 207–48.

Margalit, Avishai. *The Ethics of Memory.* Cambridge: Harvard University Press, 2004.

Morgenbesser, Sidney. "Scientific Explanation." In *International Encyclopedia of the Social Sciences*, edited by David Sills, vol. 14. New York: Macmillan, 1968.

Nozick, Robert. *Anarchy, State, and Utopia.* New York: Basic Books, 1974.

Parsons, Graham. "The Incoherence of Walzer's Just War Theory." *Social Theory and Practice* 38, no. 4 (October 2012): 663–88.

Pfaff, Tony. *Development and Reform of the Iraqi Police Forces.* Carlisle: Army War College Press, 2008. https://ssi.armywarcollege.edu/pubs/display.cfm?pubID=840.

"Protocol Additional to the Geneva Conventions of 12 August 1949, and Relating to the Protection of Victims of International Armed Conflicts (Protocol I)." June 8, 1977. The United Nations. https://www.un.org/en/genocideprevention/documents/atrocity-crimes/Doc.34_AP-I-EN.pdf.

Rawls, John. *A Theory of Justice.* Cambridge: Harvard University Press, 1971.

Shany, Yuval. "Back to the 'Ticking Bomb' Doctrine." *Lawfare*, December 27, 2017. https://www.lawfareblog.com/back-ticking-bomb-doctrine.

Vattel, Emer de. *The Law of Nations.* Edited by Béla Kapossy & Richard Whatmore. Indianapolis: Liberty Fund, 2008.

Walzer, Michael. *Obligations: Essays on Disobedience, War, and Citizenship.* Cambridge: Harvard University Press, 1970.

———. *Just and Unjust Wars.* 1st ed. New York: Basic Books, 1977.

———. *Just and Unjust Wars.* 3rd ed. New York: Basic Books, 2000.

———. *Just and Unjust Wars.* 5th ed. New York: Basic Books, 2015.

———. "Response to McMahan's Paper." *Philosophia* 34, no. 1 (January 2006): 43–45.

CHAPTER 3

Territory, Self-Determination, and Defensive Rights

Margaret Moore

This chapter argues that the right to defend territory is grounded, at least in the first instance, in the value of collective self-determination for the people living on the territory. It may therefore be read as supportive of Michael Walzer's claim in *Just and Unjust Wars* that the fundamental norm or value of the international order is that of collective self-determination. The argument provided for this view is not necessarily linked to just war theory. Its focus is on the appropriate way to think about rights over territory. According to this argument, in the context of territorial rights, defensive rights over territory emerge at the second-order level.

The justificatory argument for rights over territory, and the institutions and practices associated with jurisdiction over a territory, is rooted in the value of collective self-determination. It is this value that justifies rights to jurisdiction over a territory, to noninterference in the institutions and practices of self-determination, and, by extension, second-order

M. Moore (✉)
Political Studies Department, Queen's University, Kingston, ON, Canada
e-mail: moorem@queensu.ca

G. Parsons and M. A. Wilson (eds.), *Walzer and War*,
https://doi.org/10.1007/978-3-030-41657-7_3

rights to defense. I argue, more controversially, that the value of collective self-determination has to refer to the people living in the territory, and not simply the "self-determination" of the state. This makes my view different from both the traditional international law self-determination argument that focuses on the rights of states, and from justice accounts, which locate defensive rights solely in terms of the protection of individual human rights. It is however compatible with Walzer's appeal to collective self-determination as a fundamental principle of the international order, and, most crucially, his insight that the value of self-determination has to be realized by the "people" and not merely the state, although I offer a somewhat different argument for this claim. I recognize, at the end of the chapter, that this understanding of the "self" that is "self-determining" has implications for other elements of our understanding of justified war, but I do not discuss these implications at length.

Justice, Self-Determination, and Just War Theory

Before I begin, let me be clear what this chapter does and does not do and how it might be linked to a wider argument within just war theory. The argument of this chapter is not primarily addressed to a wider discussion of the appropriate way to think about just war theory and how to link these values with *jus in bello* and *jus ad bellum* principles. I do not try to integrate self-determination with an account of justice for a complete theory of just war. Rather, my focus is on how we should think about the right of collective self-defense, and why that right requires us to interrogate the territorial aspect of the state, and to rethink the appropriate holder of the right of self-determination.

There are two common justifications offered by those who are not pacifists for defensive rights in war: one is rooted in the value of self-determination and is typically linked to the rights of states and the importance of territorial integrity; the other is rooted in justice, and involves the defense of basic human rights, which is used both to legitimate state power and defensive war. One could of course view the first value (self-determination) as an aspect of justice, on a capacious account of what justice is, or claim to support both justice and self-determination but make the latter entirely dependent on whether the state is just and so give primacy to the value of justice. In this chapter, I distinguish between justice and self-determination views, and argue that each has a distinctive contribution to our understanding of individual and state rights, and, connected to this, to defensive war.

My argument, though, departs from both justice and self-determination accounts in significant ways. Most accounts of self-determination associate self-determination with the rights of states. In conventional just war theory, identified with Grotius, Pufendorf, and Vattel, reflection on armed conflict is primarily rooted in a vision of the world as consisting of sovereign political communities. The rights of national self-defense are primarily rights held by states. Sovereigns are the primary, morally relevant entity in war, and this seems to capture at least one aspect of war: that it is in defense of states that armies go to war, and particularly the defense of political values such as self-determination and territorial integrity. Moreover, while individual soldiers since Nuremberg have had to be self-reflective about the moral status of their actions, and take responsibility for them, there is still an unmistakable hierarchical structure to armies; soldiers are often trained to act together as a unity, which makes sense on the view that the soldier fights on behalf of his or her state, and that in war, unlike individual combat, states are an important, decision-making collective agent.

Arguably, beginning with Walzer, but exemplified clearly in recent theories about war, such as Cecile Fabre's[1] and Jeff McMahan's,[2] the moral framework for thinking about war has shifted to the language of justice and individual human rights. This new move has a number of real advantages: it links the moral justification of war to the generally accepted language of human rights, and it can explain the right of defensive war in terms of resistance to the vital interests of individuals that aggression typically threatens. This shift has had a considerable effect on our understanding of the normative principles that underlie war and also structures our understanding of humanitarian intervention and third-party duties.

Both forms of justification have serious limitations. On the one hand, the traditional statist argument seems inadequate to explain the role of the individual soldier, who after all is the one who must fight in the war.[3] On the other hand, the focus on justice also seems not to address some important elements of war. It is true that justice is an important value, and sufficiently robust to justify violence in its defense; but it's perhaps not very helpful to proceed in our discussions of just war theory as if we can clearly distinguish between just and unjust sides, and therefore just and unjust combatants, and the various rights and duties that line up on these sides. That picture certainly describes the Second World War, when Allied powers, who were largely liberal and democratic regimes, fought a defensive war against an egregiously unjust, indeed murderous and genocidal, aggressive Nazi regime. But in most wars, both sides feel that they have some justification on their side—justice even—and, in many cases, the issue between them could be more accurately cashed out in terms of defending their institutional independence or protecting the perceived vital interests of their political community. In this chapter, then, I focus on the value of collective self-determination, which I take to be distinct from appeals either to justice or to state functions and the goods that the state provides. I do not deny the importance of these other values, but this chapter argues that territorial rights (including the defense of territorial rights) are linked to the value of collective self-determination.

Some Preliminaries: Why Territory? What Is Territory?

Let me begin by explaining why in this chapter I focus on territory and on territorial rights. Our usual conception of justified (that is, defensive) war has a strong territorial component: aggression against the territory of another state constitutes an act of war, regardless of whether anyone is killed in the taking of the territory. This is a point that has been forcefully made by David Rodin, to point out that we cannot conceive of war as simply analogous to individual self-defense.[4] We are not entitled to kill a harmless trespasser on our property; what then would entitle us to respond to a bloodless territorial aggression with a war which would predictably kill many people on both sides, including probably innocent civilians? We need an account of rights over territory to explain this, because defense of territory is not reducible to, or analogous to, individual self-defense.

If we are to understand why the defense of territory is conceived of as so important that it can legitimate war, which predictably involves killing, we need to consider the question of what justifies territory. This is not straight-forward since most political theory, until very recently, has focused on the relation between state and citizen—the entitlements and responsibilities of the citizen to state, and vice versa—but very little about what justifies the geographical domain of the state, or how to draw justified (or legitimate) boundaries between distinct territorial units.

To address this question of the basis for rights over territory, some clarifications are in order. What is territory? What kinds of rights are we thinking about when we talk about territorial rights? Territory, as I understand it, is the geographical domain of political or jurisdictional authority. It is a *political* concept and so distinct from land, which is a geographical notion: land is the part of the earth's surface that is not covered by water. Of course, most land is claimed by a state, and so also is territory, but there could be unclaimed land or land that is contested between two states. Further, the territorial domain of the state also extends to the airspace above and to the sea offshore, so is not coextensive with land. Territory, then, is more than topology, but includes the idea of political authority.

Territory is also distinct from property, which we normally understand as a cluster of rights, liberties, powers, and immunities that, when held together with respect to a material thing, represent a form of "ownership." There are however some close analogies between the concept of "property" and the concept of "territory." Like property, the territorial right-holder that has claims over territory (e.g., an agent such as the state) typically doesn't have just one single right but a cluster of different rights, possibly including rights to jurisdiction, rights to control the flow of goods and people across borders, rights to natural resources within the territorial domain, and rights to defend these rights by military means. Like property, the appropriate justification for "territorial rights" is at the level of the system of territorial states, just as, with property, it is with the system of property holdings.[5]

What do we mean by a normative *theory of territory*? It is now almost universally accepted among theorists working on territorial rights that a normative *theory* of territory is a theory of the appropriate, normatively defensible relationship between the state, the people, and land.[6] Any theory of territory has to explain how these three elements are related and to justify the particular configuration. It is a normative theory because it is aimed at *justifying* the authority of the state, both over people and over the territory that it controls. And any theory of territory will have to explain or justify the rights normally associated with territory—the right, if any, to resources, defense, jurisdiction, and so on.

There are two standard justifications for territorial rights, which mirror the justifications above for defensive war: (1) self-determination and

(2) justice. In the next section, I will explain the problem with the justice defense, at least as it applies to territory and the defense of territory, as part of an argument in favor of appealing to the value of self-determination to justify control over territory.

TERRITORIAL RIGHTS AND JUSTICE

My central question in this chapter is what justifies defensive rights, which is related to, but distinct from, the question of what justifies territory. In this section, though, I will begin by analyzing a justice-based argument for territory, and then expand the focus to the implications for defensive rights.

The justice-based argument for territory derives from Kant and is perhaps the dominant view about what justifies territorial rights. On this view, political communities have territorial rights because they implement justice. For Kant, people who live in close proximity to one another, and therefore cannot avoid interacting, are morally obliged to enter the civil condition and acknowledge a political authority whose coercive law can guarantee their property rights. The justification for the authority's exercise of those rights is simply that it thereby replaces "a state *devoid of justice*" with "a rightful condition."[7]

Modern heirs to Kant adopt the same form of argument—that justice grounds territorial rights—but they are more explicit in adopting the language of rights to characterize the just condition. As Allen Buchanan has argued, "any wielder of political power over a territory" must, if it is to be legitimate, do a "credible job of protecting at least the most basic human rights of all those over whom it wields power."[8] Anna Stilz's argument adopts a similar form: a state's claim to territory requires a system of law that "rules in the name of the 'people', by protecting basic rights and granting the people a voice in defining them."[9] Lea Ypi lists as "essential criteria" for legitimacy "the ability to guarantee the rule of law; to protect basic human rights; and to provide sufficient opportunities guaranteeing citizens' democratic participation."[10] All three theorists focus on justice, defined in terms of upholding basic human rights, though they do also suggest the importance of a democracy. This is clear in the passage above from Stilz and Ypi; but Buchanan also argues that where "institutional resources allow for democratic authorization," full legitimacy then requires "all persons to participate as equals in the public processes for determining who shall wield political power," that is, some form of democracy.[11]

Let us, for present purposes, set aside the democratic requirement, because both Stilz and Buchanan are pretty careful in the language surrounding the question of whether, to hold legitimate rights to territory, the state must be organized democratically. Buchanan, and Stilz at least in the 2011 article on territorial rights, both focus on the justice (basic human rights protection) requirement.

This human rights argument is extremely plausible as a requirement for holding territorial rights in part because it is consistent with our intuitions about the minimum requirements of state action, consistent too with much human rights literature, and is especially compelling as an aspect of just war theory, since war is a brutal affair and requires very strong justificatory arguments. The value of justice is a strong candidate to explain why it is permissible to defend, violently, any aggression on the territory of the state.

It is, however, doubtful that *territorial rights* should be grounded in justice considerations, at least as that is ordinarily understood.[12] There are at least three problems with this otherwise compelling argument. First, this argument isn't adequate, at least not adequate as a complete justification, because, while it defends a territorial state system, it doesn't defend or define the precise *territory* or domain of the state. It tells us that the state ought to be ordered territorially, but not where the state's territory ought to be. To answer this question, which is usually dubbed "the particularity question," we need to connect particular states with particular geographical areas. This is necessary to address territorial conflicts, such as when two or more states claim the same piece of land, or, in the case of secession, to define the boundaries of the seceding unit, or to sort out claims to the seabed or the High Arctic or Antarctica, which require us to think about the principles on which boundaries should be drawn. The answer to the particularity question, which is not provided by this argument, would also explain why we are justified in protecting the territory of our state, but not any just state.

We can also question the argument due to its counter-intuitive implications. Stated briefly, this argument seems to strip many—perhaps all—states in the past, and many current states of rights over their territory.

Why is that a problem? The problem is that, while justice is an important, indeed arguably the central criteria *for a legitimate government*, there are counter-intuitive implications attached to making territorial rights contingent on justice. Consider the fact that, in the past, states were rarely just: they rarely protected human rights, even on a noncontroversial understanding of what that involves, and were also rarely democratic.

But we often think that there was something wrong with taking land, as many imperial powers did, from their colonial subordinates, often justifying their rule over "less civilized" populations in terms of their potentially morally superior rule. The requirement that territorial rights track the justice of states has the clear implication that all states in the past did not have rights to their territory. That would mean that more just states could be justified in taking over the territory of less just (or unjust) states, because the unjust state did not have rights over that territory in the first place. Do we really believe that nineteenth-century Morocco had no rights over the territory that we now identify with Morocco?[13] Do we really want to say that the British Empire did not violate territorial rights in India because the princely rulers there were unjust? Do we really think that the only wrong of colonialism was that it institutionalized hierarchical relations of domination and subordination but that the taking of territory was not an additional wrong?[14]

This is not just a backward-looking problem about how to theorize the wrong of colonialism. Many states today are unjust. If territorial rights are contingent on justice, then the conclusion that most contemporary states have no legitimate claim to the territories they govern seems unavoidable. The authors above are aware of this, and attempt to set the bar fairly low, with unclear language on the democratic requirement and focusing on the violation of basic or minimal lists of human rights. Yet even a basic human rights condition seems to disqualify many of them (as Stilz admits, citing Zimbabwe, Iran, Sudan, China, and North Korea as examples).

On what grounds then can we explain why justice-promoting states should be prevented from annexing or colonizing justice-deficient ones? This leads us directly in the realm of just war theory and how this connects to rights over territory. To see the problem, let's consider one important response to the challenge above, which has been developed primarily by Allen Buchanan and Lea Ypi.

Ypi implicitly acknowledges the difficulty of setting a bar of justice for defining a legitimate holder of territorial rights. However, she responds to this problem by laying heavy stress on the *de facto* possession of territory, whatever its origins, and then coupling this with the proviso that full territorial rights can only be established by states subjecting themselves to an international political authority that will adjudicate all territorial claims. This solution draws inspiration from Kant, but this procedural solution—that states are conclusively (as opposed to provisionally) entitled to whatever the global association says they are—does not tell us what we should do now, and why we should accord provisional territorial rights to states that do not meet the bar of even minimal justice, since the "conclusive" territorial rights solution seems very far in the future. This "solution" appears to allow egregiously unjust states to continue to be egregiously unjust by conferring on them many powers, while upholding an ideal that looks like it will not be realized any time in the future. And this seems to strip the justice argument of the power and intuitive plausibility that I argued above was its main recommendation.

Buchanan deals with the problem (that on his argument many current states are not entitled to their territory) by appealing to considerations within justice theory itself: he points out that a state cannot gain rights over territory if they do so unjustly; they must not unjustly displace some other group, mustn't usurp an already legitimate state. But this doesn't really address the problem that we are confronted with. Is it justified on this argument to usurp the authority of an illegitimate state? Presumably, because the state in question is not legitimate, it has no legitimate authority and, therefore, usurpation is not an issue. However, both Buchanan and Stilz are also at pains to emphasize that aggression is itself unjust, so is disallowed on their principles. This appears to be a partial answer: the previous political order was not legitimate but the replacing state cannot be legitimate if it usurps or aggresses against the previous state. This seems to enable justice theorists of territorial rights to explain the wrongness of annexation.

It is, however, much more difficult to show why a just state could not gain territorial rights from a much less just state if they annex its territory through victory in a defensive war. This of course was precisely the situation of the Allied Powers who occupied Germany in 1945, a case addressed by Stilz.[15] To resist the conclusion that the Allies could legitimately incorporate the divided territory of Germany within their various political projects, thereby gaining rights of jurisdiction, resources, and so on, Stilz invokes the idea of a German "people" who hold meta-jurisdictional rights over the territory in question. I think appealing to this is exactly right—and it's a similar move to the one made in a somewhat different context by both Walzer in his discussion of just war and by myself in my book on territory.[16] However, it's not clear that a *justice* theory has the conceptual resources to make this move, because the appeal here is to considerations outside of justice, such as self-determination. It is to this that I now turn.

Territorial Rights and Self-Determination

In this section, I will advance the argument for territorial rights rooted in the value of realizing collective self-determination rather than justice. However, this argument cannot easily be married to the justice account above because it requires us to view *the people* as the appropriate holder of territorial rights, and to do so through a coherent account of the relationship between government, territory, and people. In making this argument, I think in some sense I am following Walzer, who also appeals to the concept of self-determination in *Just and Unjust Wars*, where he suggests, following John Stuart Mill, that self-determination is "the right of a people 'to become free by their own efforts, if they can.'"[17] He also argues, in responding to critics of his theory, that "the real subject of my argument is not the state at all but the political community that (usually) underlies it."[18] The argument developed here follows this structure, but unlike Walzer, I conceptualize the people as a collective agent without appealing to any kind of "cultural community" or to an "inherited culture" that is shared among the group.[19]

Let us return to the case of the territorial rights of the German people in occupied Germany in 1945. This surely is a meta-jurisdictional right to be self-determining which is held by the German people themselves in a way that is disconnected, at least in the first instance, from the governing regime. At least the thought must be that the Nazi regime (and the institutions and practices of the state associated with it), which was egregiously unjust—indeed genocidal—and aggressive, could and ought to be replaced and restructured in important ways, but that there is still value in ensuring that the people have the possibility to be self-determining and thereby create for themselves rules, practices, and institutions to organize their collective life together, presumably in line with basic justice.

If that is the thought, then at least three elements need to be further explicated, which I will briefly summarize here. First, there is the idea that the people themselves be the primary right-holder, and this requires that we can identify the people as a collective agent in a way that is distinct from, and conceptually independent of, the state itself. Second, there is a challenge linking the people with land so as to connect it to the geographical domain on which they are entitled to organize their collective lives and be self-determining. Thirdly, we need to explain the value that would be realized, which, I argue, is the value of self-determination.

The first idea is to identify the people as the territorial right holder; or, to be more precise, the holder of a meta-jurisdictional right to be collectively self-determining in a specific geographical domain. This is a challenge. It's much easier to attribute territorial rights to the state: the state is a standard kind of collective agent, with a decision-making mechanism, such that we can attribute choices or decisions to it that are independent of the choices and decisions of any individual member of the state. It is however much more difficult to attribute collective agency to "the people" in a way that isn't circular and doesn't fall back on the state as the mechanism by which "the people" speak. I propose however that we can describe "the people" as the collective agent if (1) a large majority of people are in a relationship with one another that involves a shared political commitment to establish rules and practices of self-determination; (2) they have the political capacity to establish and sustain institutions of political self-determination; and (3) they possess an objective history of political cooperation together, through for example participating in state or sub-state institutions, or even through mobilizing and participating in a resistance movement. The relationship speaks to the fact that it cannot be a momentary encounter; it must be temporally extended—both with a history and with (in normal cases) the expectation of a future—and it realizes moral goods that are intrinsic to that relationship. A "people" so described can be an agent in so far as it makes sense to attribute actions and projects and plans to it that are independent of the actions of any of its constituent members, and it also satisfies both the individuation condition (i.e., explains how one people can be distinguished from another) and the continuity condition (i.e., explains how a people can be identified over time while still changing) which are important desiderata of a collective agent.[20]

How can we identify the territory of "the people" so defined? Here the basic idea is that we can appeal to the idea that individuals and "peoples" have rights to land, which help to define the territorial right. I will not spend much time on this, in part because there is convergence by all the competing theories of territory on the idea that rights attach to individuals who live on and are settled on land.[21] There is a moral right of residency which attaches to individuals and has three components: a general liberty right to settle in an unoccupied area; a right of non-dispossession, by which I mean a right to remain, at liberty, in their homes and communities and not to be removed from the place of one's projects, aims, and relationships; and a right of return, when an individual has been unjustly dispossessed of the land on which s/he has a right to reside. But it would be wrong to think of place-related rights as attaching only to individuals, since individuals are not isolated and atomistic but operate within a structure of relationships that give meaning to their life and have collective identities that are integral to their sense of who they are as well as collective aspirations as members of these groups. So in addition to (and indeed inextricably linked to) the idea of a right of residency is a group right of occupancy, where groups in question—a people—have rights to place that are forged not simply independently by individuals living in a place, but by individuals as members of a collective, whose members share a geographical location with one another, and whose locus is defined by the activities and projects central to that relationship.

Finally, what value is served by conferring territorial rights (and specifically the right of meta-jurisdictional authority) on peoples so defined over the areas that they occupy? It seems that the primary answer is that of self-determination. Although this is a recognized legal right, enshrined in Art. 1, par. 2, and Article 55 of the United Nations Charter, I assume that there is a moral (and not merely legal) right to collective self-determination. This moral right follows from the idea that political communities are valuable in part because they are spaces in which members co-create their own political project and together implement their own conception of justice. Institutions of political self-determination give expression to the communities in which people live. They express people's identities, and they are an important forum in which collective autonomy can be expressed, and people can shape the context in which they live and realize their political aspirations free of external domination.

The moral value of self-determination does not inhere in the fact that through it people create objective justice; rather, the process of making the rules that govern a people's collective existence is itself morally valuable. People who exercise collective self-government have the institutional mechanisms to shape the conditions of their existence, and their future together, and are thereby more autonomous—or experience a different (collective) dimension of autonomy that is distinct from individualized autonomy.

TERRITORIAL RIGHTS AND DEFENSIVE RIGHTS

Let us now turn to the implications of this conception for our understanding of justified (defensive) war. Any theory of defensive rights has to provide an account of what agents are permitted to do in defense of their rights, and war poses a particular challenge because of its dualist character: it is, as Fabre helpfully reminds us, "waged by groups *ad bellum* and fought by individuals *in bello.*"[22] Marrying the group and individual elements is very challenging indeed.

One strategy, discussed above, is to describe states' rights to defend their territory as a collective analogue of the right to individual self-defense.[23] This strategy that has been critiqued by Rodin and is puzzling because it requires a further account of what is so valuable about the state. One might think that this shouldn't be too hard to provide—we can always associate the state with various goods (peace and stability). The problem here is that a justification that is so strong that it would permit some people to be sacrificed in defense of state sovereignty would also, it seems to me, attribute greater importance and value to the collective entity than the individuals who are subject to it, and so open the door to fascism.

The alternative, reductive strategy—which is associated with McMahan, Fabre, and other liberal and cosmopolitan accounts of war—explains war by references to the rights of individuals, and especially to our widely held intuition that we have an individual right of defense against attackers. Earlier I claimed that this strategy generates a right to defend oneself against aggression (of one's individual rights), but it also assumes that we can know clearly who is an aggressor and who is a victim, who is unjust and who is just, which is problematic in many cases.

How can this account, rooted in individual rights and justice considerations, generate a right of self-defense for unjust states? Some have argued that it cannot, but that this is a virtue of the account. Brian Orend, for example, argues the right to wage war (even defensive war) can only be had by legitimate regimes—legitimate here being understood as a minimum threshold of justice for the state being recognized as an international actor.[24] However, following from my argument about territorial rights above, it seems that there are at least two distinct legitimacy questions. The first is whether the government is legitimate vis-à-vis its citizens, a question that is answered in terms of either democratic legitimacy or protecting human rights. Almost all individualist accounts of defensive war focus on the protection of human rights; indeed, the reductionist strategy does so by conceiving of war as reducible to individual self-defense (of one's rights). The second legitimacy question is whether the state has legitimate occupancy over its territory. Since an attack on the territory of the state constitutes an act of war and seems not reducible to individual rights (especially when no loss of life is involved), I argued that we need an account of rights *over territory* as well as over persons. I also suggested that that argument had to be conceptualized, not in individualist terms or justice terms, but in terms of the value of collective self-determination which can be legitimately exercised on territory that the group legitimately occupies (in the sense that it does not displace another group that occupies that area). However, the right of collective self-determination is held not by the state, but by the people who have a kind of meta-jurisdictional right on the land that they occupy to be the ones who create and sustain the institutions of self-determination in that place and over their collective lives.

This gives us the conceptual resources to respond to the defensive rights held by illegitimate states. It opens up the possibility that a state can be illegitimate in the first respect (on justice or democratic criteria) but legitimate in the second respect (in terms of its possession of territorial rights), or vice versa. What is important for the argument of this chapter, however, is my claim that the second plank of legitimacy—the legitimate occupancy of territory over which people exercise their collective rights to self-determination—is what explains how an illegitimate state (in the first sense) might nevertheless have a right of self-defense. This right is grounded in the peoples' rights over territory, which is itself further grounded, not in justice considerations, but in collective self-determination.

This argument makes better sense of our intuition that even rights-denying states may have a right of self-defense. Consider the example posed (and addressed) by Fabre: that of the Soviet Union during the Second World War. On any plausible description of justice, the Soviet Union under Stalin was not a justice-abiding state: it violated individual rights, to life and liberty, did not protect the rule of law, and was responsible for the capture and murder of millions of people through its policies. Does such a state, an illegitimate state, have defensive rights? Is it a legitimate actor that ought to be able to protect itself when attacked? Can a justice-based account of state legitimacy recommend defensive rights for states that are illegitimate in the sense that they are not rights-protecting?

Fabre asks and then answers this very question and it is worth examining her response at length. At the end of a long section justifying defensive rights in an account of individual human rights, and justifying states' moral right to govern in terms based in the protection of these rights, Fabre then poses the question of "the grounds upon which—if any at all—illegitimate states can have the right to wage a war of collective self-defense."[25] I agree with her question and her conclusion but think that the argument needs to be fleshed out more precisely in terms of legitimate authority over territory.

Her first move is to argue that citizens "are under an obligation to obey the government only if their fundamental rights are thereby better protected by those directives than if they disobeyed."[26] But while this question of political obligation is relevant to the question we are considering, it's not a precise answer to the question posed. What we need to know is whether an illegitimate state has a right of self-defense, understood as a right to defend itself in war, on an individualist/reductionist account of the rights in question. It is hard to see how justice/rights theorists of war can show that it can. This is because defensive rights are attributed to states on account of their legitimacy, which is itself cashed out in terms of the protection of human rights.

Fabre then goes on to provide a more direct answer, using the example of the USSR during the Second World War:

> That the Soviet regime was illegitimate is absolutely beyond question. But it does not allow us to conclude that Germany did not violate the rights to sovereignty, territorial integrity, and life, of Soviet citizens, and that Stalin and his henchmen therefore did not have the right (acting on behalf of those citizens) to take the steps necessary to repel the invasion.[27]

In this passage, Fabre appeals to "sovereignty" and "territorial integrity." But it is hard to see how sovereignty or indeed territorial rights can be derived from her individualist paradigm, especially if the state is not protecting individual rights.

This is a similar problem to the one faced by Stilz when she considered whether in 1945 the Allied powers, who were democratic, justice respecting, and fighting a defensive war were entitled to the territory of Germany. And as Stilz discovered in that discussion, the most straightforward argument that makes sense of the view that they were not so entitled is one that appeals to an understanding of territorial rights, rooted in the value of the collective self-determination of peoples.

This type of analysis also seems to apply to defensive rights. Does an unjust state, like the Soviet Union, have a right to defend itself? Like Fabre, I agree that it may have the right, and not merely because I want to endorse precautionary principles in the design of the international order such that we should be careful not to license aggression or encourage boundary-changes (although I also believe this). The most straightforward and obvious reason is that there is something valuable about collective self-determination. People are entitled to defend themselves when their territorial rights, which are necessary for collective self-determination, are threatened. However, the right to defend territory is held by peoples, understood as a collective agent in the sense discussed earlier, and only secondarily by states, as the instruments of these peoples, in cases where state institutions, boundaries, policies, and practices are consonant with the identity and aspirations of individuals *as members of collectives* that aspire to realize collective self-determination.

CONCLUSION

In this chapter, I have argued that the holder of territorial rights—and particularly jurisdictional rights—is the people who are in legitimate occupancy of a territory, rather than the state. This is why a state, even a state that is rights-violating, may have the right to protect itself in a war; and why justice-protecting states are not entitled to the territory of justice-deficient states. States acquire defensive rights when it is seen by its members as a vehicle, even perhaps an imperfect vehicle, for their self-determination.

In arguing for the value of collective self-determination to understand defensive rights, the chapter can be taken as a partial vindication of Walzer's view that political self-determination is an important value in international society; but I do so, not by arguing directly in terms of the relationship between individual and collective rights and values, but by arguing that peoples have a collective right of self-determination over the territory that they legitimately occupy. This is not directly connected to justice, but is an important element in any adequate account of defensive rights, the wrongs of annexation, and so on.

If we accept the view of the justification for territorial rights and defensive rights outlined above, we open up the possibility that the collectives that individuals value (their sense of peoplehood) may not map fully on to the current state order. They *may* map on to the world of states, because many states have facilitated relationships of trust and of shared identity through their institutions and practices; but where they have not, it is hard to see why the self-determination of the state is itself valuable. This means that we cannot simply and crudely appeal to the importance of territorial integrity of states as a value whenever the "territorial integrity" of states is threatened. It is, for example, relevant to the issue of the violation of territorial rights whether the unity of states is threatened by a secessionist movement within the state, or whether the unity of the state and the territorial rights associated with this is threatened by an external aggressor.

Another implication of the argument advanced here is that the use of force may be permissible both to realize rights of self-determination and to protect it—although in both cases the use of force has to meet a high bar of justification, and the good achieved has to be significant in order to meet the proportionality requirement (to justify the killing that inevitably follows). I cannot discuss the full implications of this revision here, but it is not surprising that a full theory of justified defensive war that incorporates the value of self-determination of peoples would have effects on other elements of a normative theory of war.

NOTES

1. See Cecile Fabre, *Cosmopolitan War* (Oxford: Oxford University Press, 2012).
2. See Jeff McMahan, *Killing in War* (Oxford: Oxford University Press, 2009).
3. Seth Lazar, "Introduction," in *The Morality of Defensive War*, eds. Cecile Fabre and Seth Lazar (Oxford: Oxford University Press, 2014), 1–10.
4. David Rodin, *War and Self Defense* (Oxford: Clarendon Press, 2002).
5. Cara Nine, *Global Justice and Territory* (Oxford: Oxford University Press, 2012).
6. David Miller, "Territorial Rights: Concept and Justification," *Political Studies*, 60, no. 2 (2012): 252–68.
7. Immanuel Kant, *The Metaphysics of Morals*, trans. Mary Gregory (Cambridge: Cambridge University Press, 1996 [1797]), 90.
8. Allen Buchanan, *Justice, Legitimacy, and Self-Determination: Moral Foundations for International Law* (Oxford: Oxford University Press, 2004), 247.
9. Anna Stilz, "Nations, States, and Territory," *Ethics* 121, no. 3 (2011): 578.

10. Lea Ypi, "The Permissive Theory of Territorial Rights," *European Journal of Philosophy* 22, no. 2 (2014): 300.

11. Buchanan, 256.

12. There are two important links between territorial rights and justice. One is that the limits of some of these rights are defined by justice. The second is that serious and egregious injustice can result in forfeiting territorial rights. I make this last point without argument, but it seems to me that individual rights can be subject to forfeiture and the same should be true of collective rights. However, this is not a grounding argument: rather the conditions that justify forfeiture operate as a constraint on the argument. Moreover, it's difficult to attribute the conditions for forfeiture to "a people." Regimes or states or individual members of a "people" can be unjust but it's not obvious that individual injustice or injustice by the regime or injustice by the state would cause the people to forfeit their rights. I think there are some conditions that would satisfy the attribution requirement, but they are difficult to meet, and as I go on later to argue was not even met by Nazi Germany.

13. See Ayelet Banai, "The Territorial Rights of Legitimate States: A Pluralist Interpretation," *International Theory* 6, no. 1 (2014): 140–57.

14. See Margaret Moore, "Justice and Colonialism," *Philosophy Compass* 11, no. 8 (2016): 437–46.

15. Stilz, 590–91. For a critical appraisal, see Margaret Moore, "Which People and What Land? Territorial Right-Holders and Attachment to Territory," *International Theory* 6, no. 1 (2014): 121–40.

16. Moore, *A Political Theory of Territory* (New York: Oxford University Press, 2015).

17. Michael Walzer, *Just and Unjust Wars: A Moral Argument with Historical Illustrations*, 5th ed. (New York: Basic Books, 2015), 88.

18. Walzer, "The Moral Standing of States: A Response to Four Critics," *Philosophy & Public Affairs* 9, no. 3 (1980): 210–11.

19. Ibid.

20. Moore, *A Political Theory of Territory*.

21. See, for example, Moore, "Which People and What Land?"; Moore, *A Political Theory*; Stilz, "Nations, States, and Territory"; and Walzer, *Spheres of Justice: A Defense of Pluralism and Equality* (New York: Basic Books, 1983), 43.

22. Fabre, 54.

23. See Emer de Vattel, *The Law of Nations* (Indianapolis, IN: The Liberty Fund, 2008).

24. Brian Orend, *The Morality of War* (Peterborough, ON: Broadview Press, 2006), 34ff.

25. Fabre, 70.

26. Ibid., 71.

27. Ibid.

BIBLIOGRAPHY

Banai, Ayelet. "The Territorial Rights of Legitimate States: A Pluralist Interpretation." *International Theory* 6, no. 1 (2014): 140–57.

Buchanan, Allen. *Justice, Legitimacy, and Self-Determination: Moral Foundations for International Law*. Oxford: Oxford University Press, 2004.

de Vattel, Emer. *The Law of Nations*. Edited by Béla Kapossy and Richard Whatmore. Indianapolis: Liberty Fund, 2008 [1758].

Fabre, Cecile. *Cosmopolitan War*. Oxford: Oxford University Press, 2012.

Grotius, Hugo. *The Rights of War and Peace, Including the Law of Nature and of Nations*. New York: Cosimo Classics, 2007 [1625].

Kant, Immanuel. *The Metaphysics of Morals*. Translated by M. Gregor. Cambridge: Cambridge University Press, 1996 [1797].

Lazar, Seth. "Introduction." In *The Morality of Defensive War*, edited by Cecile Fabre and Seth Lazar, 1–10. Oxford: Oxford University Press, 2014.

———. "Responsibility, Risk, and Killing in Self-Defense." *Ethics* 119, no. 4 (2009): 699–728.

McMahan, Jeff. *Killing in War*. Oxford: Oxford University Press, 2009.

Miller, David. "Territorial Rights: Concept and Justification." *Political Studies* 60, no. 2 (2012): 252–68.

Moore, Margaret. *A Political Theory of Territory*. New York: Oxford University Press, 2015.

———. *Ethics of Nationalism*. Oxford: Oxford University Press, 2001.

———. "Justice and Colonialism." *Philosophy Compass* 11, no. 8 (2016): 437–46.

———. "Which People and What Land? Territorial Right-Holders and Attachment to Territory." *International Theory* 6, no. 1 (2014): 121–40.

Nine, Cara. *Global Justice and Territory*. Oxford: Oxford University Press, 2012.

Orend, Brian. *The Morality of War*. Peterborough, ON: Broadview Press, 2006.

Pufendorf, Samuel von. *On the Duty of Man and Citizens According to Natural Law*. Edited by J. Tully. Cambridge: Cambridge University Press, 1991 [1673].

Rodin, David. *War and Self-Defense*. Oxford: Clarendon Press, 2002.

Simmons, A. John. "On the Territorial Rights of States." In *Social, Political and Legal Philosophy: Philosophical Issues*, edited by Ernest Sosa and Enrique Villanueva, 300–26. Malden, MA and Oxford: Blackwell, 2003.

Stilz, Anna. "Nations, States, and Territory." *Ethics* 121, no. 3 (2011): 572–601.

Walzer, Michael. *Just and Unjust Wars: A Moral Argument with Historical Illustrations*. 5th ed. New York: Basic Books, 2015.

———. *Spheres of Justice: A Defense of Pluralism and Equality*. New York: Basic Books, 1983.

———. "The Moral Standing of States: A Response to Four Critics." *Philosophy & Public Affairs* 9, no. 3 (1980): 209–29.

Ypi, Lea. "The Permissive Theory of Territorial Rights." *European Journal of Philosophy* 22, no. 2 (2014): 288–312.

CHAPTER 4

Rethinking Humanitarian Intervention: Interests and Consequences

Jennifer M. Welsh

Introduction

When reading, and re-reading, Chapter Six of *Just and Unjust Wars*, one is struck by how Michael Walzer's discussion of humanitarian intervention now sits within the longer trajectory of this practice over the past half century. At the time of the first edition, written at the height of the Cold War, humanitarian intervention was a rare phenomenon, subject to moral debate, and—in the view of most international lawyers—prohibited by the legal framework regulating the use of force as set out in the UN Charter. But already by the third edition, at the turn of a new century, Walzer acknowledged that the issues he examined under the rubric of "intervention" had migrated from a peripheral concern into the very center of ethical debates about military force. Indeed, he went as far as to suggest that "the greatest danger most people face in the world today comes from their own states," and that the "chief dilemma of international politics is whether people in danger should be rescued by military forces from the outside."[1] The prefaces to the fourth and fifth editions (in 2006

J. M. Welsh (✉)
McGill University, Montreal, QC, Canada
e-mail: jennifer.welsh@mcgill.ca

© The Author(s) 2020
G. Parsons and M. A. Wilson (eds.), *Walzer and War*,
https://doi.org/10.1007/978-3-030-41657-7_4

51

and 2015, respectively) primarily address the fall-out from the 2003 war against Iraq and the particular challenges associated with asymmetric warfare, but they were also composed against a backdrop of efforts to increase the will to intervene in extreme situations of mass killing or humanitarian emergency—most notably through the rise of the principle of the "Responsibility to Protect" (RtoP). While Walzer demonstrated some sympathy for these efforts, his staunch opposition to the 2011 NATO-led intervention in Libya,[2] and his initial skepticism about the wisdom of inserting Western forces into the civil conflict in Syria,[3] indicate that he ultimately clung to a restrictionist position on humanitarian intervention—reserving it for the most extreme instances of "one-sided" atrocity crimes.[4]

In what follows, I discuss the ethics of humanitarian intervention in light of how it was practiced during what we still refer to awkwardly as the "post-Cold War period"—the heady days of liberal internationalism. Of course, some might reach the conclusion that nothing at all has changed since the first edition of *Just and Unjust Wars*: humanitarian intervention is still relatively rare (despite the assertions of some of its critics), subject to intense ethical contestation, and circumscribed by the Charter and broader international law—even after the development of RtoP. But I argue that some features of our moral discussion of humanitarian intervention *have* changed in light of that practice, largely as a result of more intense reflection on two issues: the role of state interests in motivating and shaping humanitarian intervention, and the need to (seriously) consider consequences in overall judgments of its legitimacy. As it turns out, Walzer was already pointing us in this direction.

Humanitarian Intervention's Long History

Before turning to concentrate on contemporary international relations, let me briefly gaze backward, to what comes *before* Walzer's own seminal "intervention" into the debate on the use of force for humanitarian purposes, in order to position his work along a broader spectrum. As a new wave of historical literature has emphasized over the past two decades, ethical and political debates about the legitimacy of military action by external actors to address humanitarian suffering in another state have been intimately bound up in the very constitution and evolution of modern international society. From at least as early as the sixteenth century, princes and state leaders deployed armed force in other territorial jurisdictions not just in response to armed attacks or other existential threats, but also to address what they publicly decried as the appalling acts of foreign sovereigns. The late sixteenth-century Elizabethan intervention in support of the Dutch revolt against the tyrannical rule of the King of Spain—which extended for more than two decades in a variety of financial, material, and military forms—was motivated, as historian David Trim explains, by protests against "Spanish treatment of the population of the Netherlands in general, not just of the various types of Protestants."[5] In a similar way, when Oliver Cromwell intervened in the Savoy in 1656 on behalf of the Vaudois, his expression of religious affinity to fellow Protestants was magnified by concerns over their inhumane treatment at the hands of the Duke of Savoy. He "conceived of the Vaudois," in Trim's words, "as fellow suffering *human beings* rather than simply types of Protestant martyrheroes."[6]

At the same time, key Protestant thinkers of the sixteenth and seventeenth centuries, such as Alberico Gentili and Hugo Grotius, drew upon Roman views about war and peace in ways that, as Richard Tuck demonstrates, left "the door wide open to...humanitarian intervention."[7] Through an intricate combination of Protestant political theory and Roman attitudes to war, Gentili reasoned that while private individuals could not legitimately rise up with force against a tyrannical sovereign—given concerns about endorsing any right of active resistance—an outside sovereign had the right to take up arms on their behalf. He therefore reached the curious conclusion that Queen Elizabeth I's intervention in the Netherlands was legitimate, even if the Dutch revolt was illegitimate.[8] Grotius's writings on the subject of internal dissent and external intervention, in *De Jure Belli ac Pacis*, largely conformed to Gentili's arguments. When contemplating the question of "Whether we have a just Cause for War with another Prince, in order to relieve his Subjects from their Oppression,"[9] he answered with the same combination of non-resistance theory and the right of third-party states to wage war on others' behalf. He also defended a more expansive right of just punishment, grounded in an analogy between individuals and states. Just as individuals in the state of nature enjoyed not only the right to defend their own life but also "the right of chastisement" prior to entering civil society, so too did sovereigns have a right not merely to defend themselves and repel injury but also to punish others' grievous violations of the law of nature.[10] Grotius then went on to outline a range of such violations that sovereigns had a right to punish by war, including acts of piracy, cannibalism, and the excesses of tyranny against a subject population.

As noted by scholars of international relations, the right of war to punish tyranny and rescue populations from oppression was not explicitly articulated by sixteenth- and seventeenth-century theorists in terms of an exception to a sovereign right of non-intervention; this more modern concept was to feature in state practice and discourse much later.[11] To be sure, sovereign authority was understood at this time, particularly in the writings of Thomas Hobbes, to imply both external independence as well as internal supremacy.[12] And while Grotius allowed for war to be waged on behalf of the oppressed, he also cautioned against rulers interfering in each other's affairs, "lest by intruding into each other's Provinces they should quarrel among themselves."[13] Such fears inspired later and more direct articulations of a sovereign right of non-intervention, buttressed by Emerich de Vattel's normative defense of state liberty. But Grotius' own conception of sovereignty did not entail that states had a *duty* to refrain from intervening in each other's affairs—thus making him, as R.J. Vincent suggests, a precursor to, rather than author of, the principle of non-intervention.[14] Similarly, while the Peace of Westphalia did represent a shift toward the centralization and territorial demarcation of political authority into states, it did not instantly enshrine a modern international society governed by principles of sovereign equality and non-interference.[15]

As Vincent goes on to explain, there are two principal reasons why Grotius did not couple his right of sovereignty with an explicit rule of non-intervention as a means of expressing respect for that sovereignty. The first relates to issues of terminology. Grotius simply had no conception of intervention as a distinct practice. The external dimension of sovereignty was conceived and expressed in Grotius' era "not in terms of a right of nonintervention and its exceptions but in terms of a right to wage war and its limitations."[16] Any act of violence by one state upon another was for Grotius (as it was for other early Just War theorists) an act of war. Second, and more importantly, while one of Grotius' seminal contributions was to conceive of a rule-governed international society, he theorized a universal community of *humankind*, in which natural law applied directly to individuals, as well as states. It was only later, in the nineteenth century, that international law would come to understand international society as composed exclusively of sovereign states with hard-wired rights of non-intervention to protect their particular practices of rule and (to use Walzer's words) forms of "common life." But following the logic of Grotius, if an individual is as much a subject of international law as is a state, and if in any dispute an individual's cause can be regarded as just, then external action on behalf of oppressed individuals becomes "not only permissible, it is also honourable."[17]

In sum, despite the image portrayed by the "Westphalian myth"—of a state system post-1648 that was marked by self-contained units of political authority concerned with questions of external rather than internal legitimacy—there were numerous instances of intervention in the affairs of individual sovereign territories to constrain tyrants, respond to violence meted out against particular religious groups, or simply to punish extreme "princely behaviour." Nonetheless, given the gathering strength of a counteracting norm of non-intervention in intra-European relations,[18] and the value that was increasingly placed on its protection of diversity and autonomy, intervening princes and states were more likely to seek a change in a target's policy or behavior, rather than to change the governing authority itself.[19] These were acts of policy correction, not regime change.

The power of non-intervention as a brake on transgressions of sovereignty was also buttressed by the more general rise of positivism in international law. If the law regulating the relations among sovereign states was to emanate from either their express consent (in the form of treaties) or a discernible pattern of practice (in the development of custom), then attempts to ground state rights—or duties—in an immutable law of nature became much more controversial. Indeed, Vattel rejected Grotius' endorsement of the use of force to punish or correct violations of the law of nature, given his skepticism about states' (or individuals') ability to evaluate the actions of other states as right or wrong. Sovereign states, as equal and independent bodies, could not in Vattel's theory "set themselves up as judges over one another."[20]

Walzer's writings on intervention build on this Vattelian legacy, rather than a Grotian one. First, as we see in the early pages of Chapter Six of *Just and Unjust Wars*, there is a clear delineation between war and intervention. Although contemporary analysis often blurs the distinction—think, for example, of the Kosovo "War" of 1999—Walzer conceives of war (and particularly aggressive war) as a crime that merits a response, while intervention is a practice that can in very exceptional cases be legitimate. He shares the Vattelian conception of intervention as a (temporary) transgression of a jurisdiction, designed to reshape or alter "the domestic arrangements or...conditions of life" in a target state. And like any transgression, which breaks a conventional pattern of relations, it "always has to be justified."[21] And second, while Walzer suggests that the rights of territorial integrity and political sovereignty enjoyed by states "derive ultimately from the rights of individuals," his legalist paradigm does not follow Grotius in recognizing individuals as legitimate subjects of international rules and principles. States, not individuals, are the members of his international society.[22]

Following the spirit of the Vattelian paradigm, the legitimate grounds for the use of force gradually narrowed over the course of the late eighteenth and nineteenth centuries as older practices were increasingly deemed illegitimate.[23] In particular, though humanitarian intervention did develop into a coherent *political* notion in the nineteenth century, and was practiced widely by the ancestors of modern-day liberals in crises such as the Greek War of Independence, or the persecution of Christian minorities in the Ottoman Empire,[24] these cases were not generally considered by prominent international lawyers as constituting a legal exception to the hardening rule of non-intervention.[25] Moreover, these responses to massacre and atrocities were not based on a broad philosophy of "secular universalism," or a general call to come to the aid of those who were oppressed, but rather, as the historian David Rodogno argues, on threats to particular religious and ethnic groups.[26] By the early twentieth century, intervention was legally sanctioned only in situations of civil war where clear lines could be drawn between a ruler and his people; it could not be justified as a defense of the rights of the oppressed in other jurisdictions against their sovereign. Most international lawyers, as Walzer notes in *Just and Unjust Wars*, placed the question of humanitarian intervention outside the realm of law altogether, describing it as a matter of politics, policy, or morality.

But the ambiguous status of humanitarian intervention in the nineteenth century—and beyond—was not only a matter for international lawyers. As I have suggested elsewhere,[27] it also stemmed from a set of ethical and political concerns that have continued to shape debates about its standing and legitimacy in the twentieth and twenty-first centuries. These can be roughly grouped into problems related to *motives, consistency, scope,* and *participation*.

The first issue arises from the frequent and unavoidable presence of mixed motives in state action: how can we condone the practice of humanitarian intervention, it is sometimes asked, if interveners have additional motives—beyond humanitarian ones—for employing military force? If there are additional purposes lurking behind action to "save strangers," don't these taint the whole exercise and shape the way interveners act on the ground? The second and related problem is that of inconsistency: why intervention on behalf of the Ottoman Greeks, but not to save Ottoman Armenians? Or, to take a more recent example, why military action to protect Kosovar Albanians but not the victims of the Janjaweed militia in Darfur? Former British Prime Minister Tony Blair once quipped that "just because we can't intervene everywhere doesn't mean we shouldn't act where we can." But the rationale behind the choices that would-be interveners make has often been questioned, as they seem to mount compelling cases to intervene where it is "easy," but appear to leave strategically important allies free from outside interference. "When friendly states commit atrocities," laments one recent critic, "the great powers are wont to look away, offer political cover, or even provide material assistance."[28] Indeed, the selectivity with which powerful states have intervened has been one of the most common concerns motivating opposition to legitimizing the practice of humanitarian intervention.

The third source of concern is one of scope. If a case can be made that armed intervention is required to address a humanitarian emergency, the questions that quickly follow are what kind of military action and what level of force are appropriate. Are humanitarian objectives best served by a sharp and short show of force or do they require a more comprehensive and sustained commitment by outside powers—which in turn could embroil interveners in a long-term campaign? In the contemporary era, this dichotomy between "surgical strike" and "quagmire"[29] has played out most prominently in debates over whether air power alone can protect populations, and condemnations of the way in which the risk aversion of Western states leads to a privileging of force protection over the minimization of civilian casualties.[30] Walzer himself, in a later essay called "The Politics of Rescue," decried the tendency of modern politicians to prioritize the costs to their own soldiers and to themselves, rather than ensuring the appropriate level of force is directed at the perpetrators of atrocities.[31] But worries about how to define and contain the scope of humanitarian intervention have a longer history. The fear of stationing a large army in Asia Minor constrained European powers from responding decisively to the 1909 massacre of Armenians in Adana, just as the reluctance to deploy significant numbers of American forces acted as a break on U.S. intervention under President Obama, just over a century later, in the Syrian civil conflict.

The final issue that frequently features in debates about humanitarian intervention relates to participation: who has the right to act in the "interests of humanity"? Writing just prior to the First World War, French international lawyer Antonine Rougier insisted that not just any old power, no matter how capable, could respond to a violation of the laws of humanity. In order to minimize the risk of self-serving interventions by powerful states, unilateralism had to be outlawed and collective approval made obligatory.[32] In fact, Martha Finnemore highlights the multilateralization of military action as one of the key ways in which the beliefs about the use of force have changed over the past two and half centuries.[33] But multilateral mechanisms only function when consensus is possible: what about those instances in which collective agreement is either unavailable, or too time-consuming to achieve? Despite the frustrations associated with multilateral processes, most states in international society have continued to insist upon them as a means of placing checks and balances on military intervention and taming the unilateral adventures of great powers.[34] It is precisely because the use of coercive means in a society of formally equal members is so controversial that states have sought to subject those means to a form of "rational-legal authority."[35]

Justifying Humanitarian Intervention in the Age of the UN Charter

Walzer's arguments about humanitarian intervention were crafted in a context in which the UN Charter circumscribes much of the legal and political—if not necessarily moral—discussion of the practice. But despite the fact that the Charter established clear limitations on the use of force, effectively outlawing aggression, it did not directly address the question of whether states can use military force to address a humanitarian crisis occurring within the sovereign jurisdiction of another UN member state. The provisions of Article 2 (4) reflect the strong post-war commitment to delegitimizing acts of war outside the context of self-defense and to transferring any authorization for coercive collective security measures to the newly established Security Council.[36] Yet, at the same time, the experiences of genocide and disproportionate uses of force against populations during the Second World War inspired many state representatives to advocate for the promotion and protection of human rights as one of the core purposes and principles of the new international organization. These twin forces resulted in what many portray as an irreconcilable conflict between two core principles of the United Nations system: sovereignty and human rights.[37] The former suggests that states should enjoy sovereign equality—defined internally as exclusive jurisdiction within a territory and externally as freedom from outside interference—while the latter indicates that individual rights are inalienable and transcend sovereign frontiers.

Walzer's carefully constructed revision to the legalist paradigm attempts to take both sets of imperatives seriously, though there are vocal critics who believe that sovereignty fares much better than human rights under Walzer's account. By drawing on the reasoning of John Stuart Mill, he also inserts into the mix a principle that was to gain increasing traction as the membership of international society expanded to incorporate newly decolonized states: the self-determination of peoples. Walzer begins Chapter Six of *Just and Unjust Wars* by setting a high bar on what counts as a legitimate foreign intervention, given the moral weight he attaches to self-determination. His conception of this principle insists that we should presumptively respect local politics and communal ways of life: self-determination is not equivalent to political freedom, nor the institutions and arrangements that protect a community from outside interference, but rather refers to the *process* by which a community comes to have those institutions and arrangements. Self-determination, following Mill, is "the right of a people to become free by their own efforts," and "nonintervention is the principle guaranteeing that their success will not be impeded or their failure prevented by the intrusions of an alien power."[38]

But exceptions there must be—just as Vattel, writing more than two centuries before Walzer, believed both that duties of assistance, on grounds of shared humanity, could legitimize intervention to save tyrannized subjects, and that external states could intervene in situations of civil war when a political community had become so ruptured that belligerent parties effectively became two nations.[39] Walzer, like Vattel, strives to make his exceptional instances of legitimate intervention "as much like non-intervention as possible," by designing them as temporary efforts to restore well-functioning sovereign polities. With respect to cases of humanitarian crisis, Walzer comes to his defense of intervention through further reflection on what "real" self-determination requires, observing that in cases of massacre or enslavement there can be no meaningful self-determination—and thus no communal process for outsiders to respect. External actors are effectively engaged in rescue, rather than intervention in a sovereign jurisdiction, and their action comes closer—in his view—to a form of law enforcement.[40] Walzer also demonstrates his commitment to self-determination by arguing that intervening states should "enter, to some degree, into the purposes of [oppressed] people," even if their task is not to fully realize those local aims. This appears a demanding requirement, given that external actors may not—and indeed often do not—fully share the agenda of those they are seeking to assist, particularly in instances in which oppressed populations are seeking to secede from their parent state. Nonetheless, Walzer maintains that, at the very least, a legitimate humanitarian intervention entails that interveners not prevent local purposes from being achieved. "One cannot intervene on their behalf," he writes, "and against their ends."[41]

More controversially, Walzer also suggests that military victory over those engaged in oppression is "morally necessary," since those who "initiate massacres lose their right to participate in the normal….processes of domestic self-determination."[42] This argument veers onto the contested terrain of whether so-called regime change is, or should be, the ultimate purpose of humanitarian intervention. On first glance, it certainly seems to rule out what many contemporary proponents of the principle of the Responsibility to Protect call for (and certainly called for in the case of Libya in 2011[43])—namely, a limited, or what others have less charitably called an "immaculate intervention,"[44] that focuses solely on short-term civilian protection and remains politically neutral in the broader outcome of a conflict. Walzer's insistence on military victory over the oppressors also fails to address a reality he acknowledges in later writings: that not all situations involving calls for humanitarian intervention feature identifiable tyrants—whereby it is relatively straightforward to "rescue the people in trouble from their troublers"[45]—but rather are marked by intense and long-standing inter-ethnic conflicts, or state failure, in which the victim/victimizer paradigm is less easy to apply. What we have in these cases, in a twist on Hobbes, is a "murderous war of some against some,"[46] where a single identifiable evildoer is illusive.

Walzer's other unusual move is to defend *unilateral* intervention in situations in which acts are being committed that, in his now famous words, "shock the moral conscience of mankind." He writes in his Preface to the third edition that "any state that can stop them, should stop them—or, at the very least, has the right to do so."[47] For Walzer, morality "is not a bar to unilateral action" if there is no available alternative.[48] In fact, he goes on to suggest that United Nations-sponsored action may not necessarily have the moral superiority to unilateral action that so many theorists and lawyers believe. "States don't lose their particularist character merely by acting together," he writes. "If governments have mixed motives, so do coalitions of governments."[49] Walzer has consistently held up three Cold War-era unilateral interventions as examples of effective and legitimate actions to save populations from conscience-shocking acts: India's intervention in East Pakistan in 1971, Tanzania's intervention in Idi Amin's Uganda in 1979, and Vietnam's intervention against Pol Pot's regime in Cambodia in 1979. While he fully recognizes that these "neighborhood" interventions might have entailed old rivalries and new ambitions, as well as humanitarian objectives, he believes their effectiveness in bringing about positive humanitarian outcomes outweighs concerns about unilateralism. Waiting for the United Nations to offer its approval is not always an option.

It is important to note, however, that in some ways it was the UN itself that helped to pave the way for a more acceptable form of humanitarian intervention—or at least a form that was compatible with the views of its member states (especially in the Security Council) as the Cold War was ending. Another way of interpreting the Charter is to recognize the ways in which it left open the possibility of interventions for humanitarian purposes through the directives of the Security Council. The provisions containing collective obligations for the maintenance of international peace and security suggest that sovereignty is not a general and absolute barrier to action. And although Article 2 (7) of the Charter is normally taken as *the* definitive statement of non-intervention, the final phrase of that same article allows for enforcement actions under Chapter VII. This opening, combined with the provisions of Article 39 and 42, gives the Council the right to define what constitutes a threat to international peace and security and to decide on the appropriate type of military action—should it be deemed necessary to counter that threat.

The Security Council was typically reluctant to adopt an expansive definition of threats to peace and security for most of the Cold War period, for reasons that cannot be fully elaborated here. But following the end of the superpower standoff, its members began to utilize the power they always had in theory, to take a broader approach in defining threats to peace and security when dealing with a series of situations involving humanitarian crises. This was particularly visible with respect to the Council's response to the plight of Kurds and Shiites in Northern Iraq in 1991, the famine in Somalia in 1992, the destructive civil war in the Balkans during the 1990s, and the post-referendum violence in East Timor in 1999. All of these situations gave rise to Security Council authorized actions to address various forms of humanitarian crisis. This accumulated practice indicated that the Council had come to see, in the words of one of its resolutions on the protection of civilians in armed conflict, "flagrant and widespread violations of international humanitarian and human rights law in situations of armed conflict" as a threat to the peace.[50] It also revealed at least toleration, if not always active support, among member states for UN-authorized military actions with an expressly humanitarian purpose.

This more activist posture by the Security Council coincided with, and in many ways was facilitated by, three broader features of the international landscape. The first is what is now referred to (nostalgically by some) as the liberal internationalist moment in post-Cold War world politics—a time when Western leaders were confident and bold about promoting the spread of liberal democratic norms, including, when necessary, by force. This was also a period in which leadership from liberal democratic states led to the creation of new institutions, such as the International Criminal Court, which put individual security and not just state security at the heart of international relations. The second feature was regional developments in Africa that attempted to respond to an expected withdrawal of the two superpowers from the continent, and that emphasized the need for African states themselves to take a more proactive and collective approach to maintain peace and security in their "neighborhood." Article 4 (h) of the 2001 African Union's Constitutive Act, which is cited by some as a precursor to the imperative associated with the Responsibility to Protect,[51] thus called upon members of the union to respond collectively in "grave circumstances"—by which it meant the commission of war crimes, crimes against humanity, or genocide. And the final feature was the so-called CNN effect, in which global and instantaneous access to information heightened popular awareness of humanitarian crises and made the case for intervention easier to mount (even if it did not always result in timely or effective action).[52]

While this was undoubtedly a more permissive context for arguments in favor of humanitarian intervention, it is crucial to recognize the very particular conditions that underpinned it. The dominance of Western states aided both the development and diffusion of norms related to human rights, criminal accountability, and atrocity crimes. Moreover, these states were searching for new forms of political legitimacy and "moral author-ity" to replace the ideologically driven politics of the Cold War.[53] But more broadly, humanitarian intervention has always been facilitated by these kinds of material and ideational "hierarchies." This was as true of the early post-Cold War period as it was of the mid-nineteenth century.[54] Although the edifices of some moral philosophers do not bend to these realities of power, Walzer was all too aware of them, and built them into his evolving writing on humanitarian intervention. In "The Politics of Rescue," written in 1994, his list of appropriate candidates for the task of humanitarian intervention is largely dominated by the United States and its allies. Yet he also presciently muses that it is "hard to say how respon-sibility passes on, when the obvious candidates refuse its burdens."[55]

Arguing About Humanitarian Intervention

So how did this period—which we might say reached its nadir in Libya in 2011, and was buried in the rubble of Aleppo under siege in December 2016—affect how we now pass moral judgment on humanitarian inter-vention? There are two ways we can begin to answer this question. The first is to look at the contribution of the principle of the Responsibility to Protect. The second is to examine the impact of actual interventions (and non-interventions) on our moral intuitions.

The Development of RtoP

Seen from one perspective, the two decades between 1991 and 2011 appear to have offered answers to some of the outstanding questions con-nected to humanitarian intervention that were raised by Walzer in the preface to his Third Edition. The first relates to the lack of clarity around the threshold for activating the right of humanitarian intervention. "How much killing is 'systematic killing,'" he asks, and how "bad do things have to be on the other side of the border to justify a forceful crossing?" And second, revisiting long-standing debates about participation, Walzer asks who should carry out a humanitarian intervention. He notes the general problem that intervention, even if justified and necessary, is "an imperfect duty." It doesn't belong to any particular agent. Although someone ought to intervene, "no specific state in the society of states is morally bound to do so."[56] Yet if responsibility is left diffuse, philosophers tell us, it is eas-ier for actors to shirk their obligations, thereby creating a collective action problem. "The more potential rescuers there are," writes James Pattison, "the less the likelihood of the chances of actual rescue."[57]

The principle of the Responsibility to Protect, endorsed by all heads of state in government in 2005 at the World Summit, went some way toward trying to resolve these two problems. Article 138 of the Summit Outcome document acknowledges the primary responsibility of individual sovereign states to protect their own populations from atrocity crimes, and to prevent both their commission and incitement. The subsequent paragraph, Article 139, commits the international community (working through the United Nations) to take collective action, "on a case-by-case basis," using diplomatic, humanitarian and—if necessary—forceful means in situations where national authorities "are manifestly failing to protect their populations" from such crimes. This paragraph also affirms the commitment of the international community to assist states in building the capacity to protect their populations, and to act before crises fully develop.

RtoP's first contribution, then, was to try to specify the conditions under which rescue by the international community—whether through military or non-military means—should be considered. During the 2005 negotiations, states agreed to circumscribe the scope of RtoP, expressly limiting it to four specific *crimes*: genocide, crimes against humanity, war crimes, and ethnic cleansing. This list was similar to those crimes which had been identified in both the 1998 Rome Statute and the 2001 Constitutive Act of the African Union, and therefore reflected a reasonably robust consensus on the acts that constituted the kind of exceptional circumstances that RtoP was designed to address. This formulation also added greater precision to the original notion of "large scale loss of life," that had been set out in the original 2001 Report of the International Commission on Intervention and State Sovereignty (ICISS).[58] While still controversial to those who wish that a broader set of violations could also activate the principle, the definition in the Summit Outcome has become the authoritative interpretation within the United Nations system. It also seems to conform to Walzer's own understanding of actions that "shock the conscience of mankind."

Second, RtoP tries to move away from a discretionary model or right of intervention, toward employing the more demanding idea of a shared responsibility. The notion of *protection* shifted the focus from the claims or rights of intervening states, to the victims of suffering in need of assistance.[59] Furthermore, the moral concept of *responsibility* enlarged the circle of protective actors available to prevent or respond to atrocity crimes.

Each and every state—along with other actors in the international community—therefore has a responsibility to protect.

In setting out this proposition, the principle of RtoP nevertheless created a tier of responsibilities: the primary responsibility of national authorities, the supportive responsibility of the international community to assist states in meeting their protection obligations, and the remedial responsibility of the international community in situations of "manifest failure." In those situations in which coercive means are to be used to implement the RtoP,[60] Article 139 of the Summit Outcome also tried to remedy the "imperfect duty," by requiring that the UN Security Council authorize any military action for humanitarian purposes through its collective security provisions. This intergovernmental consensus on how the coercive dimension of RtoP should be operationalized reflects a continuing concern about unilateralism and thus rests firmly upon multilateral authorization. As Michael Doyle has therefore noted, RtoP can be seen as "both a *license for* and a *leash against* forcible intervention": it legitimizes greater international concern for atrocity-crime situations that occur (or are imminent) inside a state's sovereign jurisdiction, but insists that any coercive response to such situations must be undertaken through "case by case" decisions of the Security Council.[61] But Walzer's lingering worry about multilateralism—that it might not produce timely or effective responses to mass atrocity—remains as relevant as ever.

The Impact of Recent Cases

Moral and political debate on humanitarian intervention has also been profoundly shaped by prominent cases of intervention and non-intervention. This is no more apparent than in Walzer's own writing over the decades, both in the different editions of *Just and Unjust Wars* and in his regular contributions to *Dissent* magazine. His active engagement with the crises of the Cold War and post-Cold War periods has generated what one observer has called a "principled pragmatism," rather than a dogmatic adherence to specific tenets of Just War theory.[62]

In the past decade, ethical reflection on the use of force for humanitarian purposes has been particularly marked by growing concerns about the role of interests in motivating the resort to force, as well as the unforeseen consequences of employing military means; both have combined to limit (or some would say, further limit) the practice of humanitarian intervention. As a consequence, despite the continuing power of individual-centric

rather than state-centric notions of security, and the breadth of the consensus on the need to treat atrocity crimes as matters of *international* (as
opposed to domestic) concern, the presence of a case for humanitarian
intervention today is much less likely to translate into an actual choice to
intervene than it would have in the 1990s or 2000s.

Let's begin with interests. One of the most refreshing aspects of
Walzer's writings on humanitarian intervention, from the perspective
of a political scientist, is that he takes a clear-eyed stance toward the
presence—and potentially productive role—of state interests. His preface
to the third edition is firm on this point: "There is no such thing as a
pure will in political life. Intervention cannot be made to depend upon
the moral purity of its agents."[63] In addition, he mounts the pragmatic
argument that humanitarian intervention might be more effective, and
timely, if neighboring states with concrete interests drive the process of
rescue. This lack of concern for purity of motive is consistent with his
deviation from many other thinkers in the Just War tradition, for whom
"right intention" plays a prominent role in legitimizing the use of force.

Second, as suggested earlier, Walzer cautions us against assuming that
multilateralism does away with particularism or the influence of certain
national interests. "The politics of the UN is no more edifying than the
politics of many of its members, and the decision to intervene, whether it
is local or global, whether it is made individually or collectively, is always
a political decision. Its motives will be mixed; the collective will to act
is sure to be as impure as the individual will to act."[64] This plurality of
purposes, and of the motivating power of interests, was clearly present
in the Security Council's authorization, through Resolution 1973, of
"all necessary measures" to protect civilians in Libya in the spring of
2011.[65] Yet the manner in which disillusionment with the use of force in
Libya gradually coalesced, as more classified information about the case
became publicly available, illustrates how suspicion about mixed motives
can come to dominate subsequent moral and political judgments about
the legitimacy of humanitarian intervention.

The Libyan intervention has also been delegitimized by influential negative assessments about both its short-term and long-term consequences.
The critique of its short-term impact relates to the alleged "creative use"
of the Security Council's imprimatur by NATO forces to target members
of the Qaddafi regime. Once the initial bombing campaign achieved the
objective of preventing the further advance of Qaddafi's forces on Beng-
hazi, NATO widened its list of targets to include more controversial sites

(such as buildings hosting senior political officials in the Libyan chain of command) and some countries in the coalition began providing key support to fighters from the Libyan opposition—in apparent contravention of Security Council resolutions.[66]

These tactical moves by the NATO-led mission sparked intense criticism of the intervention and claims that the legally mandated objective of civilian protection had been overtaken by the broader goal of regime change.[67] For his part, Walzer had always been dubious about an intervention that seemed to lack a clear purpose. Was it designed merely to rescue an imperiled population, he asked, or to rescue a failed rebellion and facilitate the overthrow of Qaddafi? If the former, he argued, there was no case for intervention: the situation in Libya did not reach his threshold of massacre or enslavement. And if the latter, Western-led action was doomed to failure, both because it lacked sufficient Arab support and because it contravened Mill's dictum about the need for freedom to be won from the *inside*. "The overthrow of tyrants and the establishment of democracy has to be local work, and in this case," he wrote, "the locals couldn't do it."[68]

The post-facto assessments of the military campaign in Libya have therefore been dichotomous. For some, March 2011 represented a "coming of age" for RtoP and a sign that states could come together to defend humanitarian principles. As one proponent of the intervention put it: "Libya suggests that we can say no more Holocausts, Cambodias, and Rwandas—and occasionally mean it."[69] But others—especially those Security Council members who had reluctantly allowed Resolution 1973 to pass—have claimed that they were "hoodwinked" by Western powers and now insist that interventions for humanitarian purposes will always be manipulated by the powerful for their own purposes.[70] They also point to the unwillingness of Western interveners to stay the course, and establish a sufficiently robust post-intervention "footprint" to bring stability to post-Qaddafi Libya.

Walzer, of course, had some insight into these problems. On the one hand, he judged humanitarian interventions by the readiness of interveners, once the mass killing has been halted, to leave the premises. This is proof, he suggests in Chapter Six of *Just and Unjust Wars*, that their action is not just another variety of imperialism. But on the other hand, in-and-out missions create their own challenges. As he shrewdly observes in the Preface to the Third Edition, "the same motives that lead some states to refuse to intervene at all may lead others, so recent experience suggests, to move in and out too quickly. They are interested above all in avoiding or reducing the costs of intervention."[71]

Perhaps not surprisingly, it is the longer-term aftermath of the intervention in Libya—most notably the country's descent into chaos—that has had the greatest influence on moral judgments about its impact. One fierce critic of the intervention, Rajan Menon, contends that even though the reality of post-conflict rebuilding is "a protracted and frustrating business," with "malign effects on intended beneficiaries and their neighbours," too many practitioners and scholars of intervention are "so suffused with moral certainty, that they have not considered these problems in any depth."[72] Whether it is appropriate to blame the breakdown in political order in Libya and the rampant insecurity that followed on intervening forces is not for this essay to determine. Nevertheless, the lesson drawn by Menon and others has been clear: third party intervention for humanitarian purposes ultimately does more harm than good. What is more, the controversy surrounding the use of force for humanitarian purposes in Libya had a significant and measurable impact on subsequent policy-making with respect to the ongoing crisis in Syria—most notably the failure of the Security Council to act decisively to address mounting evidence of atrocity crimes.

When they invoke the Libyan precedent, contemporary scholars and policy-makers thus not only reference the age-old concern about the potential for humanitarian rationale to mask deeper and "darker" motives; they also point to the aftermath of the 2011 intervention to emphasize the costs of using military means. The forces of third-party actors always bring chaos and destruction, they contend, leaving societies less stable and more violent than they would have been without external intervention. The combined experience of Western states in Afghanistan and Iraq—military actions that were not humanitarian interventions—have only amplified the power of this lesson learned. Military action to prevent or respond to atrocity crimes is judged today not in terms of whether it meets its immediate goal, but rather in terms of whether the state in which intervention occurs becomes *generally* more stable. And when this test is applied, the conclusion invariably appears to be that the costs outweigh the benefits.

CONCLUSION

Walzer's carefully reasoned exception to the legalist paradigm, which permits an exceptional right of humanitarian intervention, is as compelling today as it was in 1977. His high threshold for the use of force is a useful standard to employ in an international system no longer dominated by liberal internationalists who are tempted by visions of regime change. In addition, his willingness to countenance unilateral intervention by those proximate to a humanitarian crisis—no matter how controversial—may prove especially relevant in a geopolitical context in which multilateral agreement (particularly within the UN Security Council) is likely to remain a rare achievement. Above all, his far-sighted observations on interests and consequences will assist other principled pragmatists in navigating an imperfect world, in which motives will never be singular and calculations about the costs and benefits of intervention will always be an imperfect science.

If we cast our eye over contemporary decision-making with respect to situations that feature atrocity crimes, the pendulum appears to have swung toward inaction. Worries about potential quagmires and the costs of full-scale intervention loom large in Western capitals and show little signs of abating—particularly if we consider the demanding standard with which interventions are judged. Walzer's commitment to action in the face of conscience-shocking crimes suggests that he should be uncomfortable with this resting place. Indeed, in his later commentary on the Syrian conflict, and the tragedy of the refugee crisis it generated,[73] he seemed to acknowledge one of the greatest risks associated with the current obsession in Western societies with the costs of military action: namely, that the costs of "doing nothing" will be systematically underplayed.[74] It is both wise and morally necessary to assess the potential for creating further harm through one's actions; but it is equally important to illuminate and evaluate the effects of *not* acting. Walzer's rich body of work on humanitarian intervention may not have solved all of its dilemmas, but it continues to help us to understand both.

NOTES

1. Michael Walzer, *Just and Unjust Wars: A Moral Argument with Historical Illustrations*, 3rd ed. (New York: Basic Books, 2000).
2. Michael Walzer, "The Case Against Our Attack on Libya," *The New Republic*, March 20, 2011, http://www.tnr.com/article/world/85509/the-case-against-our-attack-libya.
3. Michael Walzer, "Syria," *Dissent*, March 9, 2012. There was some evolution in Walzer's position, as he later mused as to whether earlier Western action in support of the rebels—before jihadi militants flocked into the country and before Russia, Iran, and Hezbollah were fully engaged—might have made a difference in limiting the duration and lethality of the conflict. See Michael Walzer, "Were We Wrong About Syria?" *Dissent*, October 30, 2013.
4. In this chapter, I use the term "atrocity crimes" to refer to the four acts commonly associated with the principle of the Responsibility to Protect, which are specified in paragraph 138 of the 2005 World Summit Outcome Document: genocide, war crimes, crimes against humanity and ethnic cleansing (United Nations 2005).
5. David Trim, "Intervention in European History, c. 1520–1850," in *Just and Unjust Military Intervention: European Thinkers from Vitoria to Mill*, eds. Stefano Recchia and Jennifer M. Welsh (Cambridge: Cambridge University Press, 2013), 35.
6. Ibid., 38.
7. Richard Tuck, "Grotius, Hobbes and Pufendorf on Humanitarian Intervention," in *Just and Unjust Military Intervention*, eds. Recchia and Welsh, 97.
8. Ibid., 104.
9. Hugo Grotius, *De Jure Belli ac Pacis*, 1625, trans. of 1646, ed. by F. W. Kelsey et al., 1925, reprint, New York, 1964. Book II, Chapter 25, section 8.
10. Ibid., Book II, Chapter 20, section 40.
11. See for example, Luke Glanville, *Sovereignty and Responsibility: A New History* (Chicago: Chicago University Press, 2013), 48–49; Martha Finnemore, *The Purpose of Intervention: Changing Beliefs About the Use of Force* (Ithaca: Cornell University Press, 2003), 10.
12. Jonathan Havercroft, "Hobbes, Bellarmine, and the Norm of Nonintervention," *Global Constitutionalism* 1, no. 1 (2012): 120–40.
13. Grotius, *De Jure Belli*, Book II, Chapter 25.
14. R. J. Vincent, *Nonintervention and International Order* (Princeton: Princeton University Press, 1974), 22.
15. For the extensive debate on whether Westphalia represented a "watershed" moment in the development of a modern international system, see

Andreas Osiander, "Sovereignty, International Relations, and the West-phalian Myth," *International Organization* 55, no. 2 (2001): 251–87; Benno Teschke, *The Myth of 1648: Class, Geopolitics, and the Making of Modern International Relations* (London: Verso, 2003); Brendan Simms, "'A False Principle in the Law of Nations': State Sovereignty, [German] Liberty, and Intervention in the Age of Westphalia and Burke," in *Humanitarian Intervention: A History*, eds. Brendan Simms and David Trim (Cambridge: Cambridge University Press, 2011); and Glanville, *Sovereignty and Responsibility*, 49–56. While a measure of religious toleration was endorsed at Westphalia as a means of preventing continued instability and bloodshed, religious affiliation was not completely relegated to the "domestic realm." Instead, as shown by Glanville, the Peace of Westphalia proclaimed in treaty law the responsibility of states to ensure the protection of their religious minorities, and it bound neighboring states to *enforce* this responsibility when necessary. The preservation of religious liberty thus became a matter of *international* responsibility, and a potential pretext for intervention.

16. Glanville, *Sovereignty and Responsibility*, 48.
17. Grotius, *De Jure Belli*, Book I, Chapter 5, Section 2; Book II, Chapter 25, Section 6. See the discussion in Vincent, *Nonintervention and International Order*, 24.
18. In relations between Europe and the non-European world, by contrast, intervention was widely practiced as a tool to reorder and "civilize."
19. Trim, "Intervention in European History," 44.
20. Jennifer Pitts, "Intervention and Sovereign Equality: Legacies of Vattel," in *Just and Unjust Military Intervention*, eds. Recchia and Welsh, 145.
21. Walzer, *Just and Unjust Wars*, 86. For other definitions of intervention as a transgression, see Vincent, *Nonintervention and International Order*, 4–10; Chris Reus-Smit, "The Concept of Intervention," *Review of International Studies* 39, no. 5 (2013): 1057–76.
22. Walzer, *Just and Unjust Wars*, 53, 61. For further comment on Walzer's individualism, both its limits and potential, see the discussions by David Luban, Margaret Moore, and Graham Parsons in Chapters 2, 3, and 11, respectively, of this volume.
23. See Finnemore, *The Purpose of Intervention*. As an example, Finnemore demonstrates that while states had previously intervened legitimately to collect debts owed to their nations by other states, this practice was largely eliminated by the early twentieth century.
24. See Finnemore, *The Purpose of Intervention*; Gary Bass, *Freedom's Battle: The Origins of Humanitarian Intervention* (New York: Knopf, 2008); and David Rodogno, *Against Massacre: Humanitarian Interventions in the Ottoman Empire, 1815–1914* (Princeton: Princeton University Press, 2011).

25. Simon Chesterman, *Just War or Just Peace? Humanitarian Intervention and International Law* (Oxford: Oxford University Press, 2001), 35–44.
26. Rodogno, *Against Massacre*, 11.
27. Jennifer M. Welsh, "Humanitarian Intervention," in *The Oxford Handbook of International Security*, eds. Alexandra Gheciu and William Wohlforth (Oxford: Oxford University Press, 2018), Chapter 31. The discussion on motives, scope, consistency and participation is drawn from this chapter.
28. Rajan Menon, *The Conceit of Humanitarian Intervention* (New York: Oxford University Press, 2016), 99.
29. John Macmillan, "Intervention in the Modern World," *Review of International Studies* 39, no. 5 (2013): 1039–56.
30. For a discussion of risk aversion in the case of the Kosovo war of 1999, see Edward N. Luttwak, "Give War a Chance," *Foreign Affairs* 78, no. 4 (1999): 40–41.
31. Michael Walzer, *Arguing About War* (New Haven: Yale University Press, 2004), 67–68.
32. Antoine Rougier, *La theorie de l'intervention d'humanite* (Paris: A. Pedone, 1910).
33. Finnemore, *The Purpose of Intervention*, 17.
34. Stefano Recchia and Jennifer M. Welsh, "Introduction," in *Just and Unjust Military Interventions*, 4.
35. Finnemore, *The Purpose of Intervention*, 21.
36. Chesterman, *Just War or Just Peace?* 48–49.
37. Thomas G. Weiss, *Humanitarian Intervention* (Cambridge: Polity Press, 2012), 24.
38. Walzer, *Just and Unjust Wars*, 88.
39. For more discussion of Vattel's exceptions to the principle of non-intervention, see Pitts, "Intervention and Sovereign Equality," 145–48.
40. Walzer, *Just and Unjust Wars*, 104.
41. Ibid.
42. Ibid., 106.
43. See, for example, Gareth Evans, "R2P Down but Not Out After Libya and Syria," *Open Democracy*, September 9, 2013, https://www.g-l-f. org/site/global_leadership_foundation/assets/pdf/evans_-_r2p_down_ but_not_out_after_libya_and_syria.pdf. See also Sarah Brockmeier, Oliver Stuenkel, and Marcos Tourinho, "The Impact of the Libya Intervention Debates on Norms of Protection," *Global Society* 30, no. 1 (2015): 113–33.
44. George Friedman, "Immaculate Intervention: The Wars of Humanitarianism," *On Geopolitics*, April 5, 2011, https://worldview.stratfor.com/ article/immaculate-intervention-wars-humanitarianism.
45. Walzer, *Arguing About War*, 70. I have written more fully elsewhere about the difficulties in maintaining a strict dichotomy between victims

and perpetrators in contemporary instances of atrocity crimes. See Jennifer M. Welsh, "The 'Narrow but Deep Approach' to Implementing the Responsibility to Protect: Reassessing the Focus on International Crimes," in *Reconstructing Atrocity Prevention*, eds. Sheri P. Rosenberg, Tibi Galis, and Alex Zucker (Cambridge: Cambridge University Press, 2016), 81–94.

46. Walzer, *Arguing About War*, 70.
47. Walzer, *Just and Unjust Wars*, xii.
48. Ibid., 107.
49. Ibid.
50. United Nations Security Council, "The Protection of Civilians in Armed Conflict," UN doc. S/Res/1296 (April 19, 2000).
51. See, for example, Alex J. Bellamy and Edward C. Luck, *The Responsibility to Protect: From Promise to Practice* (Cambridge: Polity, 2018).
52. Larry Minnear et al., *The News Media, Civil War and Humanitarian Action* (Boulder: Lynne Reinner, 1999).
53. I develop these points more fully in the Introduction to Jennifer M. Welsh, ed., *Humanitarian Intervention and International Relations* (Oxford: Oxford University Press, 2004), 1–2.
54. John Macmillan, "Intervention in the Modern World," *Review of International Studies* 39, no. 5 (2013): 1039.
55. Walzer, *Arguing About War*, 79.
56. Walzer, *Just and Unjust Wars*, xv, xiii.
57. James Pattison, *Humanitarian Intervention and the Responsibility to Protect: Who Should Intervene?* (Oxford: Oxford University Press, 2010), 9.
58. *The Responsibility to Protect, Report of the International Commission on Intervention and State Sovereignty* (Ottawa: IDRC, 2001).
59. Ibid., 15.
60. It is important to underline that while RtoP took a narrower approach to defining the scope of its application—situations featuring atrocity crimes—it advocated a broader set of measures (including non-coercive means) for its implementation.
61. Michael Doyle, *The Question of Intervention* (New Haven: Yale University Press, 2015), 110.
62. Chris Brown, "Michael Walzer," in *Just War Thinkers from Cicero to the 21st Century*, eds. Daniel R. Brunstetter and Cian O'Driscoll (London: Routledge, 2017), 205–15.
63. Walzer, *Just and Unjust Wars*, xiii.
64. Ibid., xvi.
65. The Resolution was passed with 10 votes in favor and 5 abstentions (China, Russia, Brazil, India and Germany).
66. Roland Paris, "The 'Responsibility to Protect' and the Structural Problems of Preventive Humanitarian Intervention," *International Peacekeeping* 21, no. 5 (2014): 569–603.

67. Alan Kuperman, "NATO's Intervention in Libya: A Humanitarian Success?" in *Libya, the Responsibility to Protect and the Future of Humanitarian Intervention*, eds. Aidan Hehir and Robert Murray (New York: Palgrave Macmillan, 2013), 191–221.
68. Walzer, "The Case Against Our Attack on Libya."
69. Weiss, *Humanitarian Intervention*, 172.
70. Doyle, *The Question of Intervention*, 14; Brockmeier et al., "The Impact of the Libya Intervention Debates on Norms of Protection," 123.
71. Walzer, *Just and Unjust Wars*, xiv.
72. Menon, *The Conceit of Humanitarian Intervention*, 14.
73. Walzer, "Were We Wrong About Syria?".
74. Bashar Haydar, "The Bias Against Intervention," paper presented to the Symposium on "Humanitarian Intervention and the Responsibility to Protect," American University of Beirut, January 26, 2017.

BIBLIOGRAPHY

Adler-Nissen, Rebecca, and Vincent Pouliot. "Power in Practice: Negotiating the International Intervention in Libya." *European Journal of International Relations* 20, no. 4 (2014): 1–23.

Annan, Kofi. *In Larger Freedom: Toward Development, Security and Human Rights for All*. UN doc. A/59/2005, March 21, 2005.

———. *Report of the Secretary-General Pursuant to General Assembly Resolution 53/35: The Fall of Srebrenica*. A/54/549, November 15, 1999.

Ban Ki-Moon. *Report of the Secretary-General on Implementing the Responsibility to Protect*. UN doc. A/63/677, July 23, 2009.

Bass, Gary. *Freedom's Battle: The Origins of Humanitarian Intervention*. New York: Alfred Knopf, 2008.

Bellamy, Alex J. "From Tripoli to Damascus? Lesson Learning and the Implementation of the Responsibility to Protect." *International Politics* 51, no. 1 (January 2014): 23–44.

Brockmeier, Sarah, Oliver Stuenkel, and Marcos Tourinho. "The Impact of the Libya Intervention Debates on Norms of Protection." *Global Society* 30, no. 1 (2015): 113–33.

Chesterman, Simon. *Just War or Just Peace? Humanitarian Intervention and International Law*. Oxford: Oxford University Press, 2001.

Doyle, Michael. *The Question of Intervention*. New Haven: Yale University Press, 2015.

Evans, Gareth. "The Responsibility to Protect: An Idea Whose Time Has Come… and Gone?" *International Relations* 22, no. 3 (September 2008): 283–98.

————. *The Responsibility to Protect: Ending Mass Atrocity Crimes Once and for All.* Washington: Brookings Institution, 2008.

————. "The 'RtoP' Balance Sheet After Libya." Available at http://www.globalr2p.org/publications/205. Accessed June 30, 2013.

Finnemore, Martha. *The Purpose of Intervention.* Ithaca: Cornell University Press, 2004.

Grotius, Hugo. *De Jure Belli ac Pacis.* Translation of 1646 edition by F. W. Kelsey et al. 1925. Reprint, New York, 1964.

Haydar, Bashar. "The Bias Against Intervention." Paper presented to the Symposium on "Humanitarian Intervention and the Responsibility to Protect." American University of Beirut, January 26, 2017.

Holzgrefe, J. L., and Robert Keohane. *Humanitarian Intervention: Ethical, Legal and Political Dilemmas.* Cambridge: Cambridge University Press, 2003.

Independent International Commission on Kosovo. *The Kosovo Report: Conflict, International Response, Lessons Learned.* Oxford: Oxford University Press, 2000.

International Commission on Intervention and State Sovereignty. *The Responsibility to Protect: Report of the International Commission on Intervention and State Sovereignty.* Ottawa: International Development Research Corporation, 2001.

Jones, Bruce. "Implementing 'In Larger Freedom'." In *Irrelevant or Indispensible? The United Nations in the 21st Century,* edited by Paul Heinbecker and Patricia Goff. Waterloo: Wilfred Laurier University Press, 2005.

Keene, Edward. "International Hierarchy and the Origins of the Modern Practice of Intervention." *Review of International Studies* 39, no. 5 (December 2013): 1077–90.

Kuperman, Alan. "NATO's Intervention in Libya: A Humanitarian Success?" In *Libya: The Responsibility to Protect and the Future of Humanitarian Intervention,* edited by Aidan Hehir and Robert Murray, 191–221. New York: Palgrave Macmillan, 2013.

MacMillan, John. "Intervention in the Modern World." *Review of International Studies* 39, no. 5 (2013): 1039–56.

McGovern, Alison, and Tom Tugendhat. *The Cost of Doing Nothing: The Price of Inaction in the Face of Mass Atrocities.* London: Policy Exchange, 2017. Available at www.policyexchange.org.uk.

Mill, J. S. "A Few Words on Non-Intervention." In *Dissertation and Discussions: Political, Philosophical, and Historical,* vol. III, 2nd ed., 153–78. London: Longmans, 1875.

Minnear, Larry, Colin Scott, and Thomas G. Weiss. *The News Media, Civil War, and Humanitarian Action.* Boulder: Lynne Reinner, 1999.

Paris, Roland. "The 'Responsibility to Protect' and the Structural Problems of Preventive Humanitarian Intervention." *International Peacekeeping* 21, no. 5 (2014): 569–603.

Recchia, Stefano, and Jennifer J. Welsh, eds. *Just and Unjust Military Intervention: European Thinkers from Vitoria to Mill.* Cambridge: Cambridge University Press, 2013.

Rieff, David. "R2P, R.I.P." *The New York Times*, November 7, 2011. https://www.nytimes.com/2011/11/08/opinion/r2p-rip.html.

Roberts, Adam. "The United Nations and Humanitarian Intervention." In *Humanitarian Intervention and International Relations*, edited by Jennifer M. Welsh, 71–97. Oxford: Oxford University Press, 2004.

Rodogno, Davide. *Against Massacre: Humanitarian Interventions in the Ottoman Empire, 1815–1914.* Princeton: Princeton University Press, 2011.

Shaw, Martin. *Civil Society and the Media in Global Crises.* London: Pinter Press, 1996.

Strauss, Ekkehard. "A Bird in the Hand Is Worth Two in the Bush—On the Assumed Legal Nature of the Responsibility to Protect." *Global Responsibility to Protect* 1, no. 3 (January 2009): 291–323.

Stuenkel, Oliver, and Marcos Tourinho. "Regulating Intervention: Brazil and the Responsibility to Protect." *Conflict, Security and Development* 14, no. 4 (2014): 379–402.

Thakur, Ramesh. "Freedom from Fear." In *Irrelevant or Indispensable? The United Nations in the 21st Century*, edited by Paul Heinbecker and Patricia Goff, 115–30. Waterloo: Wilfred Laurier Press, 2005.

Trim, David. "Intervention in European History, c. 1520–1850." In *Just and Unjust Military Intervention: European Thinkers from Vitoria to Mill*, edited by Stefano Recchia and Jennifer J. Welsh, 21–47. Cambridge: Cambridge University Press, 2013.

United Nations. *Report of the Independent Inquiry into the Actions of the United Nations During the 1994 Genocide in Rwanda.* UN doc. S/1999/1257, December 16, 1999.

———. *2005 World Summit Outcome.* UN doc. A/Res/60/1, September 16, 2005.

United Nations Human Rights Council. *Report of the International Commission of Inquiry on Libya.* UN doc. A/HRC/19/68, 2014.

United Nations Security Council. *Protection of Civilians in Armed Conflict.* UN doc. S/Res/1296, April 19, 2000.

Waltz, Kenneth. *Man, the State, and War: A Theoretical Analysis.* New York: Columbia University Press, 1959.

Walzer, Michael. *Arguing About War.* New Haven: Yale University Press, 2004.

———. *Just and Unjust Wars.* 3rd ed. New York: Basic Books, 2000 [1977].

———. "Syria." *Dissent*, March 9, 2012.

————. "The Case Against Our Attack on Libya." *The New Republic*, March 20, 2011. http://www.tnr.com/article/world/85509/the-case-against-our-attack-libya.

————. "Were We Wrong About Syria?" *Dissent*, October 30, 2013.

Weiss, Thomas G. *Humanitarian Intervention*. Cambridge: Polity Press, 2012.

Welsh, Jennifer M. *Humanitarian Intervention and International Relations*. Oxford: Oxford University Press, 2004.

————. "Humanitarian Intervention." In *The Oxford Handbook of International Security*, edited by Alexandra Gheciu and William Wohlforth, chapter 31. Oxford: Oxford University Press, 2018.

————. "Norm Contestation and the Responsibility to Protect." *Global Responsibility to Protect* 5, no. 4 (2013): 365–96.

Welsh, Jennifer M., and Maria Banda. "International Law and the Responsibility to Protect: Clarifying or Expanding States' Responsibilities?" *Global Responsibility to Protect* 2, no. 3 (2010): 213–31.

Winfield, Percy H. "The History of Intervention in International Law." *British Yearbook of International Law* 4 (1922–1923): 131–34.

War, Collective Responsibility, and Contemporary Challenges to Democracy

Sally J. Scholz

Michael Walzer's account of collective responsibility for unjust wars draws on a principle he takes from J. Glenn Gray's philosophical memoir. The principle states: "The greater the possibility of free action in the communal sphere, the greater the degree of guilt for evil deeds done in the name of everyone."[1] Walzer works with this principle and explores the opportunities for free action in the communal sphere prior to and during a democratic regime engaging in an unjust war. Using the Vietnam War, he addresses the obligations of democratic citizens who voted for the war or "who cooperated in planning, initiating, and waging it" as well as those who failed to vote or voted against the war. Although brief, his analysis offers some careful thinking about responsibility for and in war as well as the variety of methods that might be used to oppose an unjust state action. In this chapter, I reexamine his argument for a new era of warfare as well as new challenges to democracy. When democratic states take a path toward unjustified warfare, collective responsibility and individual obligations of citizenship expand in complexity. Contemporary

S. J. Scholz (✉)
Villanova University, Villanova, PA, USA
e-mail: sally.scholz@villanova.edu

G. Parsons and M. A. Wilson (eds.), *Walzer and War*,
https://doi.org/10.1007/978-3-030-41657-7_5

challenges to democracy, such as an increased focus on national security and an unceasing distribution of media presented as news, demand a reexamination of collective responsibility for unjust war and citizen obligations when democratic states act unjustly.

A fairly robust literature on the topic of democracy and collective responsibility for war has emerged in the wake of the Vietnam era and the subsequent wars in Iraq and Afghanistan. This literature may be parsed according to those accounts that address collective liability for unjust actions of individuals within the collective,[2] political authority in democratic regimes that act unjustly,[3] and individual citizen obligations in the face of unjust collective action.[4] Joel Feinberg rather famously catalogues "collective responsibility" in his essay by that name. His categories of analysis influenced Walzer: liability without contributory fault, liability with noncontributory fault, contributory group fault (collective and distributive), contributory group fault (collective but not distributive).[5] Walzer's account covers these nuances, but I would like to suggest that the account he offers in *Just and Unjust Wars* is unique in how it connects the individual to the collective. Walzer introduces the responsibility to work with others to resist or protest injustice. It is not enough merely to vote against an unjust war; Walzer holds that people armed with adequate knowledge and information are also charged with increased responsibility to oppose an unjust war.

My interest in this chapter is the responsibility and guilt of democratic citizens in a democratic regime that wages an unjust war. Although relevant to collective responsibility and democratic citizenship obligations, such topics as unjust aggression emerging from nondemocratic states or nonstate actors,[6] challenges to civilian immunity and the principle of discrimination,[7] *post bellum* reparations owed to victims of aggression, and *jus in bello* will be addressed only tangentially.

Before turning to Walzer, I illuminate Gray's comment and the context in which it was made. Adopting that comment as a principle, in the second section I trace Walzer's unpacking of the expectations of democratic citizenship given the prospect or potential of an unjust war. The third section reflects on some of the contemporary challenges to democracy with the aim of highlighting the continuing relevance of Walzer's work.

A Citizen-Soldier's Guilt

J. Glenn Gray was a counter-intelligence officer during World War II. His philosophical memoir was written fourteen years after the war and draws on his war journals, revealing his personal experiences as well as his contemporaneous reflections. *The Warriors* is a moving postwar philosophical reflection on some of the most central questions of war: Love, death, guilt, enmity, and peace. Walzer's approach throughout *Just and Unjust Wars* is to use insight from war memoirs and historical accounts of specific wars or battles. Working with Walzer then requires that we respect his approach and be cautious of abstract principles—"illuminations and resolutions" to arguments—not rooted in lived experience. He explains in the postscript to the fifth edition of the book, in relying on abstract principles "I worry that the illumination and resolutions won't ring true to the people I have always tried to address, for whom war is a primary subject and a personal experience."[8] Given this aim, Gray's discussion of individual and political guilt aids in developing a richer understanding of Walzer's account of collective responsibility.

The principle that interests Walzer appears within a much longer discussion of collective guilt from the soldier's perspective. Gray asks one of the most important questions of collective guilt and responsibility: "Why can men do together without conscience things that would torment them unendurably if done singly?"[9] Gray distinguishes individual guilt, political guilt, and metaphysical guilt. He also differentiates the politically conscious soldier from the majority of soldiers who "let the conscience sleep."[10] The latter generally do not consider or feel guilt at the actions of the state of which they are instruments. The soldier whose conscience remains asleep accepts the cause of the war and its justification. He or she finds fulfillment in enacting the will of the state and serving as an instrument in its struggle. The former, the politically conscious soldier, cannot help but feel remorse at war's devastation. Even in just wars, the politically conscious soldier is aware that some innocent people will be killed, that the soldiers he or she is fighting did not choose their cause any more than he or she chose his or hers, and that war, no matter its reason, entails evil.

Political guilt is the concept that concerns us here. Political guilt is guilt that one feels by virtue of being a member of a state that acts in one's name. It is guilt as a member of a political body, guilt that is engendered by the actions of the collective whole. The body politic and the government are separable in theory but political guilt rests also on the realization that a democratic government acts on the authority of the body politic.[11] Political guilt concentrates on the action or inaction of those in whose name the democratic government or state acts.

Immediately preceding the statement that guides Walzer's argument about collective responsibility, Gray discusses the guilt felt by a politically conscious soldier:

> Insofar as his political guilt is in direct relation to his freedom, he will become conscious of what he has done or failed to do to promote or hinder the humanizing of military or political means and objectives. He will be certain at all events that he has not done enough. On this or that occasion he has been silent when he should have spoken out. In his own smaller or larger circle of influence he has not made his whole weight felt. Had he brought forth the civil courage to protest in time, some particular act of injustice might have been avoided. Whatever the level of influence the soldier commands, from the squad or platoon to the command of armies, in some manner he is able to affect the course of group action.[12]

This rich passage reveals quite a lot about political guilt. Political guilt presumes the ability of an individual to influence the course of events, even if in only small or incremental ways. Gray is sanguine about the power of individuals to create change or influence a "smaller or larger circle"; he asserts the need to "recognize our individual freedom and consequent responsibility for our deeds in war and peace."[13] Gray also suggests that it is incumbent upon citizens—and in this case citizen-soldiers—to retain the role of humanizing the body politic even in spite of coordinated efforts to dehumanize or instrumentalize the individual citizens, soldiers, or opponents. The soldier-as-citizen feels as an individual even while he or she acts as a part of a whole. As Gray states, as an individual, the citizen-soldier is "certain…he has not done enough"; this feeling results not from a failure of the individual to act, but rather because one *feels* as an individual. In spite of the mismatch between what one feels and the power of one's actions, one's actions do have power. Protest, persuasive dialogue, courageously taking a stand, exemplify some of the means the citizen-soldier might use both to affect the course of events and to assuage guilty feelings, to respond to the voice of conscience with "I did something."

In the paragraph where Walzer takes his inspiration, Gray is still focusing on the soldier and whether the politically conscious soldier hails from a relatively free state or a totalitarian state. In other words, the passage comes from a discussion of the burden of guilt felt by soldiers. I quote here again the line that Walzer cites as well as the instructive subsequent passage:

> *The greater the possibility of free action in the communal sphere, the greater the degree of guilt for evil deeds done in the name of everyone.* Still, the degrees of guilt are impossible to assess for anyone else, and hardly any two people share an equal burden of communal guilt. The soldier may have been too young as a civilian to have exerted much influence on events or he may have been too poorly informed or confused to know where his political duty lay. As a soldier, he may be in too isolated or insignificant a location to make effective use of his freedom. No citizen of a free land can justly accuse his neighbor, I believe, of political guilt, of not having done as much as he should to prevent the state of war or the commission of this or that state crime. But each can—and the man of conscience will— accuse himself in proportion to the freedom he had to alter the course of events.[14]

I want to highlight three parts of this passage. First, Gray is consistent here and throughout *The Warriors* that guilt, albeit communal in some regard, is experienced as an individual feeling and that no one may judge the degree of guilt of another. Each person shares it differently based on the action that that individual's freedom permitted. Walzer does not agree with this assessment and makes explicit his position that it is possible to judge and assign responsibility to others.[15] Notably, he shifts from Gray's more phenomenological account of degrees of guilt to the moral ascription of responsibility. Guilt for Walzer becomes both shame at actions done in one's name and a level of responsibility for communal or collective action. Whereas Gray accepts that neighbors do not know the content of their neighbors' intentions nor the full extent of their actions, Walzer splits the question of guilt in order to isolate at least some of the blame for collective action.

Second, the case of the soldier is distinct from the case of the citizen. Both Walzer and Gray recognize that the soldier is also a citizen, but that their work as soldiers may compromise their freedom as citizens. The lack of information about politics and the war effort contributes to a structural incapacitation on the part of the soldier.[16] The citizen—especially a citizen of a democratic regime—in contrast, has a slightly better ability to act, depending on the quality and extent of information in the citizen's possession. Walzer and Gray agree on this point.

Finally, Gray emphasizes self-blame and the individual's use of his or her own power to alter the course of collective action. In addition to whether individuals may judge the guilt of another, Walzer and Gray part ways over the sort of blame that one can attribute to oneself. Gray is hesitant to overestimate an individual's ability to change the course of events, saying, "For the deeds of my fellow men, specifically my fellow countrymen, my responsibility cannot be a public or legal one, for it is too dependent on my estimate of my ability to hinder criminal acts and of my inner consent to their commission."[17] For Gray, then, self-blame is tied to the individual's response to his or her conscience. The ability to halt collective action is outside of the individual's control except insofar as he or she participates in the collective action.[18] Walzer takes the relation between guilt and freedom in a slightly different direction than Gray by using guilt as an invitation to scrutinize responsibility for collective actions. He includes the ability to ascribe blame or liability to others as well as the distribution of self-blame.

This richer context of Gray's account of individual and political guilt reveals that the sentence I am calling a principle—"The greater the possibility of free action in the communal sphere, the greater the degree of guilt for evil deeds done in the name of everyone"—concerns the soldier-as-citizen, not the citizen per se. Walzer uses this principle to open a discussion of citizen responsibility, although he does not completely set aside the soldier-as-citizen. This context is especially important for thinking about what Walzer means by collective responsibility and the attribution of blame to citizens. Guilt, rather than liability, motivates the discussion, but both are present. In addition, Walzer means to capture the circumstances of war in order to reveal the limitations of accounts of responsibility articulated for civil society. Something separates war from everyday events or the mundane happenings of civil society; and conceptualizing collective responsibility in the context of war must convey that. In the postscript to the fifth edition of *Just and Unjust Wars*, Walzer identifies three features that mark the uniqueness of war: (1) "the circumstances of war are intensely coercive"[19]; (2) "war is an intensely collective and collectivizing experience"[20]; and (3) "war is a world of radical and pervasive uncertainty."[21] Accounts of collective responsibility for war must reflect the coercive, collectivizing, and uncertain aspects of war.

Responsibility of Democratic Citizens for an Unjust War

As I will show, Walzer unpacks multiple layers of responsibility that cover not only blameworthiness or liability for an action done in the name of the collective, but also the more difficult to attribute political guilt introduced by Gray, shared costs, and civic obligations to collectivize. This latter obligation, the obligation to collectivize, points to the power of certain well-positioned individuals to affect the availability of knowledge about a pending war and to influence the collective moral response in light of the political possibilities by uniting with others. I begin by focusing, with Walzer, on shared costs of state action because they accrue to all citizens equally, and then move on to discuss collective responsibility understood as blameworthiness of citizens for an unjust war of a democratic state.[22]

Importantly, much of Walzer's discussion of collective responsibility falls within the discussion of punishment and reparations after an unjust war. Reparations and collective punishment are among the few *post bellum* obligations that Walzer mentions in *Just and Unjust Wars*.[23] By situating his account of collective responsibility within a discussion of reparations and punishment after the war, Walzer also reaffirms his contention that civilians are not appropriate targets of war. Without getting sidetracked by the question of the moral equality of soldiers, it is important to acknowledge Walzer's position with regard to soldiers who oppose the war and citizens who hawkishly pursue it.[24] Walzer draws the line for targeting during war very clearly between soldier and civilian, regardless of their support for the war. He suggests a parallel to the moral equality of soldiers for civilians: "With reference to the actual fighting, as I have already argued, civilians on both sides are innocent, equally innocent, and never legitimate military targets."[25] Noting that during war we cannot make the distinction between soldiers who are innocent and civilians who deserve to be targeted, he argues that during war "individuals are incorporated into both of these collectives [soldiers and citizens] without regard to their personal and moral standing."[26] But there is a different line drawn for assessing the responsibility or guilt for unjust aggression in war's aftermath. The cost of reparations are shared universally on the basis of citizenship status. Walzer explains, "They [civilians] are, however, political and economic targets once the war is over; that is, they are the victims of

military occupation, political reconstruction, and the exaction of repara-
tive payments."[27] In making this distinction—between citizens as targets
during war and citizens as political and economic targets after the war—
Walzer is implicitly distinguishing forms of collective responsibility. Members of the political collective are liable for the costs of the unjust actions
of their state. They participate in the state and carry the burden of that
authorization.[28] They may not, however, be liable for the war itself (and
hence ought not to be targeted).

Membership in a political community accords citizens certain rights
but those rights carry a cost when the political community acts unjustly.
The costs should be distributed equitably and are not limited to the current generation of citizens.[29] This burden provides some of the justificatory force for individuals assuming more responsibility for affecting the
course of events when they have the means to do so. If the burden for
a state's unjust aggression is borne by all, then individuals will accept
and assume their own individual responsibility more readily. As Walzer
explains,

> costs are distributed through the tax system, and through the economic
> system generally, among all the citizens, often over a period of time extend-
> ing to generations that had nothing to do with the war at all. In this
> sense, citizenship is a common destiny, and no one, not even its oppo-
> nents (unless they become political refugees, which has its costs, too) can
> escape the effects of a bad regime, an ambitious or fanatic leadership, or an
> overreaching nationalism. But if men and women must accept this destiny,
> they can sometimes do so with a good conscience, for the acceptance says
> nothing about their individual responsibility. The distribution of costs is
> not the distribution of guilt.[30]

Walzer's move here is telling. He rightly notes that citizens do have some
ability to participate or not in the actions of their government, or to
accept with or without resistance or protest the unjust actions of their
government, army, or comrades. Walzer separates the individual responsibility from the collective responsibility. The former pertains to one's own
direct actions in perpetrating or resisting injustice. The latter, in the context of reparations, pertains to the common destiny or shared costs of
members of a political community.

He also distinguishes the feelings of shame that one might feel at the
actions of the community from the responsibility or blame (individual

or collective) for those actions. "It might be better to say of loyal citizens who watch their government or army (or their comrades in battle) doing terrible things that they feel or should feel ashamed rather than responsible—unless they actually are responsible by virtue of their particular participation or acquiescence."[31] Walzer's distinctions are tied to Gray's account of political or collective guilt. Using the case of a "conscientious German," Walzer explains that we would expect such a person to feel shame at the actions of the German soldiers, but that responsibility for those actions need not be attributed to him "unless there was something he should have done, and could do, in the face of the horror."[32] This last phrase invites much greater speculation. Although shame is individual, political guilt is shared. Political guilt accrues to each citizen when their state acts unjustly. Is there something that an individual citizen could have done, should have done? Might the tide of horror have been altered in any way?

Walzer thinks so, at least for typical citizens, and he gives a thorough account of individual responsibility within the collective to substantiate his view. Using Gray's dictum—"The greater the possibility of free action in the communal sphere, the greater the degree of guilt for evil deeds done in the name of everyone"[33]—Walzer maps out an account of responsibility for individuals within a state. It is here that he makes the slight shift from assessing guilt after an unjust war to addressing the possibility for individual actions to affect the course of events prior or during a conflict.[34] Inspired by Gray's reflections and his own interpretation of them, Walzer asserts, "the more one can do, the more one has to do."[35] Although authoritarian regimes are not without some possibilities for free action, the principle draws attention to the free action of citizens in a democratic regime.

In cashing out this principle for a democratic regime, Walzer argues that three factors affect the attribution of responsibility: (1) the nature of the democracy, (2) an individual's place in the democratic order, and (3) the individual's pattern of political activities.[36] A perfect democracy is going to distribute the political power and the political responsibility equitably such that policies enacted in the name of the state are, in effect, policies enacted in the name of the citizens. Citizens in a perfect democracy would understand the importance of their participation, even if they do not live up to their democratic obligations all of the time.

Even in perfect democracies, however, a unanimously supported referendum is all but impossible. The citizens of a perfect democracy that decides to engage in an unjust war, then, may be divided into three classes. The first group are those citizens who support the war in concrete ways. In considering who is responsible for an unjust war, Walzer identifies "all those men and women who voted for it and who cooperated in planning, initiating, and waging it."[37] This excludes the soldiers in their role as soldiers but includes them as citizens if they voted for it.[38] Those citizens who vote for the war or otherwise cooperate are "guilty of the crime of aggressive war."[39] Walzer further supports his position in the postscript to the fifth edition saying, "aggressive war is indeed a crime, but it isn't the crime of the ordinary soldiers who fight it. The criminals are the men and women, mostly men, the political and military leaders who consult together and decide, let's say, to attack a neighboring country."[40] Blameworthiness, which might inform moral, social, or even legal punishment, is not shared equally. Those who supported the war with their votes, cooperated in planning it, or took the lead in waging the war are surely blameworthy for the unjust actions of the collective.

The second group or class of citizens are those "who voted against the war or who refused to cooperate in the waging of it."[41] This group, according to Walzer, cannot be blamed for the war. This does not, however, mean that they bear no responsibility at all with respect to the war. They might be blameworthy for failing to take positive actions of resistance—protests, marches, public assemblies, etc.—that could have affected the vote. These failures do not make them guilty of the unjust war but do make them guilty of not doing some simple, nonburdensome acts in order to try to stop the act of aggression. Walzer, then, appeals to two standard principles of morality. The first is explicit: the principle of the Samaritan according to which, "if it is possible to do good, without risk or great cost, one ought to do good."[42] The second is implicit, "one ought to prevent harm to others when it is within one's power to do so without harming oneself." Given the case of war, one's ability to do good is paired with one's ability to prevent quite serious harm, the harm that will undoubtedly affect innocent people on both sides of the hostilities. It is worth pausing here to see that there is something else important going on in this section of *Just and Unjust Wars*.[43]

To these two standards of morality, a third is implied by Walzer: one ought to seek to change the will of the collective when it is within one's power to do so. This is what might be called a duty to collectivize intentionally and differs from the second principle in two key ways. First, preventing harm to others when it is possible to do so without harming oneself implicates the moral actor in a direct relation to the harm-producing event. Seeking to change the will of the collective, in contrast, is an indirect route that only sometimes aims at preventing harm. That is, to say that one ought to seek to change the will of the collective when it is within one's power to do so is to call upon individuals to engage with others: to build a knowledge base, to collect and disseminate information, to articulate opinions in contexts where others may hear and potentially be persuaded, and many more activities. Undertaking these activities may be with the intended purpose of preventing harm (to the collective self or to others) but the activities themselves do not directly prevent harm. Secondly, the principle to prevent harm addresses individual morality, while the duty to collectivize intentionally addresses social morality; the former obliges the individual to act, the latter obliges the individual to act in a way that coordinates with others to collectivize, to seize the power that emerges from uniting with others.

Walzer elides the harm done by a political community with the harm done in the citizen's own name, even though, of course, the moral life of the individual is distinct from the moral status of the collective. Given that the harm is one's own insofar as one is a member of a collective (the political body), and given that one ought to prevent harm when one has the ability to do so, individuals who oppose the war have some obligation to make that opposition known. But Walzer clearly does not leave this obligation as a simple action on the part of the individual. Posting a sign in one's yard in opposition to a war or, the electronic equivalent today, posting a message on social media identifying oneself as a member of the opposition are acts of an individual citizen and some such identifiable opposition (including voting in opposition) is required of the individual who opposes a war. But those actions alone do not fulfill any of the three moral principles at work here. Democratic decision-making, even in a perfect democracy, is not merely a matter of tallying the votes, viewpoints, or opinions of constituent citizens. Democracy involves dialogue with one another, and that dialogue is required for potentially altering the course of events. Of course, a perfect democracy is not realistic so Walzer waits until his discussion of a less than perfect democracy before suggesting three specific duties of citizens in opposition to war.

The third, and perhaps the most troubling, group of citizens in an unjust war are those who did not vote either because they did not wish to take sides or because they were lazy. What do we say about these people? Walzer suggests ("is inclined to say") that they are blameworthy but "not guilty of aggressive war." Note that this is a matter of properly distinguishing citizen roles for a decision taken by a political community.

Citizens who fail to vote are blameworthy for failing to act on their democratic civic obligations and for failing to decide—to take a stance—within that democracy.[44] They are not directly blameworthy for the aggressive war. They are blameworthy for failing to recognize their obligations in and to a collective, and to acknowledge the responsibility such membership entails. Being a citizen in a community is not a passive position. Although the ambivalent or lazy citizen is not blameworthy for the war, they are blameworthy for failing to see and act on the ties that bind them to others in a collective. Those ties do not generally require heroic action (for the citizen) or even public action or awareness-raising and protest. However, the ties that bind citizens in a collective do mean that individual participants must understand that the government acts on the authority of the collective whole, that that collective whole has power, and that individuals within the collective whole play a role in maintaining the authorization of the state, raising questions to affect the course of the state, or challenging the state when or if the citizens decide it has gone astray.[45]

Each of these classes of citizens—those who support the unjust war, those who oppose the war whether merely by voting or also through protest, and those who fail to decide—presume a democratic regime wherein citizen power is equitably distributed and met with respect from governing officials. In other words, they presume a perfect democracy:

> Here, assuming still that the community is a perfect democracy, it looks as if a citizen is blameless only if he takes back his name. I don't think this means that he must become a revolutionary or an exile, actually renouncing his citizenship or loyalty. But he must do all he can, short of accepting frightening risks, to prevent or stop the war. He must withdraw his name from this act (the war policy) though not necessarily from every communal action, for he may still value, as he probably should, the democracy he and his fellow citizens have achieved. This, then, is the meaning of Gray's maxim: The more one can do, the more one has to do.[46]

Notice that the authorization of the state in Walzer's perfect democracy allows for the removal of a dissenting individual's authorization. The nature of the dissenting action is thus contingent on what role one has in a democracy and the pattern of political activities.

Leaving aside the perfect democracy, Walzer acknowledges the difficulty of ascribing responsibility in regimes where information is mediated or controlled by distant officials, imperfect distribution systems, or self-interested media conglomerates. He carves out a space where individual members of an imperfect democracy might be faulted for having bad faith as citizens or for being duped into ignorance of the state's actions but are not blameworthy for an aggressive war.[47] However, as Walzer explains, not every citizen may be so excused for being caught up in patriotic zeal and naïve trust of governmental bodies. There is a significant class of individuals we can expect to have the requisite information and knowledge, as well as the tools of critical awareness (a healthy distrust), which would allow them to make conscientious decisions about the state's actions. These are what Walzer calls the "foreign policy elites." They share particular obligations to oppose aggressive war.

Foreign policy elites, because they have access to the appropriate knowledge, are "at least potentially blameworthy" for aggressive war "unless they join the opposition."[48] Importantly, this expansive group of foreign policy elites includes not just politicians at the national level but also local politicians, religious leaders, corporate executives, and intellectuals. "To say that [they are blameworthy if they fail to oppose the war] is to presume upon the knowledge they have and their private sense of political possibility."[49] Even allowing for the possible effects of "false beliefs, misinformation, or honest mistakes," Walzer "insist[s] that there are responsible people even when, under the conditions of imperfect democracy, moral accounting is difficult and imprecise."[50]

The two powers—knowledge of foreign policy and private sense of political possibility—are intimately tied and in many ways inseparable, but I suggest that the private sense of political possibility is perhaps the more important of the two for three reasons. First, a private sense of political possibility is a recognition of one's own power or role in the acquisition of appropriate knowledge regarding foreign policy. It is, second, an acknowledgment that that knowledge itself imbues the individual with responsibility. And, third, a private sense of political possibility is an active hope that inspires one to act, to recognize that one's own power could influence the course of events in a state.[51] Responsibility is measured not by causal efficacy of one's actions—Walzer is not employing consequentialist reasoning here—but by the obligation assigned to one's role in a democracy.

In his account of the obligations of foreign policy elites, those things that are "morally required of the men and women who are trained to perform them," Walzer offers three practical tasks. His lens is his own position acting in opposition to the war in Vietnam: "we must describe as graphically as one can the moral reality of war, talk about what it means to force people to fight, analyze the nature of democratic responsibilities."[52] All three presume the ability to perform them, including the requisite training and knowledge. Notice that the obligation is not to stop an unjust war, it is to collectivize intentionally: to affect the availability of knowledge of foreign policy for others and to stress the political possibilities for morality, thereby bringing more citizens into the circle of "foreign policy elites." Walzer also recognizes that these are duties performed in the relative safety of a war fought on distant lands and within a democratic regime where acting on these tasks does not subject the agent to unnecessary risk (or risk at all).

The justification for the moral obligation to collectivize intentionally marks Walzer's account as distinct from other discussions of collective responsibility. I am suggesting that we can identify in Walzer's account not only shared collective costs, individual and collective liability or blameworthiness, and individual and collective guilt, but also an individual responsibility to act with others. The content of the duty to collectivize is less clear but we can see from some of his other work[53] a focus on argument and discussion that indicates a commitment to acting on one's knowledge in a way that informs others.[54] Importantly, the obligation to collectivize intentionally does not require foreign policy elites who oppose a war to lead protest movements, but it does suggest that through the actions of sharing their information with the intent of exposing the moral horror of the state in its path toward unjust aggression, the foreign policy elites likely persuade others and gradually create a collective resistance.[55] Citizen led protests and marches are one mechanism of resistance. They may not be effective in the end, but they are a minor inconvenience for the resisters that carry the potential to stop a major harm when a democratic regime is considering waging an unjust war. Protests and other activities meant to persuade and collectivize demonstrate the activity of doing what one can in the face of state action authorized by, but not endorsed by, the citizenry.[56]

Are the non-elites absolved of responsibility? Do the normal civic obligations of citizenship tell us anything about their responsibility for an unjust war? Citizens who are not among the foreign policy elites have civic obligations. Some of those obligations are heightened or augmented during times of war. The non-elites maintain the obligations to participate in democracy, which entails at least some minimal information gathering and knowledge building as well as dedicated commitment to uphold the rights of all citizens.[57] In the anticipation of or during war, this obligation is heightened. By listening to the arguments of the state as well as the arguments of the leaders in opposition, they exercise part of their civic obligations. They exercise another part of their civic obligation when they "take sides."[58] As noted earlier, Walzer expects leaders and citizens "will respect the disagreements of their fellow citizens" as they fulfill their obligation to argue about going to war.[59]

CHALLENGES TO DEMOCRACY

As we have seen, Gray's reflections on World War II served as an inspiration for Walzer's influential book in the wake of the Vietnam war. Walzer's just war position reflects his own commitment to articulate moral reasoning for a democratic people. As he explains in the preface to the third edition,

> only in democratic states are citizens able to join the argument, freely and critically. This book was written for them in the belief that just war theory is a necessary guide to democratic decision-making....The stakes are high when we debate whether to send soldiers into battle...Leaders and ordinary citizens need to worry about, argue about, event fight (nonviolently) about what to do.[60]

Subsequent theorists have similarly taken inspiration from Walzer in the aftermath of the invasion of Iraq in 2003 by a coalition of forces led by the United States. Once again, foreign policy elites, regular citizens, and soldiers-as-citizens were confronted with the potential reality that their state might be acting unjustly in their name. Nearly two decades later, the international community continues to struggle with threats of aggressive action from leaders of democratic states. It might be argued, however, that the nature of the democracies has changed rather profoundly in the decades since Walzer wrote his account of collective responsibility. Two significant facets of that change may be described as an increased focus on national security and a saturation of media.

The state in western democracies more thoroughly took on the guise of protector after the terror attacks of September 11, 2001, directing the so-called legitimate use of force internally as well as externally. National security—rather than welfare, human rights, and education—dominated the political discourse. This focus on national security and responding to terror brought about radical shifts in the experience of democracy for citizens. Privacy, individual rights, and political participation were in varying ways transformed, compromised, or eroded. Also notable during this era is the increased spending on the military (especially in the United States), often at the expense of basic infrastructure improvements, increased funding for education, and creative welfare programs for the most vulnerable among us.[61] The challenges to democracy accompanying the focus on national security range from heightened state power, isolationism, increased socioeconomic inequality, and widespread distrust.

The second major change in the last two decades is the change in media. News from around the globe is available within seconds of an event occurring and in a never-ending cycle. However, that news is often presented and consumed in a skewed fashion. Individual citizens tend to rely on their preferred news provider or social networks to receive news of their own state without global perspective, and experience tragic or fear-inducing events in a disproportionate saturation. Moreover, social media networks and algorithms curate news and information in a way that reinforces consumer's ideological perspectives rather than exposing them to a variety of perspectives and an array of information sources. One is reinforced in one's own position without attaining a greater understanding of other positions. Rather than deliberation, social media actually facilitates a series of insular or egoistic announcements.

The new media environment creates information loops that isolate the spheres of influence within modern democracy. Citizens who receive information only from sources which share their ideology find they understand situations vastly different than those who consume news from opposing networks or sources. At the same time, communication arguably has never been easier. Social media, at least on the surface, appears to bring people together and facilitate discussion that seems to resemble democratic deliberation.

But what do the pervasive news cycles, ideological feedback loops, and social media do to democracy? Recall that Walzer rests the moral obligations of foreign policy elites on the knowledge they have and their private sense of political possibilities. In many democratic regimes, the distance between the political leaders and the people seems to be widening. So too, it might be argued that the foreign policy elites are further from the majority of the people in a number of measures, especially income. However, the distance between foreign policy elites and ordinary citizens might also be collapsing with the availability of news and information.

Perhaps it could be argued that the availability of foreign policy information via the news cycle expands the number of Walzer's foreign policy elites. The availability of information means that many more of us can make decisions about whether a state's actions are just or not. On the other hand, the quality of the information received and the dialogue that ensues ought to be questioned.

As in *Just and Unjust Wars*, in *Spheres of Justice* Walzer asserts that "democracy puts a premium on speech." He briefly considers the possible uses of technology to disseminate information to the citizenry with the hope of obviating the influence that comes from persuasive mechanisms such as compelling talent or social deference to wealth or family. Walzer was rather prescient in his diagnoses of democracy and technology in *Spheres of Justice*. He considers the possibility of modern technology facilitating "push-button referenda on crucial issues."[62] Although Twitter and Facebook are not quite the pure information purveyors that he envisioned, they might be a semblance of what he suggests. The problem, of course, is that we don't merely get information; instead the presentation of facts and figures itself shapes the audience's reasoning. Walzer concludes by saying that such uses of technology, rather than facilitating simple equality in the vote, are "another example of the erosion of value—a false and ultimately degrading way of sharing in the making of decisions."[63]

Elsewhere in his writings, Walzer describes democracy as "a way of allocating power and legitimating its use—or better, it is the political way of allocating power."[64] This new political landscape suggests the need for further reflection about citizen obligations and collective responsibility. Walzer favors a strong form of participation that makes arguments central.[65] It is more significant to be part of the conversation, to try to influence the discussion and the debates, than to merely vote. "Democracy requires equal rights, not equal power. Rights here are guaranteed opportunities to exercise minimal power (voting rights) or to try to exercise greater power (speech, assembly, and petition rights)."[66] The citizen is obliged at least minimally to vote, especially on those matters that carry some consequences. Exercising greater power through assembly or speech is a guaranteed right; in the context of a democratic regime pursuing an unjust war, these powers too ought to be practiced. In order to counter the influence of feedback loops, citizens should seek multiple sources of information and listen to the views of those who oppose them.

As Walzer notes, there is no definite conclusion in democratic politics. Even if citizens who oppose the war do not attain the power to influence the decision to go to war, that is not the end point. "No citizen can ever claim to have persuaded his fellows once and for all." Argument, the activity that is so central to democracy, continues: "The citizen must be ready and able, when his time comes, to deliberate with his fellows, listen and be listened to, take responsibility for what he says and does."[67] When the subject is an unjust war, the obligations of citizenship require putting interests of the state over at least some personal interests—to realize that the state acts on the authorization of citizens, and to vote, to participate, to argue, and to organize.

The civic obligation to collectivize intentionally is under threat by national trends and social trends that pull people apart. Simultaneously, democratic regimes threaten aggression as a "negotiating tactic" on a regular basis. Given these challenges to democracy, individual citizens would do well to remember Walzer's motivating dictum: "The more one can do, the more one has to do." Collective responsibility requires thinking proactively about our democratic rights and obligations, exercising them in small and large ways: voting, listening, arguing in a way that collectivizes rather than factionalizes. Collective responsibility holds democratic citizens responsible for policies, strategies, and actions conducted in their name. But more to the point, it empowers the citizen to take action, to form collectives that have the power to influence governments.

Conclusion

Strictly speaking, the citizens resisting the unjust aggression done in their name commit neither civil disobedience nor have dirty hands.[68] They act on their rights in a democracy. Democracy's freedom not only allows the citizen to speak but requires that he or she do so if he or she has information that might influence others.

Do people have an obligation to oppose an unjust war? Walzer's response is a qualified yes. Those with sufficient knowledge that the war is unjust should vote against it and otherwise make their opposition known. In addition, as we have seen, foreign policy elites who oppose an unjust war should make multiple and varied efforts to convince others to also oppose the war. Those citizens in a democratic regime who are not counted among the foreign policy elites also have regular citizenship responsibilities that oblige them to hear and seek to understand the positions of their fellow citizens, to understand the relation between the citizens (as individuals and as collective) and the government, to claim their own power in influencing the knowledge-base or ideas of others, and to claim their own power in authorizing the state.

Gray focuses on the inescapable feeling of guilt: "Even if he did not consciously will them and was unable to prevent them, he cannot wholly escape responsibility for collective deeds."[69] Walzer takes it a step further to attribute blame, but his position is also full of hope at the political possibilities of individual citizens. Nonetheless, if our state engages in unjust aggression, even if we did not consciously will it and even if we believe we did everything in our power to oppose it, the guilt will remain. And it should. As Gray says,

> We may call it social and political or collective guilt; it is not essentially different for the civilian than for the soldier, and it is inescapable. No matter how self-contained and isolated in spirit the man of conscience may feel, he cannot avoid the realization that he is a participant in a system and an enterprise whose very essence is violence and whose spirit is to win at whatever cost.[70]

The guilt plays the all-important role of keeping citizens in a democracy active, of ensuring that our rights are protected and our authority remains a power in our hands.

Walzer's method serves as a reminder: "wars and battles are not 'cases' to which the law and morality of everyday life can be applied; by definition, they don't take place in civil society."[71] I have argued that Walzer's account of collective responsibility is much richer and more nuanced than is often acknowledged. His account includes not only collective liability or blameworthiness for harms done by the state but also collective costs and collective guilt. Moreover, using the dictum inspired by Gray, "The more one can do, the more one has to do," Walzer articulates a citizen obligation to collectivize intentionally. To keep war out of civil society, individual actors and the collective whole must do their part to maintain civil society and our right to argue against attempts to manipulate the collective will into endorsing unjust aggression in our name.

Notes

1. J. Glenn Gray, *The Warriors: Reflections on Men in Battle* (Lincoln: University of Nebraska Press, 1959), 199. Quoted in Michael Walzer, *Just and Unjust Wars*, 2nd ed. (New York: Basic Books, 1992), 298.
2. E.g., Peter French, ed., *Individual and Collective Responsibility* (Cambridge: Schenkman, 1972); Larry May, *The Morality of Groups* (South Bend: University of Notre Dame Press, 1987); and Howard McGary, "Morality and Collective Liability," *The Journal of Value Inquiry* 20 (1986): 157–65.
3. E.g., Massimo Renzo, "Political Authority and Unjust Wars," *Philosophy and Phenomenological Research* 99, no. 2 (2018): 311–335; Anna Stilz, "Collective Responsibility and the State," *The Journal of Political Philosophy* 19, no. 2 (2011): 190–208.
4. E.g., Virginia Held, "Can a Random Collection of Individuals Be Morally Responsible?" *Journal of Philosophy* 67, no. 14 (1970): 471–48; Lisa Rivera, "Citizen Responsibility for War in Imperfect Democracies," *Dialogue* 48 (2009): 813–40.
5. Joel Feinberg, in *Doing and Deserving* (Princeton: Princeton University Press, 1970), 233–51.
6. Cf. Michael Walzer, "The Moral Standing of States: A Response to Four Critics," *Philosophy and Public Affairs* 9, no. 3 (1980): 209–29.
7. See Seth Lazar, "Just War Theory: Revisionists Versus Traditionalists," *Annual Review of Political Science* 20 (2017): 37–54 for an overview of the revisionist critiques.
8. Michael Walzer, *Just and Unjust Wars*, 5th ed. (New York: Basic Books, 2015), 337. For more discussion of Walzer's method, see David Luban's chapter in this volume.
9. Gray, *The Warriors*, 168.
10. Ibid., 183.
11. Walzer, "The Moral Standing of States."
12. Gray, *The Warriors*, 198.
13. Ibid., 168.
14. Ibid., 199; emphasis added.
15. Michael Walzer, *Just and Unjust Wars*, 2nd ed., 298.
16. Walzer offers a defense of this in his postscript to the fifth edition: "Given the circumstances of war, soldiers have a right to be wrong, and they have a right to think that they may be wrong, and to defer to the decisions of (let's say) their democratically elected leaders. They also have a right to think that though they should oppose the war as citizens, they are bound to fight it as soldiers....And, finally, soldiers have a right to refuse to fight in a war they believe to be unjust; in cases like the Nazi war effort...refusal

is certainly the best response. But it is an act of heroism, and it can't be morally required; unheroic conduct isn't criminal conduct" (Walzer, *Just and Unjust Wars*, 5th ed., 345).

17. Gray, *The Warriors*, 202.

18. Self-blame, or guilt as Gray uses the term, is an important philosophical concept and one worthy of much study. Hannah Arendt, who wrote a preface for the second edition of Gray's book, famously analyzed the collective guilt of Germans in World War II.

19. Walzer, *Just and Unjust Wars*, 339.

20. Ibid., 340.

21. Ibid., 344.

22. Following Walzer, the guilt of soldiers-as-soldiers and soldiers-as-citizens is largely left aside, although the latter is implicated in what is said about the obligations of democratic citizenship.

23. It is not until much later that he endorses a more complete account of *post bellum* obligations. See Michael Walzer, *Arguing About War* (New Haven: Yale University Press, 2004); Walzer, "The Aftermath of War: Reflections on *Jus Post Bellum*," https://berkleycenter.georgetown.edu/events/the-aftermath-of-war-reflections-on-jus-post-bellum, 2010.

24. Walzer, *Just and Unjust Wars*, Chapter 3.

25. Ibid., 296.

26. Ibid., 342–43.

27. Ibid., 296–97.

28. Anna Stilz makes a similar argument using the distinctions of "blame responsibility" and "task responsibility" (Stilz, "Collective Responsibility and the State," *Journal of Political Philosophy* 19, no. 2 (April 2011): 205–6). Stilz does not cite Walzer but her discussion is inspired by responsibility for unjust wars and the cost of reparations. In contrast, see Endre Begby, "Collective Responsibility for Unjust Wars," *Politics* 32, no. 2 (2012): 100–8.

29. Brian Orend disputes Walzer's careful distinction here. Walzer is distinguishing the burden of reparations which falls as a "common destiny" to all citizens from the culpability for the unjust war, which falls only to those who voted for it or who failed to vote but not to those who actively opposed the war. Orend argues that sharing the tax burden among all citizens "fails to respect the discrimination principle during war termination" (Brian Orend, *The Morality of War* [Peterborough: Broadview Press, 2013], 203).

30. Walzer, *Just and Unjust Wars*, 297.

31. Ibid.

32. Ibid., 298.

33. Gray, *The Warriors*, 199.

34. Walzer draws this insight both from the assessment of shared costs and the analysis of guilt.

35. Walzer, *Just and Unjust Wars*, 301. Walzer is not appealing to a principle of causal efficacy, as Rivera, "Citizen Responsibility for War in Imperfect Democracies," argues. The principle bridges the guilt/responsibility divide and in doing so is better understood in deontological rather than consequentialist terms.

36. Walzer, *Just and Unjust Wars*, 299.

37. Ibid.

38. As he explains, we vote as individuals but soldiers fight as "members of the political community, the collective decision having already been made" (ibid., 299, footnote; see also Chapter 3). This, of course, is what has been called the "moral equality of soldiers" and puts Walzer at odds with some scholars working in the just war tradition today. (For a nice overview of the debate, see Mark Wilson, "Michael Walzer," in *Encyclopedia of the Philosophy of Law and Social Philosophy* [New York: Springer, 2018].) It is certainly courageous for individual soldiers to refuse to fight in situations they deem to be unjust but "sharing combat risks with their countrymen" should be tolerated. Walzer adds a caveat however: "we should expect opponents of the war to refuse to become officers or officials" (*Just and Unjust Wars*, 299–300, footnote).

39. Ibid., 300.

40. Ibid., 339.

41. Ibid., 300.

42. Ibid.

43. Gray offers a slightly different assessment because he is most concerned with what the politically conscious soldier feels. See Gray, *The Warriors*, 198.

44. Walzer further notes that in this assessment of their blameworthiness, he differs from Gray who states that citizens cannot blame their fellow citizens for not doing as much as he or she could to stop the war. Gray holds that one can blame oneself but not others; Walzer is here appealing to the collective nature of a moral community and affirming the ability to blame others.

45. Walzer, "The Moral Standing of States," 1980.

46. Walzer, *Just and Unjust Wars*, 301.

47. Ibid.

48. Ibid., 302.

49. Ibid.

50. Ibid., 303. Walzer does not simply dismiss "ordinary citizens" as having "so little influence over events leading to unjust wars that we cannot hold them retrospectively responsible for unjust wars" as Rivera suggests ("Citizen Responsibility for War in Imperfect Democracies," 815). On the

contrary, Walzer acknowledges the less than ideal conditions for various participants in a democracy and associates their responsibility with where they are situated, what roles they play and political activities they engage, and the nature of the democracy in which they participate.

51. See also the role of hope or "historical possibility" in Michael Walzer, *The Company of Critics* (New York: Basic Books, 1988), 17.

52. Walzer, *Just and Unjust Wars*, 303.

53. Michael Walzer, *Spheres of Justice* (New York: Basic Books, 1983).

54. Elsewhere I discuss Walzer's important work on critique (Walzer, *Interpretation and Social Criticism* [Cambridge: Harvard University Press, 1987]; *The Company of Critics*). The critic seeks to articulate the values present in common complaints, to give them power and to envision a different future (*The Company of Critics*, 16–17). Within movements to create social change, critique plays a crucial role to help orient and reorient participants for the cause. See Sally Scholz, *Political Solidarity* (State College: Penn State Press, 2008), Chapter 3.

55. I thank the editors for noting a similarity here between Walzer's view and Iris Young's view (see esp. Young, *Global Challenges* [Cambridge: Polity, 2007]).

56. Walzer chastises oppositional movements for the infighting that characterizes so much of oppositional politics (e.g., *The Company of Critics*, 22). The duty to collectivize must accommodate dissent without that dissent becoming self-defeating.

57. Maintaining citizen rights is at least one way to curtail pernicious attempts on the part of the government to abridge citizen power thereby creating the structural conditions for unjust government-led aggression. (Harry van der Linden discusses structural injustices in "Iris Young, Radical Responsibility, and War," *Radical Philosophy Review* 17, no. 1 [2014]).

58. Walzer identifies the taking of sides as especially important in modern democracy (*The Company of Critics*, 17).

59. Walzer, *Just and Unjust Wars*, 3rd ed. (New York: Basic Books, 2000), xvi.

60. Ibid.

61. Max Roser, "Democracy," *Our World in Data*, https://ourworldindata.org/democracy based at the University of Oxford.

62. Walzer, *Spheres of Justice*, 306.

63. Ibid., 307.

64. Ibid., 304.

65. Hence he favors caucuses over primaries because it closes the gap between leaders and voters; local leaders have to discuss their positions with voters in a caucus and voters don't just show up to vote, they engage in the hard work of deciding.

66. Walzer, *The Spheres of Justice*, 309.

67. Ibid., 310.
68. Michael Walzer, "Political Action: The Problem of Dirty Hands," *Philosophy and Public Affairs* 2, no. 2 (Winter 1973): 160–80.
69. Gray, *The Warriors*, 197.
70. Ibid., 195.
71. Walzer, *Just and Unjust Wars*, 5th ed., 337.

BIBLIOGRAPHY

Begby, Endre. "Collective Responsibility for Unjust Wars." *Politics* 32, no. 2 (2012): 100–8.
Feinberg, Joel. *Doing and Deserving*. Princeton: Princeton University Press, 1970.
French, Peter, ed. *Individual and Collective Responsibility: Massacre at My Lai*. Cambridge, MA: Schenkman Publishing, 1972.
Gray, J. Glenn. *The Warriors: Reflections on Men in Battle*. Lincoln: University of Nebraska Press, 1959.
Held, Virginia. "Can a Random Collection of Individuals Be Morally Responsible?" *Journal of Philosophy* 67, no. 14 (1970): 471–81.
Lazar, Seth. "Just War Theory: Revisionists Versus Traditionalists." *Annual Review of Political Science* 20 (2017): 37–54.
May, Larry. *The Morality of Groups*. South Bend: University of Notre Dame Press, 1987.
McGary, Howard. "Morality and Collective Liability." *The Journal of Value Inquiry* 20 (1986): 157–65.
Orend, Brian. *The Morality of War*. 2nd ed. Peterborough: Broadview Press, 2013.
Renzo, Massimo. "Political Authority and Unjust Wars." *Philosophy and Phenomenological Research*. Online Early View (2018). https://doi.org/10.1111/phpr.12487.
Rivera, Lisa. "Citizen Responsibility for War in Imperfect Democracies." *Dialogue* 48 (2009): 813–40.
Roser, Max. "Democracy." *Our World in Data*. https://ourworldindata.org/democracy based at the University of Oxford. Accessed March 29, 2019.
Scholz, Sally. *Political Solidarity*. State College: Pennsylvania State University Press, 2008.
Stilz, Anna. "Collective Responsibility and the State." *Journal of Political Philosophy* 19, no. 2 (2011): 190–208.
Van der Linden, Harry. "Iris Young, Radical Responsibility, and War." *Radical Philosophy Review* 17, no. 1 (2014): 45–62.
Walzer, Michael. *Arguing About War*. New Haven: Yale University Press, 2004.

———. *Interpretation and Social Criticism.* Cambridge: Harvard University Press, 1987.

———. *Just and Unjust Wars.* 2nd ed. New York: Basic Books, 1992.

———. *Just and Unjust Wars.* 3rd ed. New York: Basic Books, 2000.

———. *Just and Unjust Wars.* 5th ed. New York: Basic Books, 2015.

———. "Political Action: The Problem of Dirty Hands." *Philosophy and Public Affairs* 2, no. 2 (Winter 1973): 160–80.

———. *Spheres of Justice.* New York: Basic Books, 1983.

———. "The Aftermath of War: Reflections on *Jus Post Bellum.*" 2010. https://berkleycenter.georgetown.edu/events/the-aftermath-of-war-reflections-on-jus-post-bellum. Accessed July 25, 2018.

———. *The Company of Critics.* New York: Basic Books, 1988.

———. "The Moral Standing of States: A Response to Four Critics." *Philosophy and Public Affairs* 9, no. 3 (1980): 209–29.

Wilson, Mark. "Michael Walzer." In *Encyclopedia of the Philosophy of Law and Social Philosophy.* New York: Springer, 2018. https://doi.org/10.1007/978-94-007-6730-0_317-1.

Young, Iris Marion. *Global Challenges.* Cambridge: Polity, 2007.

CHAPTER 6

Peacebuilding and Counterinsurgency: Alternatives to the Moral Dilemma of War

Lisa Sowle Cahill

I

This chapter proposes that even morally justified war and other uses of armed force[1] always involve moral agents (individual and collective) in irreducible moral dilemmas because war entails the killing of human beings. An irreducible moral dilemma exists when no matter what course of action an agent chooses, and despite the fact that the agent acts for a greater good, that agent is simultaneously responsible for causing evil and so incurs guilt. Refusal to choose or inaction would still involve the agent in responsibility for evils that could have been averted, or goods realized, by action. Michael Walzer refers to this kind of dilemma as "the problem of dirty hands," and suggests that it is an inevitable part of the role of a politician.[2] I want to suggest that irreducible moral dilemmas are a much more pervasive reality in human moral experience, even when we are "doing the right thing."[3] And, I will argue, killing is always such a moral dilemma.

L. S. Cahill (✉)
Boston College, Chestnut Hill, MA, USA
e-mail: cahilll@bc.edu

© The Author(s) 2020
G. Parsons and M. A. Wilson (eds.), *Walzer and War*,
https://doi.org/10.1007/978-3-030-41657-7_6

105

Therefore, I will conclude, it is a *moral obligation* to avoid war, end war, and reduce killing in war—even just war—by nonviolent means as far as possible. After clarifying further why war is a moral dilemma, I will argue that the just war approaches of Augustine and Aquinas are inadequate because they attempt to resolve this dilemma and fail. I will propose further that they do tacitly recognize that killing in war could be a moral dilemma, and I will draw on Michael Walzer to make this case explicit, although Walzer argues that killing is a moral dilemma only when it targets noncombatants. Again drawing on Walzer, I borrow his critique of double effect to present nonviolent conflict transformation as an obligatory alternative to war. Finally, I will propose that peacebuilding overlaps with the military counterinsurgency mission in that both employ this alternative for moral as well as pragmatic reasons.

The basic and universal wrongness of killing, no matter what the circumstances, can be based on religious teaching, such as the New Testament love command, or the idea that all persons are created in God's image. The U.S. Catholic bishops warn, "the possibility of taking even one human life is a prospect we should consider in fear and trembling."[4] Yet the bishops believe that the duty to respect all human lives derives from basic human dignity, not only Christian teaching. And so do I. Addressing the immunity of noncombatants and the moral equality of soldiers, the philosopher Seth Lazar argues that all people have "moral status." Moreover, the inherent moral status of human beings is generally recognized, even though "explaining this is no easy task."[5] In a recent book on human equality, Jeremy Waldron takes up the challenge, arguing that natural human equality is based on a range of complex capabilities such as love, reason, and moral agency, not realized to the same degree or in the same way in every individual. Basic equality is not lost on account of wrongdoing.[6]

Seth Lazar says that people can lose their right not to be killed when they pose an unjustified threat. However, I would describe such a situation differently. When someone poses a lethal threat to others, killing may be warranted to protect other human lives. Yet because all human beings have equal basic moral status and dignity, deliberately killing a human person, even for a justified cause, is always at the same time a violation of their dignity. A moral dilemma arises precisely when an agent is morally obligated to undertake an action that on the whole is just; yet the action involves some aspect which is an objective violation of justice, such as the abrogation of an individuals' dignity or rights. Yet external observers or judges should refrain from imputation of blame to (or infliction of punishment on) the agent, if the action was on the whole just, if the good accomplished was also morally obligatory, if the wrong done was significantly less than the wrong avoided, and if there were no morally preferable alternatives.

Therefore, even in the rare instance in which killing may be seen as just and necessary, it is still a moral dilemma, and is properly accompanied not only by regret but remorse.[7] The agent who kills bears moral culpability and guilt for his, her, their, or its actions, and is obligated to take remedial, compensatory, and preventive measures. While I believe this is true even when killing combatants, it is even more obviously true when noncombatants become casualties of war, as they inevitably do. But even if one does not accept the premise that killing unjust aggressors constitutes a moral dilemma, war itself may be characterized as a moral dilemma for numerous reasons: justice and injustice can exist on both sides, characterizations of war as just or unjust are always interested not disinterested, putatively just wars can achieve no more than imperfect justice,[8] wars inevitably kill noncombatants, wars destroy basic conditions of human security and leave lasting personal and social "wounds,"[9] few combatants intentionally serve an unjust cause,[10] and few political leaders and political communities responsible for fomenting unnecessary wars are brought to justice. For all these reasons, war is never purely "just."

II

Augustine and Aquinas are the two most important influences on Christian just war thinking. However, I maintain that they do not satisfactorily resolve the conflict between killing and the duty to respect the dignity of every person, captured most saliently for them in the command of Jesus to love both neighbors and enemies. While Augustine commendably sees love as always operative in the Christian life, in every circumstance,[11] he inconsistently (and implausibly) argues that killing in just war is an expression of love for the one killed; and that a peace-seeking inward intention of love can be personally separated from, yet militarily expressed by, an outward action of killing.[12] If this were true, veterans of war would not be experiencing so many cases of post-traumatic stress syndrome and "moral injury," which can follow from the clash of soldiers' moral values with what they are required to do in war.[13] It is evidently not the case that a soldier can readily separate personal intention from outward action, or resolve dire moral conflicts in this manner, as Augustine proposes.

While Aquinas commendably stays away from making killing an act of love, defining right intention and just cause in terms of the "common weal," he maintains that only the clergy must always abide by the love command, while the laity may set it aside for the sake of the common good.[14] By taking away from warriors the obligatory force of the love command, at least when necessary for the common good,[15] Aquinas also eliminates the pressure to think about the moral and Christian meaning of "dirty hands"—applied by Walzer to cases in which an agent acts rightly for the greater good, but wrongly in relation to a moral rule or obligation that was in the process sacrificed. The paradigm case for Walzer is a politician whose role demands that he or she prioritize the greater good for the community and its survival.[16]

In contrast to the majority just war tradition, both Augustine and Aquinas give hints of an underlying worry that perhaps just war theory may be incapable of resolving the moral dilemma of war after all. Augustine seems to recognize that moral dilemmas exist. Similarly to Walzer on "dirty hands," he refers to a hypothetical judge whose role requires him to mandate torture, as doing "numerous and important evils" because "human society...compels him to this duty." Although he calls this judge "blameless," he also says true happiness eludes him, which is significant because for Augustine true virtue is the necessary and sufficient condition of happiness.[17] Augustine reiterates that even when politics and government accomplish the closest thing to "tranquility of order" that is historically possible, political life and certainly war are still full of happiness-destroying "miserable necessities" from which the judge prays to be delivered.[18] In the same vein, he refers to even just wars as full of "great evils" and lamentable "misery."[19]

Aquinas uses an early version of the principle of double effect to argue that defensive killing is justified as long as an equal or greater good (saving life), not the killing itself, is the primary object of the agent's intention.[20] As Walzer notes, this use of double effect in the just war tradition much "too easily" reconciles moral prohibitions (even absolute moral prohibitions) with "the legitimate conduct of military activity."[21] Interestingly though, in writing about the nature of evil (not killing specifically), Aquinas also asserts that "if evil is always or in most cases associated with the good intrinsically intended, the will is not excused from sin, although the will does not intrinsically intend the evil." He says that if a woodsman in a remote area kills someone with a falling tree, he is morally off the hook for this unforeseen accident. But shooting to kill is presumably not excused because of the relative certainty of death.[22] The possibility of a genuine moral dilemma raises its unseemly head in this concession.

The implicit recognition by Augustine and Aquinas of the existence of moral dilemmas in war converges with the explicit argument of Michael Walzer, who maintains that in a case of "supreme emergency...one might well be required to override the rights of innocent people."[23] Walzer defines a supreme emergency as the grave and immediate endangerment of the survival of a political community. I don't think this is enough, as political communities with long historical roots, traditions, narratives, and values can bear distorted fruits, as illustrated for example by the massacre of Bosnian Muslims by the Christian nationalist Serbs at Srebrenica. The same might be said of white nationalism in the U.S. today or even National Socialism. Objectively speaking, there's no supreme emergency when the survival of a radically unjust political community is endangered.

What really must be at stake in a supreme emergency is the victory of a morally monstrous evil greater than the morally monstrous act of killing innocent people. This is why many people draw an absolute line against torture but not killing. Torture attacks the moral core of a person in a way killing does not, making torture too a morally monstrous evil. In this vein, Walzer tacitly expands and deepens his own definition of supreme emergency, by specifying that Nazism was a threat not only to a political community, but to "everything decent in our lives," as "evil objectified in our world," a "threat to human values" (not only to a political community) that was "radical" and imminent.[24] Walzer's concept of a supreme emergency asserts the existential reality of grave, morally compromising dilemmas that cannot be avoided or resolved.

The verdict Walzer offers on the compromising roles of military commanders and political leaders, in light of the possibility of supreme emergencies, applies as well, I believe, to the role of the ordinary soldier who is expected to kill morally equal oppositional combatants[25] and to engage in actions in which risk to civilian lives is foreseen and certain. Walzer says that such agents have "dirty hands, though it may be the case that they had acted well and done what their office required." "They have killed unjustly, let us say, for the sake of justice itself," and they "bear a burden of responsibility and guilt."[26] They should not be legally responsible, according to Walzer; nor in my view should they be blamed or condemned as individuals, so that those really responsible (which may include heads of state and society at large) can evade disapprobation and hypocritically reaffirm their values.[27] What should then be done?

Here let us turn to Walzer's use of the principle of double effect, which he sees as reducing the moral justification of doing things like killing non-combatants to a simple criterion of proportionality.[28] What is important about Walzer's revision of double effect in the war context is that when an evil effect like "indirectly" killing noncombatants is contemplated, the agent must take "due care" to avoid the risk, and minimize the evil, accepting greater risks to combatants, if necessary.[29]

I hold that this is true of all killing in war, as well as of destruction of social infrastructure, means of livelihood, and natural environment; a "burden of responsibility and guilt" accrues in such cases, just as with the "dirty hands" of military and political officials. When an agent is confronted with irreducible moral dilemmas, guilt cannot be avoided, and the proper response is not only regret but remorse.[30] Therefore, these dilemmas should be prevented, forestalled, or circumvented by every means possible. This is a moral obligation.

A more morally appropriate, effective, compensatory, and solidaristic alternative to violent force is to actively promote initiatives that circumvent or remedy the damage done by war and constructively point the way to a more just and less violent future. Indeed, Augustine lights the way to such alternatives in a recently translated collection of letters he wrote to fellow bishops in North Africa, networking to lobby for the amelioration of imperial policies on things such as capital punishment, slavery, onerous taxes, and refugees.[31] That Augustine also pressed for humane and restorative practices in the wake of war (today known as *jus post bellum*[32]) is suggested by his counsel to the general Boniface: "You must be a peacemaker, even when you go to war, and help those whom you defeat to know the importance of maintaining peace...Mercy must be shown to those who have been defeated or captured, especially when they pose no threat to the future peace."[33]

III

Peacebuilding (also known by terms such as Just Peace and Just Peace-making[34]) is a salient alternative to the use of armed violence by political authorities. Peacebuilders use nonviolent means to resist unjust power, to transform conflicts, and to instigate broad social momentum favoring change. Nonviolent civil resistance and conflict mediation are not utopian and can be effective, as several reports from the USIP have shown.[35] Peacebuilding is recognized and promoted by the United Nations, the

United States Institute of Peace, and religious entities such as the World Council of Churches and the Roman Catholic Church.[36] The Catholic Peacebuilding Network, with which I have been involved as a theological consultant, has worked especially in the Great Lakes region of Africa, Colombia, and Mindanao, the Philippines.[37]

The USIP gives quite a comprehensive definition of peacebuilding, though most initiatives focus concretely on one or a few of these goals:

> Originally conceived in the context of postconflict recovery efforts to promote reconciliation and reconstruction, the term peacebuilding has more recently taken on a broader meaning.... it also includes conflict prevention in the sense of preventing the recurrence of violence, as well as conflict management and postconflict recovery. In a larger sense, peacebuilding involves a transformation toward more manageable, peaceful relationships and governance structures—the long-term process of addressing root causes and effects, reconciling differences, normalizing relations, and building institutions that can manage conflict without resort to violence.[38]

Peacebuilders often work in the midst of conflict situations, networking and building bridges in local communities, to bring hostile parties together through sharing of experiences and hopes, or to work for a common goal or project, such as safe passage in and out of a village, education for children, or a delimited "zone of peace" in which no arms will be allowed. Sometimes their aim is to repair past damage sufficiently to enable restoration of cooperative social life; sometimes it is to reduce ongoing violence, or to avoid the new outbreaks likely when simmering tensions are exploited by stakeholders who feel their interests are not well-served by peace deals. A key dimension of peacebuilding is to work broadly in civil society, drawing power from the participation of local communities. Peacebuilding can be a risky business, because it can involve mediation attempts with insurgents, paramilitary, or military forces who are still armed, accustomed to killing, and far from convinced of the merits of an agreement assuring security and political rights to their adversaries.

The priority of nonviolent conflict resolution is strongly affirmed by religious leaders and faith-based activism, even when just war theory is not entirely repudiated. The use of armed force as a last resort for self-defense and in humanitarian intervention is accepted by many Christian leaders and religious social ethicists who have denounced violence as frequently self-defeating and a contributing factor to ongoing cycles of violence,[39] or who have moved to so-called "restrictive" or "stringent" just war theory.[40] This approach prioritizes negotiation, political solutions, and conflict-reduction in local communities by nonviolent methods. Pope Francis calls nonviolence a "strategy of politics for peace," citing the examples of Mahatma Gandhi and Khan Abdul Ghaffar Khan in the liberation of India; of Dr. Martin Luther King Jr. in the U.S. civil rights movement; and of Leymah Gbowee, leader of the Liberian women's peace initiative that ended the civil war and was recognized with a Nobel Peace Prize. Pope Francis claims that "nonviolent peacebuilding strategies" can engage "even the most violent parties in efforts to build a just and lasting peace."[41]

The practical feasibility of nonviolent strategies in the face of terrorism, civil wars, political violence, ethnic conflict, or other non-state armed conflict, is confirmed by social scientists working on conflict and nonviolent resistance, and in reports from the United States Institute of Peace.[42] According to Maria Stephan, the director of the Program on Nonviolent Action at the USIP, nonviolent movements "make a firm commitment to non-violent discipline, when they say, 'We are going to fight for our rights, our freedoms, non-violently. This is how it's going to be done,' it creates just a sense of focus and unity...." Moreover, when violence is used against "demonstrably peaceful protestors," repressive regimes lose support and legitimacy, which "helps to build momentum and a sense of confidence in people, even in places where protests have been squashed in the past."[43] Faith-based organizations and leaders can support such movements because they have powerful and pervasive social presence, networking with governments and with other entities in civil society, especially in the global South.

IV

Although military theory and strategy are far outside my area of expertise, I want to suggest that the concept and practice of peacebuilding overlap with some work of the United States Armed Forces, and presumably with military education at institutions such as the United States Military Academy at West Point. I see parallels between peacebuilding and the U.S. military doctrine and mission of "counterinsurgency," deriving from U.S. military experience in Iraq and Afghanistan in the mid-2000s. From a military perspective, peacebuilding as counterinsurgency begins not from a local popular movement, although it may help bolster or partner with one. Instead, it begins with the presence of U.S. military forces in other countries, both for the purpose of protecting U.S. interests and for the related goals of ending violent insurgencies and establishing or reestablishing human security and stable political institutions in the occupied or "host" country. This suggests that foreign military forces will always be at a relative disadvantage in terms of understanding local relationships, grievances, resources, and priorities, all of which are necessary to successfully defuse violence and forge cooperative partnerships with stakeholders, whether they are grassroots leaders and religious authorities, local governments, or national parties and powers.

Arguably, the mission of using diplomatic, economic, or other nonviolent means to accomplish these goals should ideally be lodged with the United Nations Peacebuilding Commission, or the United States Department of State, either of which would be better positioned than the U.S. military to send experienced civilian teams equipped with strategies of negotiation, pressure, and persuasion which would by definition be nonviolent.[44] However, due to domestic political conflict, tensions within or around U.N. initiatives, and consequent lack of funding, these alternative entities were unable to supply adequate levels of support to nonviolent strategies in Iraq and Afghanistan. Hence, nonviolent counterinsurgency tactics were a military mission born of necessity. While U.S. Army troops in Iraq, then Afghanistan, were charged with the mission of defeating armed insurgents, they learned from experience that countering violence with violence was often unsuccessful. Hence the meaning of "counterinsurgency" efforts shifted to include the burden of devising more creative approaches.

As it evolved in the work and writing of Generals Stanley McChrystal, David Petraeus, and H.R. McMaster, a military counterinsurgency response regards "information flows, collaboration, and ultimately the support of the civilian population" as "key to achieving strategic objectives." In other words, targeting suspected insurgents with deadly force, especially when there is a significant risk of killing noncombatants (as with drones) is insufficient and often counterproductive. In fact, limiting civilian casualties and avoiding other actions that alienate the population, and instead enlisting their support through social initiatives, is "part of a winning strategy" in pursuit of the political goals that military tactics were originally intended to support.[45] Even more importantly from my point of view, protecting civilians and building relationships with and among local communities is also a "moral imperative."[46] In 2010, David

Petraeus, despite acknowledged increased risk to U.S. military personnel from a policy of "courageous restraint," placed "protection of Afghan civilians and protection of service members as equal moral imperatives."[47]

The 2014 Army field manual *Insurgencies and Countering Insurgencies*, specifies that counterinsurgency entails activities such as building civil institutions; humanitarian and security assistance; and advocating that the local population, especially the next generation, be educated and empowered to participate in legal political discourse, dissent, and "political mobilization of the people." Counterinsurgents should not limit their efforts to intellectual elites, but address the root causes of conflict and violence that concern the rural poor. Counterinsurgents should also ensure access to basic services such as schools and medical treatment, according to the manual.[48] The 2018 Armed Forces Counterinsurgency manual reiterates that counterinsurgency (COIN) depends on "support of the relevant population," especially through "economic and infrastructure development" to anticipate and deter the actions of armed insurgents.[49]

Some important features of religious peacebuilding resonate with the types of initiatives carried out under the umbrella of counterinsurgency. These include the need to enlist religious leaders and communities as key social actors with the potential for constructive influence, as well as to work interreligiously. It is also essential to recognize and enhance women's role as peacebuilders, and to engage young people in building civil society and political participation. Successful peacebuilding is a multi-pronged and multilayered set of initiatives, from local and "grassroots," to midlevel and top-level governance and leadership within a national entity, to transnational organizations, and finally to international and global lines of authority, policy, resources, and influence.[50] That being said, counterinsurgency has always been controversial, precisely because it exceeds the more strictly military goal of defeating the presence of insurgents in specified territories. The aim of creating stable local governments and competent indigenous security forces, not to mention sustainable political institutions, is extremely open-ended, requiring ongoing collaboration with partners who may be unavailable or unreliable.[51] Moreover, they may have interests and objectives divergent from those of the United States.

Finally, both peacebuilding and counterinsurgency carry inherent and inescapable moral dilemmas. Joseph Felter probes a case of "courageous restraint" in which "a twenty-two-year-old platoon leader just a few months out of West Point" must decide what to do about his platoon sergeant's order to drop a bomb on a building that the platoon leader knows is a compound ordinarily occupied by an extended Afghan family.[52] The platoon leader, Lieutenant Jones, has heard instruction from commanders all the way up to General McChrystal to limit civilian casualties and protect the population. Meanwhile the platoon is taking fire, and Lieutenant Jones is already thinking about the letters he will have to write to the parents of the four soldiers wounded or killed so far. He could try to clear the building with "direct fire weapons" which would pose a much greater risk to his platoon. As Felter says, "there is a gut-wrenching guilt and responsibility that comes with this and can haunt you for a lifetime." In effect, Lieutenant Jones is in the midst of a genuine moral dilemma. There may be reasons to prefer one of his alternatives over the others, but it will still carry with it responsibility and guilt.

V

Nonviolent civil resistance and peacebuilding after conflict, even when relatively successful, come with a moral price too. Just as in Afghanistan, civilian peacebuilding requires the careful negotiation of competing needs and interests in situations where the building of trust is an uphill battle. While social trust requires that there not be impunity for human rights violations, bringing perpetrators to account may require force and can add fuel to cycles of conflict. Reparations should be paid to victims, but their suffering is frequently incommensurate with any compensation, and compensation requires resources that may be scarce and certainly will be contested. To establish democratic participation and the rule of law requires political cooperation among or between previously feuding parties; but new alliances can serve the interests of elite negotiators more than "the people," and can be disingenuously exploited by those who want to reestablish adversarial control. Similar questions can be raised about nonviolent action to avert war and other direct uses of force. Economic sanctions can cause suffering and death as effectively as killing, albeit less quickly. Persuading would-be combatants to lay down arms can demand "unholy alliances" unlikely to secure long-lasting democracy and peace. Treaties and compromise are sure to dissatisfy if not antagonize one side or another, and the cost will be borne by religious, ethnic, or racial minorities, and in every case, women—the most active grassroots peacemakers—who suffer gender-based violence even after peace accords.[53]

These dilemmas are mirrored in the difficulties counterinsurgency may have, for instance, in identifying legitimate grievances behind local populations' narratives of exploitation or oppression, then persuading the "host" nation to take effective action against underlying causes of grievances and violence.[54] Challenges become even more complex when conflicts involve ethnic groups or transnational forces that go beyond relations between national governments and populations within their borders.[55] Imperfect a strategy as it is however, peacebuilding involves agents in fewer and less extreme moral dilemmas than armed force and killing, and it is also more likely to lead to sustainable peace.

Ultimately, peacebuilding—a category in which we might include nonviolent counterinsurgency tactics—is not only morally necessary, it is humanity's best hope to move from the injustice of just wars to an enlarged sphere of just peace. War always, not exceptionally, carries grievous evils in its wake. And despite the fact that Michael Walzer once announced "the triumph of just war theory" in public political discourse about war,[56] politicians, presidents, and potentates will always invoke the language of justice to whip up popular support for unjust uses of force. Moreover, instances are rife, and perhaps increasing, of uses or proposed uses of military force simply on the basis of national interest or demonstration of national power. This does not mean that just war theory is completely irrelevant or ineffective, or that it needs to be jettisoned. As Michael Walzer concludes, just war theory "is designed to sustain a constant scrutiny and an immanent critique of war."[57] Yet I would emphasize even more than Walzer, his observation that, even if political leaders and generals speak the language of just war theory, and even if they do so sincerely and not merely rhetorically, "we still have to insist that war is a morally dubious and difficult activity."[58] It is always so, notwithstanding the merits of just war validation and immanent critique, or even the expansion of just war criteria themselves (especially *jus post bellum*)[59] to capture long-standing and wide-ranging obligations that accompany even relatively just wars. Hence the injustice of war must be the center of gravity of its moral analysis, and peacebuilding its necessary and simultaneous alternative.

NOTES

1. Wars between or among nation-states have radically declined since World War II, but the numbers of civil wars, "societal wars," and terrorist attacks have risen in the past two decades. The greatest number of deaths in armed conflicts today are civilian, from 5% at the turn of the last century to 90% in the wars of the 90s. See Mauro F. Guillén, "Wars Between States Are Down, but Civil Wars Are Up," September 6, 2016, https://www.nytimes.com/roomfordebate/2016/09/06/is-the-world-becoming-safer/wars-between-states-are-down-but-civil-wars-are-up?mcubz=0; accessed August 17, 2017 and UNICEF, "Impact of Armed Conflict on Children," https://www.unicef.org/graca/patterns.htm; accessed September 17, 2017.

2. In "Political Action: The Problem of Dirty Hands," *Philosophy and Public Affairs* 2, no. 2 (1973): 160–80, Walzer argues that the role of the politician requires "dirty hands" because the agent's primary responsibility is the greater good, even when it cannot be pursued without breaking moral rules. Walzer uses the same example as Augustine—torture. The politician acts rightly by prioritizing the greater good, for that is his or her role. However, in so doing, "he commit[s] a moral crime and he accept[s] a moral burden. Now he is a guilty man" (167).

3. This definition is potentially too expansive, applying to any choice that foregoes other options, thus trivializing the concept of a moral dilemma. Here I intend the concept to refer to any choice in which every option involves evils significant enough so that most reasonable moral agents would regard them *prima facie* as "never to be done."

4. United States Conference of Catholic Bishops, *The Challenge of Peace: God's Promise and Our Response* (Washington, DC: United States Catholic Conference, 1983), no. 40.

5. Seth Lazar, "Evaluating the Revisionist Critique of Just War Theory," *Daedalus* (Winter 2017): 119.

6. Jeremy Waldron, *One Another's Equals: The Basis of Human Equality* (Cambridge, MA and London, UK: Harvard University Press, 2017).

7. The reality of genuine moral dilemmas can be substantiated with reference to the work of philosophers Bernard Williams, Rosalind Hursthouse, and Rosemary Kellison. Its importance to the consideration of just war will be developed in relation to the work of Michael Walzer, especially *Just and Unjust Wars* and his 1973 article, "Political Action: The Problem of Dirty Hands." On the latter, see below.

8. Mark J. Allman and Tobias L. Winright, "Growing Edges of Just War Theory: *Jus ante bellum, jus post bellum,* and Imperfect Justice," *Journal of the Society of Christian Ethics* 32, no. 2 (2012): 173–91.

9. See Daniel Philpott, *Just and Unjust Peace: An Ethic of Political Reconciliation* (Oxford and New York: Oxford University Press, 2012).

10. See Walzer, *Just and Unjust Wars*, 338–46; "mostly soldiers believe their war is just, for reasons that seem sufficient to them" (345).

11. This is reflected in the "personal advice" he gives to the Christian general Boniface, whom he advises to make "daily progress" in living out Jesus' command to love God above all, and "your neighbor as yourself" (Augustine, "Letter 189, to Boniface," in *Saint Augustine: Letters*, vol. 4 [165–203], trans. Wilfrid Parsons, SND, vol. 30 of *The Fathers of the Church*, ed. Roy J. Deferrari [New York: Fathers of the Church, 1956], nos. 1–3; citing Mt 22: 37–39).

12. Augustine, "Reply to Faustus the Manichean," in *Writings in Connection with the Manichean Heresy*, trans. R. Stothert (Edinburgh: T&T Clark, 1953), XXII.76; "Letter 138, to Marcellinus," in *Saint Augustine: Letters*, vol. 3, trans. Wilfrid Parsons (Washington, DC: Catholic University of America Press, 1953).

13. Cf. David Grossman, *On Killing: The Psychological Cost of Learning to Kill in War and Society* (New York: Open Road Media, 2014); Tobias Winright and E. Ann Jeschke, "Combat and Confession: Just War and Moral Injury," in *Can War Be Just in the 21st Century? Ethicists Engage the Tradition*, eds. Tobias Winright and Laurie Johnston (Maryknoll, NY: Orbis, 2015), 169–87; and Pristo R. Hernandez, US Army Command and General Staff College, "Killing in War as a Persisting Problem of Conscience," *Journal of Catholic Social Thought* 11, no. 1 (2013): 203–28.

14. Thomas Aquinas, *Summa Theologiae*, trans. Fathers of the English Dominican Province (New York: Benziger, 1948), II-II.Q40.

15. For Aquinas (as for later Catholic social teaching), the "common good" is not the simple equivalent of the "greater good." It does not refer to the greatest good of the greatest number, but the participation of all in a just society. Thus the common good is compatible with some absolute norms against violating the rights of individuals. This heightens the problem involved in allowing killing for "the common good," a problem that Aquinas resolves (like subsequent just war tradition) in terms of the right of self-defense against an aggressor (including situations in which the aggression has already occurred but the effects remain; cf. Gregory M. Reichberg (who misleadingly refers to such situations as "offensive war"), *Thomas Aquinas on War and Peace* [Cambridge: Cambridge University Press, 2018], 276).

16. Michael Walzer, "Political Action: The Problem of Dirty Hands," *Philosophy and Public Affairs* 2, no. 2 (1973): 163, 166–68.

17. Augustine, *City of God*, trans. Marcus Dods (New York: Random House, 1950), XIX.6.

18. Ibid., XIX.6, 13, 17.

19. Ibid., XIX.7.
20. Thomas Aquinas, *Summa Theologiae*, II-II.Q64.a7.
21. Walzer, *Just and Unjust Wars*, 153.
22. Thomas Aquinas, *On Evil*, ed. Brian Davies (New York: Oxford, 2003), 1.3.15.
23. *Just and Unjust Wars*, 258 (*JUW*, 252).
24. Ibid., 252. I also have a question about whether defining and justifying supreme emergencies in advance undermines their status as extraordinary and begins to normalize them.
25. Walzer defends the moral equality of combatants against philosophical critics in a "postscript" to the fifth edition of *Just and Unjust Wars*, 338–46. I agree with what he says there.
26. Ibid., 323.
27. Walzer offers as a commendable example of national repentance "the dishonoring of Arnold Harris," for carrying out "British terror bombing during World War II," a policy authorized by Winston Churchill (*Just and Unjust Wars*, 323–25). I take Walzer's point about reestablishing the national moral framework, but this one includes hypocrisy if not impunity. At the very least it is not sufficient. The Marshall Plan might be a better, more proactive example.
28. This is not actually true of double effect as it developed over time, since it came to require that the evil effect not be the means to the good, and that the act with two effects not be one that is ruled out in advance as "intrinsically evil." Both these conditions are controversial and perhaps incoherent. But that is a side issue.
29. Ibid., 158–59.
30. I understand guilt to refer to objective blameworthiness, while remorse is a personal stance akin to repentance. Not all who are guilty experience remorse, while not all who experience remorse are objectively blameworthy. Even in a justified use of armed force, killing a human being with equal basic status is morally problematic, even if not outrightly wrong, considering the context as a whole. I see guilt and remorse as properly entailed by the killing of any human being, especially from the standpoint of the agent. In some cases, it is fair to say that the agent "did the right thing"—yet rightly experiences remorse.
31. Consult work of Robert Dodaro, for example, *Christ and the Just Society in the Thought of Augustine* (Cambridge: Cambridge University Press, 2004) and "Between the Two Cities: Political Action in Augustine of Hippo," in *Augustine and Politics*, eds. John Doody, Kevin L. Hughes, and Kim Paffenroth (Lanham, MD: Rowman & Littlefield, 2005), 99–116.
32. See Allman and Winright, "Growing Edges of Just War Theory."
33. "Letter 189: To Boniface," no. 5.

34. See Pierre Allan and Alexis Keller, eds., *What Is a Just Peace?* (Oxford and New York: Oxford University Press, 2006); Philpott, *Just and Unjust Peace* (New York: Oxford University Press, 2015); Maryann Cusimano Love, "Just Peace and Just War," *Expositions* 12 (2018): 60–71; Glen H. Stassen, *Just Peacemaking: The New Paradigm for the Ethics of Peace and War* (Cleveland, OH: Pilgrim Press, 2008); and Susan Brooks Thistlethwaite, ed., *Interfaith Just Peacemaking: Jewish, Christian, and Muslim Perspectives on the New Paradigm of Peace and War* (New York: Palgrave Macmillan, 2012).

35. See Erika Chenoweth and Maria J. Stephan, *Why Civil Resistance Works: The Strategic Logic of Nonviolent Resistance* (New York: Columbia University Press, 2011); Maria J. Stephan, "Adopting a Movement Mindset to Address the Challenge of Fragility," USIP *Policy Brief*, https://www.usip.org/sites/default/files/Fragility-Report-Policy-Brief-Adopting-a-Movement-Mindset-to-Address-the-Challenge-of-Fragility.pdf; accessed September 18, 2017; and Maria J. Stephan, Sadaf Lakhani, and Nadia Naviwala, "Aid to Civil Society: A Movement Mindset," USIP *Special Report*, February 23, 2015, https://www.usip.org/publications/2015/02/aid-civil-society-movement-mindset; accessed September 18, 2017; and on potential religious contributions, as exemplified by the Roman Catholic Church, see Maria J. Stephan, "What Happens When You Replace a Just War with a Just Peace," USIP, May 18, 2016, https://www.usip.org/publications/2016/05/what-happens-when-you-replace-just-war-just-peace; accessed June 3, 2019.

36. For an overview of religious peacebuilding, see Susan Hayward, "Religion and Peacebuilding," US Institute of Peace *Special Report* (Washington, DC: United States Institute of Peace, 2015).

37. See the website of the Catholic Peacebuilding Network, http://cpn.nd.edu/; accessed June 5, 2019.

38. Dan Snodderly, ed., *Peace Terms: A Glossary* (Washington, DC: USIP, 2013), 40.

39. See the World Council of Churches website, "Promoting Just Peace," https://www.oikoumene.org/en/what-we-do/promoting-just-peace; accessed June 3, 2019 and Pope Francis, "Nonviolence: A Style of Politics for Peace," World Day of Peace Message, 2016, http://w2.vatican.va/content/francesco/en/messages/peace/documents/papa-francesco_20161208_messaggio-l-giornata-mondiale-pace-2017.html; accessed June 3, 2019.

40. See Gerard F. Powers, "From an Ethics of War to an Ethics of Peacebuilding," in *From Just War to Modern Peace Ethics*, eds. Heinz-Gerhard Justenhoven and William A. Barbieri, Jr. (Boston: De Gruyter, 2012), 275–311; Lisa Sowle Cahill, "Catholic Tradition on Peace, War, and Just War," in *Just Peace Ethic Virtue-Based and Case-Refined*, ed. Eli S.

McCarthy (Washington, DC: Georgetown University Press, forthcoming 2019); and Lisa Sowle Cahill, "Official Catholic Social Thought on Gospel Nonviolence," April 2016, website of the Catholic Nonviolence Initiative, https://nonviolencejustpeacedotnet.files.wordpress.com/2016/05/official_cst_on_gospel_nonviolence.pdf; accessed June 4, 2019.

41. Pope Francis, "Nonviolence: A Style of Politics for Peace," no. 4.

42. See note 33 above; as well as Maria J. Stephan, "Maria Stephan on Today's Nonviolent Movements," interview, May 30, 2019, USIP website, https://www.usip.org/publications?keywords=%22Maria%20J.%20Stephan%22; accessed June 3, 2019.

43. Ibid.

44. See Maryann Cusimano Love, "What Kind of Peace Do We Seek? Emerging Norms of Peacebuilding in Key Political Institutions," in *Peacebuilding: Catholic Theology, Ethics, and Practice*, eds. Robert J. Schreiter et al. (Maryknoll, NY: Orbis, 2010), 56–91.

45. Joseph L. Felter and Jacob N. Shapiro, "Limiting Civilian Casualties as Part of a Winning Strategy: The Case of Courageous Restraint," *Daedalus* (Winter 2017): 44. See also Joseph H. Felter, "Ethical Choices in War and Peace," *Bulletin of the American Academy of Arts & Sciences* (Winter 2017): 71–75.

46. Ibid., 55.

47. Ibid., 53–54.

48. Department of the Army, FM 3-24, MCWP 3-33.5, *Insurgencies and Countering Insurgencies* (Washington, DC, May 2014), 10-7 to 10-24; https://fas.org/irp/doddir/army/fm3-24.pdf; accessed September 20, 2017. For an on-the-ground memoir by the political advisor to General Raymond T. Odierno (later Secretary of the Army), as he and General David Petraeus were developing the background to this policy in Afghanistan in 2007, see Emma Sky, *The Unraveling: High Hopes and Missed Opportunities in Iraq* (New York: Public Affairs, 2015).

49. Chairman of the Joint Chiefs of Staff, Joint Publication 3–24, *Counterinsurgency*, 25 April 2018, "Executive Summary," https://www.jcs.mil/Portals/36/Documents/Doctrine/pubs/jp3_24.pdf; accessed June 4, 2019. For a development of similar counterinsurgency "lessons," see Lt. Col. Jesse McIntyre III, "Got COIN? Counterinsurgency Debate Continues," *Military Review Online*, September 2018, https://www.armyupress.army.mil/Journals/Military-Review/Online-Exclusive/2018-OLE/Sep/Got-COIN/; accessed June 4, 2019. A peace treaty signed in 2016 by the Afghan government and the Hezb-e Islammi militant group was the result of protracted negotiations, and illustrates the interdependence of military, political, and economic goals. The treaty's success will depend on restoring political stability and reducing unemployment and economic stagnation (William Byrd, "Afghanistan's Economic Development Hinges

on the Peace Process," September 4, 2018, USIP, https://www.usip.
org/publications/2018/09/afghanistans-economic-development-hinges-
peace-process; accessed June 4, 2019).

50. John Paul Lederach, *Building Peace: Sustainable Reconciliation in Divided Societies* (Washington, DC: USIP, 1997).

51. James F. Jeffrey, "Why Counterinsurgency Doesn't Work," *Foreign Affairs*, February 16, 2015, https://www.foreignaffairs.com/articles/united-states/2015-02-16/why-counterinsurgency-doesnt-work; accessed June 4, 2019. See also Karl W. Eikenberry, "The Limits of Counterinsurgency Doctrine in Afghanistan: The Other Side of the COIN," *Foreign Affairs*, September/October 2013, https://www.foreignaffairs.com/articles/afghanistan/2013-08-12/limits-counterinsurgency-doctrine-afghanistan; accessed June 4, 2019.

52. "Limiting Civilian Casualties as Part of a Winning Strategy."

53. See for example a report on the Democratic Republic of Congo: Johanna Mannergren Selimovic et al., *Equal Power—Lasting Peace: Obstacles for Women's Participation in Peace Processes* (Johanneshov, Sweden: The Kvinna Till Kvinna Foundation, 2012), http://kvinnatillkvinna.se/en/publication/2013/04/30/equal-power-lasting-peace-2012/; accessed April 26, 2017.

54. *Counterinsurgency* 2018, 1–3.

55. Matthew Cancian, "FM 3-24-2.0? Why US Counterinsurgency Doctrine Needs an Update," Modern War Institute at West Point, Special Series, February 21, 2017, https://mwi.usma.edu/fm-3-24-2-0-us-counterinsurgency-doctrine-needs-update/; June 4, 2019.

56. Michael Walzer, "The Triumph of Just War Theory (and the Dangers of Success)," *Social Research* 69 (Winter 2002): 925–44.

57. Ibid., 942.

58. Ibid., 935.

59. See Mark Allman and Tobias Winright, "Growing Edges of Just War Theory: *Jus Ante Bellum, Jus Post Bellum*, and Imperfect Justice."

BIBLIOGRAPHY

Allan, Pierre, and Alexis Keller. *What Is a Just Peace?* Oxford: Oxford University Press, 2006.

Allman, Mark J., and Tobias L. Winright. "Growing Edges of Just War Theory: *Jus Ante Bellum, Jus Post Bellum*, and Imperfect Justice." *Journal of the Society of Christian Ethics* 32, no. 2 (2012): 173–91.

Aquinas. *On Evil.* Edited by Brian Davies. Translated by Richard Regan. Oxford: Oxford University Press, 2003.

———. *The "Summa Theologica"* ... *Literally Translated by Fathers of the English Dominican Province*. New York: Benziger, 1948.

Augustine. *City of God*. Translated by Marcus Dods. New York: Random House, 1950.

———. *Saint Augustine Letters*. Translated by Wilfrid Parsons. New York: Fathers of the Church, 1956.

Chenoweth, Erica J., and Maria J. Stephan. *Why Civil Resistance Works: The Strategic Logic of Nonviolent Conflict*. New York: Columbia University Press, 2011.

Dodaro, Robert. *Christ and the Just Society in the Thought of Augustine*. Cambridge: Cambridge University Press, 2004.

Doody, John, Kevin L. Hughes, and Kim Paffenroth. *Augustine and Politics*. Lanham, MD: Lexington Books, 2005.

Felter, Joseph H. "Ethical Choices in War and Peace." *Bulletin of the American Academy of Arts & Sciences* LXX, no. 2 (2017): 71–75.

Felter, Joseph H., and Jacob N. Shapiro. "Limiting Civilian Casualties as Part of a Winning Strategy: The Case of Courageous Restraint." *Daedalus* 146, no. 1 (2017): 44–58.

Grossman, David. *On Killing: The Psychological Cost of Learning to Kill in War and Society*. New York: Open Road Media, 2014.

Insurgencies and Countering Insurgencies. Washington, DC: Headquarters, Department of the Army; Headquarters, Marine Corps Combat Development Command, Department of the Navy, Headquarters, United States Marine Corps, 2014.

Justenhoven, Heinz-Gerhard, and William A. Barbieri. *From Just War to Modern Peace Ethics*. Berlin: De Gruyter, 2012.

Lazar, Seth. "Evaluating the Revisionist Critique of Just War Theory." *Daedalus* 146, no. 1 (2017): 113–24.

Lederach, John Paul. *Building Peace: Sustainable Reconciliation in Divided Societies*. Washington, DC: United States Institute of Peace Press, 1997.

Love, Maryann Cusimano. "Just Peace and Just War." *Expositions* 12 (2018): 60–71.

Philpott, Daniel. *Just and Unjust Peace: An Ethic of Political Reconciliation*. New York: Oxford University Press, 2015.

Reichberg, Gregory M. *Thomas Aquinas on War and Peace*. Cambridge: Cambridge University Press, 2018.

Schreiter, Robert J. *Peacebuilding: Catholic Theology, Ethics, and Praxis*. Maryknoll, NY: Orbis Books, 2010.

Stassen, Glen Harold. *Just Peacemaking: The New Paradigm for the Ethics of Peace and War*. Cleveland: Pilgrim Press, 2008.

The Challenge of Peace: God's Promise and Our Response—Pastoral Letter of the National Conference of Catholic Bishops on War and Peace. Washington, DC: United States Catholic Conference, 1983.

Thistlethwaite, Susan Brooks. *Interfaith Just Peacemaking: Jewish, Christian, and Muslim Perspectives on the New Paradigm of Peace and War.* New York, NY: Palgrave Macmillan, 2012.

Waldron, Jeremy. *One Another's Equals: The Basis of Human Equality.* Cambridge, MA: The Belknap Press of Harvard University Press, 2017.

Walzer, Michael. *Just and Unjust Wars: A Moral Argument with Historical Illustrations.* 5th ed. New York: Basic Books, 2015.

———. "Political Action: The Problem of Dirty Hands." *Philosophy and Public Affairs* 2, no. 2 (1973): 160–80.

———. "The Triumph of Just War Theory (and the Dangers of Success)." *Social Research* 69 (2002): 925–44.

Winright, Tobias L., and Laurie Johnston. *Can War Be Just in the 21st Century? Ethicists Engage the Tradition.* Maryknoll, NY: Orbis Books, 2015.

CHAPTER 7

Fighting Versus Waging War: Rethinking *Jus in Bello* After Afghanistan and Iraq

James M. Dubik

Michael Walzer's seminal book, *Just and Unjust Wars*, remains a dominant view of just war theory.[1] As one commentator observes, "It is not much of an exaggeration to say that this work has been to current just war theory what Grotius' *The Law of War and Peace* was to prior centuries."[2] Despite its significance, there is a gap in Walzer's treatment of *jus in bello*. He limits the conduct of war to fighting, but the conduct of war involves much more. Wars have to be *waged* as well as fought. Waging war—determining war aims, deciding upon strategies and policies, planning and executing campaigns, and other strategic level activities—may take place far from the battlefield, but has a huge impact on the conduct of war. This chapter describes the distinction between fighting and waging war, presents three war-waging responsibilities, and ends by suggesting five principles that govern senior political and military leaders. My focus is on war waged by the United States, especially the

---

This chapter revisits the arguments that I present in *Just War Reconsidered: Strategy, Ethics, and Theory* (Lexington: University of Kentucky Press, 2016).

J. M. Dubik (✉)
Institute for the Study of War, Washington, DC, USA

© The Author(s) 2020
G. Parsons and M. A. Wilson (eds.), *Walzer and War*,
https://doi.org/10.1007/978-3-030-41657-7_7

125

wars in Afghanistan and Iraq. While waging war is highly situation-specific, there are, nevertheless, important lessons to be learned from these cases, especially for other democracies.

THE GAP IN TRADITIONAL *JUS IN BELLO*

For Walzer, *jus in bello*'s central moral tension is between winning, defined as achieving the military objective, and "fighting well," understood as applying a set of limitations placed on soldiers and their leaders who otherwise might justify doing anything that they believe necessary to win. These limitations, which Walzer calls the War Convention, are a "set of articulated norms, customs, professional codes, legal precepts, religious and philosophical principles, and reciprocal arrangements that shape our judgments" of military conduct in war.[3] Applying the War Convention in battle makes war distinguishable from murder and massacre. "Professional soldiers," Walzer correctly explains, "remain sensitive (or some of them do) to those limits and restraints that distinguish their life's work from mere butchery....That is why...officers...will often protest commands...that would require them to violate the rules of war and turn them into mere instruments for killing."[4] Walzer describes the War Convention using five principles: The principle of noncombatant immunity[5]; the principle of double effect and double intent[6]; the principle of proportionality[7]; the principle of due care and due risk[8]; and the principle of supreme emergency, which Walzer correctly says does not apply to individual soldiers and leaders on the battlefield.[9]

These basic principles do not resolve the tension between winning and fighting well. They reveal a fundamental characteristic of *jus in bello*: in combat, soldiers and their leaders are between a rock and a hard place. While soldiers lose their right to life "simply by fighting[10];" civilian noncombatants, the innocent, do not.[11] It is the enterprise of a soldier's class that radically distinguishes the individual soldier from the civilians he leaves behind.[12] Civilian noncombatants, on the other hand, are innocent. They are not trained and prepared for fighting; they are not fighting or cannot fight.[13] We call them innocent because "they have done nothing, and are doing nothing, that entails the loss of their rights."[14]

It is this distinction between combatants and noncombatants that creates agonizing moral problems for soldiers.[15] "I have tried to argue," Walzer writes,

...that some degree of care be taken not to harm civilians—which means, very simply, that we recognize their rights as best we can within the context of war. But what degree of care should be taken? And at what cost to the individual soldiers who are involved? The laws of war say nothing about such matters; they leave the cruelest decisions to be made by the men on the spot with reference only to their ordinary moral notions, or the military traditions of the army in which they serve.[16]

This is part of the moral horror of war from which those who fight cannot escape.

Walzer then structures a theory of responsibility for the conduct of war. The "assignment of responsibility," he points out, "is the critical test for the argument for justice."[17] There can be no justice in war if there are no responsible men and women. Walzer is not concerned with legal guilt, but with moral blameworthiness.[18] Walzer establishes a central difference between political leaders who have both *jus ad bellum* and *jus in bello* responsibilities and soldiers and their military leaders who have only *jus in bello* responsibilities.

Walzer recognizes that the moral dimension of a soldier's life is complicated at the point of battle, but he believes that the *jus in bello* principles form a suitable moral framework that addresses the tension between winning and fighting well at the individual soldier level.[19] These rules provide sufficient guidance in that space between utility and necessity on one hand, which may justify "too much" killing, and the rights of the innocent on the other, which may tend toward "absolute prohibitions" against any killing.[20] The rules also demonstrate that soldiers are not mere killing machines or automatons; rather, they remain moral agents while they serve in war, perhaps the most morally ambiguous of human activities.[21]

"Being an officer," however, "is not like being a common soldier."[22] In addition to being bound by the same rules of war as are all soldiers, officers must aim at victory and attend to the needs of their soldiers as well as those of noncombatants. Officers create the climate within which soldiers fight, and this climate has an important moral dimension: it either engenders restraint and discipline or it allows laxity in both fighting skill and attention to principles of the War Convention.[23] Such laxity is morally relevant for it may result in war crimes.[24] Officers are "automatically responsible" for their soldiers. They are, according to Walzer, "presumptively guilty" with respect to any massive violations of the rules of war by those under their command. The burden of proof is on them to demonstrate innocence.[25]

Part of an officer's responsibility derives from the durability of a soldier's right to life. The status of "being able to be killed justifiably" is conditional. It applies only when one is a soldier, only during a war or other forms of hostility, and only relative to the enemy being fought. Murder is still the appropriate term for soldiers intentionally killed by a fellow soldier or leader, or by a noncombatant.

Walzer seems to recognize the durability of this right in his claim that even in war, soldiers and their officers remain moral agents; they are never mere instruments.[26] Durability is also reflected in the fact that when one becomes a soldier the state continues to exercise its responsibility to protect the rights of their citizens-who-become-soldiers through the military chain of command.[27] Walzer recognizes that "no one would want to be commanded in wartime by an officer who did not value the lives of his soldiers."[28] General Stanley McChrystal, meeting with his leaders and soldiers in a small compound in the Euphrates Valley after a series of particularly tough fights during which his unit took significant casualties, provides the perfect example of this. "Listen," he said, "this really hurts. But let me tell you what would make these [operations] hurt even more: if it is all in vain."[29] He then went on to discuss the importance of their battles within the context of the larger strategy in Iraq and explain how the nighttime raids in the Euphrates Valley were vital to the overall strategy in Iraq.[30]

General McChrystal's comments amplify that soldiers' lives matter, they are used for a purpose, their sacrifices are made to achieve higher aims, and they are not merely wasted. This responsibility derives from the fact that in liberal societies soldiers remain citizens in the democracies for which they fight, and their government retains its obligation to provide adequate care for them as its citizens. An officer's commission reflects the responsibility to exercise this obligation. Walzer acknowledges, "soldiers have every right to expect…this of [the officer] and to blame him for every sort of omission, evasion, carelessness, and recklessness that endangers their lives."[31]

Walzer puts generals in a special category. In his view, they "straddle the line" between those responsible for the war itself and those responsible for the conduct of war.[32] His claim is overstated, however. Some generals do straddle the line between officers and political leaders, but most do not. Some generals have as little to do with "the war itself" as do common soldiers or other officers. Others have significant input into consequential decisions on war policy and have responsibilities different from the generals who do not.[33]

In one sense, Walzer seems to grasp this distinction among general officers. In his discussion of the Nuremberg Trials and of the Vietnam War, for example, he lays the responsibility for war-policy decisions not only on heads of state, but also, inner circles of advisors, those who play a major role in making or executing strategy and policy, and a nation's foreign policy elite.[34] Some generals may be in this inner circle, but not many.

But, more importantly for my purposes, Walzer's distinction "between [responsibility for] the war itself, for which soldiers are not responsible, and the conduct of the war, for which they are responsible"[35] is based on an overly simplistic view of the distinction between *jus ad bellum* and *jus in bello*. His position simply does not correspond to the realities of war. At the war-fighting tactical and operational levels, military leaders are responsible much as Walzer posits, but at the strategic level, the level at which war is waged, senior political and military leaders share responsibility. War is an important means to attain a political goal—this proposition is basic to the understanding of war.[36] Fighting a war cannot be understood in isolation from its political purposes. Waging war entails identifying these purposes and devising means and ways that align with them. Hence, waging a war is essentially a political *and* military act; it is neither solely military nor solely political—especially in democratic nations. This war-waging aspect of the conduct of war is absent from Walzer's treatment of *jus in bello*.

Not recognizing that the conduct of war includes more than fighting, Walzer leaves out the mutually related responsibilities among those senior civil and military leaders who must wage war—that is, the responsibility to figure out war aims and strategy, identify and promulgate war policies, ensure that military operations are a means toward the declared aims, and make both civil and military bureaucracies work well enough that they help achieve the aims set.

The stark line that Walzer draws also results in his belief that officers "plan and organize campaigns; they decide on strategy."[37] The reality of war is that campaigns are civil–military decisions that require a robust and continual interaction between selected senior political leaders and generals. Often the decision to conduct a campaign is more a decision of civil than of military leaders. The campaigns conducted in

North Africa, Italy, and Europe in World War II; the campaign to break out of the Pusan Perimeter and conduct the Inchon Landing in Korea; the air campaign against North Vietnam; and the decisions to "surge" in Iraq in 2007 and Afghanistan in 2009—all are examples of civil–military decisions where political considerations sometimes outweighed military factors. None were planned and organized merely by officers or based solely upon military factors. Campaigns commit significant resources of a nation—troops, funds, supplies, and equipment, as well as political capital. Such decisions involve selected senior generals and political leaders in an ongoing exchange of information and discussion.

Both generals and political leaders who help shape war-waging decisions and actions associated with aligning war aims, strategy, policy, and military operations have *jus in bello* responsibilities Walzer does not address. These political leaders do not, as Walzer suggests, just decide to go to war, then hand off the responsibility to conduct that war to generals. At least some subset of political leaders help set war aims and establish strategies and policies governing the conduct of the war—strategies and policies necessary to mobilize political, economic, diplomatic, industrial, psychological, fiscal, and logistical resources necessary to achieve the war aims, conduct military operations, and execute essential, war-related non-military activities. This subset of political leaders also has responsibilities for policies that govern actions following termination of major hostilities, which sometimes include fighting—policies of occupation, temporary guardianship of a conquered nation, or other political arrangements that may result from active combat. Further, this subset of political leaders is also co-responsible for the quality of the dialogue among senior civil and military leaders that affects war's aim as well as the strategies and policies that govern that war.

Finally, executing policies—whether those associated with *jus ad bellum*, *jus in bello*, or *jus post bellum*—requires a set of governmental leaders who are sufficiently capable of generating and orchestrating the military and non-military means available in ways that increase the probability of success. Winning—as defined by achieving the strategic aims of a war through integrating military and non-military "forces" over time—requires senior political and military leaders to establish and use some sort of cooperative scheme.

In short, *jus in bello*'s strategic dimension entails the following three war-waging responsibilities: (1) *Achieve and sustain coherence*: war aims must be aligned with means as well as strategies, policies, and campaigns in order to increase the probability of achieving the aims set. (2) *Generate and sustain organizational capacity*: initial aims and decisions must be translated into actions that achieve the war aims at the least cost in lives and resources and the least risk to the innocent and one's political community. These decisions and actions must adapt to changing conditions as the war unfolds and bring the war to a successful end. (3) *Maintain legitimacy*: war must not only be initiated for the right reasons and observe the laws of war; additionally, public support must be sustained, and the proper integration of military and civilian leadership must be ensured. Executing these responsibilities sufficiently well is the second way political leaders exercise their responsibilities to their soldiers and their nation as well as the innocent put at risk by war.[38]

Some might argue that the responsibilities that I describe above are mere "strategic" responsibilities. They are that, but they also have a moral dimension because of their direct impact on the lives of the innocent, the lives of soldiers, and the life of the political community. The strategic and the moral are two sides of the same war-waging responsibility coin.

A Contemporary Illustration: Afghanistan and Iraq

The failures in Iraq and Afghanistan provide a detailed example of the importance of war-waging responsibilities in the conduct of war, how difficult it is to exercise these responsibilities, and how poor execution of these responsibilities dramatically affects the conduct of war. Lives of the innocent and of soldiers are lost in every war, and every war involves risk to the political community. Effectively waging war, however, reduces risks to individuals and the political community, and lowers the likelihood of wasting lives.

On October 7, 2001, twenty-six days following the September 11 attack on New York and Washington, DC, the United States invaded Afghanistan. President George W. Bush claims to have "felt the gravity of this decision...[knowing] the war would bring death and sorrow...." He claims his "anxiety about the sacrifice was mitigated by the urgency of the cause...We were acting out of necessity and self-defense, not revenge."[39] The country—in fact, the world—was in support.

In relatively quick order, the Taliban was routed. By the fall of 2002, the North Atlantic Treaty Organization (NATO) assumed partial responsibility for the International Security Assistance Force (ISAF), but they would not assume full responsibility until October 2006. In the interim, three strategic decisions began to erode initial success, prolong the war, and set the conditions for the return of the Taliban and strategic stalemate.

The first decision was to allow execution to precede planning and preparation. The President, in his speech delivered to a joint session of Congress on September 20, 2001, said this would be a war to punish and bring to justice those who attacked the United States, a war "against a radical network of terrorists and every government that supports them…a war on terror…that will not end until every terrorist group of global reach has been found, stopped and defeated."[40] The President corroborated the expansive nature of the war aims in his memoir, *Decision Points*, "removing Al Qaeda's safe haven in Afghanistan….destroy the Al Qaeda network….help the Afghan people liberate themselves….bring these people [Al Qaeda] to justice….change the impression that, in the words of Bin laden, Americans were paper tigers."[41] Thinking through the political, diplomatic, fiscal, organizational, and material resources necessary to achieve these war aims is not a trivial task. Yet we initiated operations in less than one month.

Without doubt, the attack on the United States justified a rapid response. The President could not allow those who attacked the United States an opportunity to do so again. However, the speed at which the United States invaded Afghanistan meant not only that resources and means were not fully aligned with aims, but also that the aims themselves were not fully debated. Further, the execution plan was, to say the least, far from fully developed. Haste at the strategic level resulted in insufficient intellectual, strategic, organizational, and logistic preparation, and affected the conduct of the war in Afghanistan from the very start. Haste also resulted in deficiencies in numbers and types of troops, confused command and control organizations, and overly compartmentalized intelligence and planning arrangements. All this contributed to the Taliban's and al Qaeda's escape into Pakistan, thus prolonging the war.[42]

The second decision was to take a "lead nation approach" to the rebuilding of Afghanistan. This approach is one that assigns a member of a coalition "the lead" for various aspects of the operation. For example, in Afghanistan Germany was responsible for training the Afghan national police, the United States for training the Afghan Army, Great Britain for the counter-narcotics mission, Italy for the reform of the justice system, and Japan for the disarmament and demobilization of the

Afghan warlords and militias. In addition, the United States continued combat operations against the remnants of Al Qaeda and the Taliban—independent from the NATO effort. Unity of purpose and cohesion of action was lost almost immediately and stayed diffused for years. Further, many of the allied nations agreed to their tasks under the assumption that they would operate in a post-hostility environment, akin to the peacekeeping mission in Bosnia and Kosovo. They quickly found that this was not the case, so their efforts were seriously impaired.

"The multilateral approach to rebuilding...was failing," writes President Bush, "there was little coordination between countries, and no one devoted enough resources to the effort....The multilateral mission proved a disappointment as well....The result was a disorganized and ineffective force with troops fighting by different rules and many not fighting at all."[43] Not only were too few troops allocated to the task, but as the President concluded, "our government was not prepared for nation building."[44] Writing about this period, Ronald E. Neumann, U.S. Ambassador to Afghanistan from 2005 to 2007, says, "I was struck by how little either the public or senior policy makers understood the complex business of implementing policy."[45]

Dov Zakheim—who, in 2002, was the U.S. Department of Defense civilian coordinator for defense activities in Afghanistan, a position that he held simultaneously with comptroller and chief financial officer at the Pentagon—reinforces Ambassador Neumann's perspective. Zakheim observes, "In the case of Afghanistan...through sins of both commission and omission, the Bush administration was often incapable of effectively implementing manifestly good policies, sound ideas, and wisely chosen goals."[46] He continues,

> The U.S. government did not engage, anywhere in any of its various departments and agencies, in extensive planning for a post-Taliban Afghanistan....The assumption was that the international community would pick up the pieces after the Taliban regime was displaced....For several years...especially in Afghanistan, there was no functional system of governance in Washington to support [those executing civil and military operations in the theater]....the reason is that, in the absence of standard government procedures and institutions to implement [wartime] policy, no one understood the importance of devising such procedures beforehand.[47]

Everything, Zakheim concluded, "turned out to be more complicated and frustrating than it might, or should, have been."[48] He goes on to say, "Even determining the size of the ground forces the nation would need to fight in Afghanistan…was a matter more of contention than consensus."[49]

The third decision that began to erode initial success thus setting the conditions for the return of the Taliban and prolonging the war in Afghanistan, was to invade Iraq. The invasion caused U.S. attention to wander from Afghanistan according to Bruce Reidel, former CIA analyst, White House counter-terrorist specialist, and Brookings Institute fellow. The result: the effort to rebuild Afghanistan stalled and the Taliban regrouped in Pakistan and staged a comeback.[50]

Turning now to the case of Iraq, the invasion and its subsequent operations provide further evidence of how war-waging decisions affect war-fighting actions.

On March 19, 2003, President Bush ordered Operation Iraqi Freedom to begin. On April 9, Baghdad was close to falling into coalition hands. The initial invasion and immediate aftermath in Iraq looked eerily similar to what was done in Afghanistan. The Iraqi regime fell as quickly as did the Taliban in Afghanistan. Then a new reality emerged. The security vacuum in Iraq—fueled by years of oppression under the Saddam regime as well as insufficient numbers of coalition forces, the destruction of the Iraqi army, and the collapse of the police—resulted in widespread kidnapping, murder, looting, and pillaging.

The U.S. Central Command, responsible for U.S. military actions throughout most of the Middle East, used three large units each commanded by a three-star general—one U.S. Army corps, one Marine Expeditionary Force, and a common headquarters in charge of the other two—to plan, coordinate, and execute the campaign to remove the Saddam regime. All three of these headquarters were withdrawn about 90 days after the initial invasion and were replaced by a single, different, three-star U.S. Army corps headquarters that would be responsible for executing the "post combat" phase of the invasion, though neither its commander, Lieutenant General Ricardo Sanchez, nor its staff participated in any of the planning or preparation for this transition. In fact, General Sanchez was only interviewed by the Secretary of Defense in April—one month after the invasion and less than two before he would assume his responsibilities in Iraq.[51]

One three-star headquarters—especially one led by a newly promoted commanding general with an understaffed headquarters—would not be able to attend properly to the combination of active combat requirements, rebuilding the Iraqi forces, the logistical tasks inherent in supporting an effort like that in Iraq at the time, and the administration of large detention operations. Nor would one headquarters be able to attend adequately to all of the tasks listed above as well as to the demands of coordination with the political, diplomatic, and non-governmental agencies that were responsible for reconstruction and humanitarian assistance.

In retrospect, Secretary Rumsfeld said that this decision was a "serious misassessment," acknowledging that the tasks assigned to Sanchez required "a large, fully staffed supporting headquarters [but what the commanding general got was]...well less than half—37 percent—of the staff he required."[52] This "misassessment" was not corrected until June 2004, one year after the initial invasion. Sanchez agreed, "It was simply too much of a burden for an Army corps headquarters to bear."[53]

This "misassessment" was preceded by others. An Office of Reconstruction and Humanitarian Assistance (ORHA) had been created hastily just prior to the invasion, in January of 2003. This organization was charged with devising and implementing the plans for the rebuilding of Iraq. The civilian who would initially become responsible for Iraqi reconstruction—Jay Garner, a retired U.S. Army three-star general—was first contacted by the Department of the Defense in January 2003, just a few months before the invasion of Iraq.[54] About 30 days prior to launching the invasion, Garner orchestrated a meeting that assembled "most of the players in the government's postwar game, including the Pentagon, State Department, CENTCOM [U.S. Central Command], the vice president's office, and [then Lieutenant General David] McKiernan's command at Camp Doha [the Kuwaiti base of the three-star headquarters responsible for planning, preparing, coordinating, and executing ground operations in Iraq]."[55] The meeting was to provide an "opportunity for each agency to pitch its ideas about how to proceed, but there was, as yet, no master strategy."[56] One general who participated in the session concluded that "The U.S. agencies were not ready, had no real understanding of what Iraq was like, and did not yet have a coherent plan....There was no clear demarcation between what would be run by the civilians and what the generals would control. The funding for the multibillion-dollar undertaking in Iraq was still up in the air, and it was ludicrous to expect that it would all come from the U.N."[57]

Just a few months later, in May of 2003, ORHA was disbanded. Garner and his staff returned to the United States. In their stead came Ambassador L. Paul Bremer and a new agency, the Coalition Provisional Authority.

In April of 2003—a month after the invasion of Iraq began—Ambassador Bremer had been contacted about the possibility of assuming the responsibilities originally given to Garner. "Over the next two weeks," Bremer writes, "I had a frenzied series of meetings at the Pentagon, struggling to get 'read in' on the situation in Iraq before my departure. Between sessions, I scrambled to assemble a staff."[58] Many on that staff were young professionals who had never worked outside the United States and would never leave Baghdad's secure "Green Zone." Many rotated in and out of their jobs in less than a year, some as short as 90 days; and many were more politically correct than professionally competent.[59] The Ambassador would hold his job for about a year, until June 2004—the same tenure as Lieutenant General Sanchez.

All this upheaval made progress that year fitful. Saddam Hussein was captured and Iraqi sovereignty was transferred to an interim government that set the conditions for drafting an Iraqi constitution and holding elections. But the insurgency grew, as did Al Qaeda's involvement in it, fed in part by the increase of foreign fighters but also by the disbanding of the Iraqi Army and the de-Ba'athification program—two Bremer-related war-waging policies. Violence from an expanding Shia militia also contributed to Iraqi insecurity and instability, as did crimes of some Iraqi Security Forces and by U.S. soldiers in the Abu Ghraib prison.[60]

In 2004, one well-known defense analyst said: "it quickly became apparent that the…administration had paid far more attention to the planning and conduct of the war than to the planning and conduct of the 'peace.'" Moreover, he continued, one of the main obstacles was "continuing division…over U.S. policy toward Iraq and the respective roles of the State and Defense Departments in formulating and implementing that policy."[61] General (retired) Jack Keane, who was then Vice Chief of Staff of the U.S. Army, said more bluntly: "the United States mission in Iraq was made all the more difficult by the administration's aversion to nation-building and its determination not to study the lessons of its predecessors. That attitude set the stage for many of the problems that were to come." Keane added "military leaders, including the Joint Chiefs of Staff, the Vice Chiefs, and General Franks share responsibility [with the political leaders at the time] for the problems in Iraq."[62] Confusion, insufficient attention, and lack of civil–military cohesion followed the initial success in Iraq, just as in Afghanistan, and the price was paid in blood for years.[63]

In the early summer of 2004, Ambassador Bremer and Lieutenant General Sanchez were replaced by Ambassador John Negroponte and General George W. Casey. Ambassador Negroponte's U.S. Embassy and its staff would replace the ad hoc Coalition Provisional Authority. To replace the lone, three-star army corps, General Casey would create a large staff commensurate with his four-star rank—the Multi-national Force, Iraq. Additionally, Casey, understanding the complexity and scope of his task, brought in three, three-star deputies: one to run combat operations (Multi-national Corps, Iraq), a second to help create the Iraqi military and police forces (Multi-national Security and Transition Command, Iraq), and a third to run the special operations in Iraq. But, over the next two years, the violence went from bad to worse.

In sum, the strategy in Iraq—pursuing extremists and reducing the military footprint with Iraqi military and police forces—was failing. In March of 2003 when the invasion of Iraq began, 75% of those polled believed that the United States had not made a mistake sending troops to Iraq, and only 23% thought sending troops was a mistake. By December 2006, the numbers were 45 and 53%, respectively. Support for the war was clearly slipping.[64] "For the first time," President Bush wrote, "I was worried we might not succeed."[65] "For two and a half years," the President continues, "I had supported the strategy of withdrawing our forces as the Iraqis stepped forward—the 'we'll stand down as they stand up' policy. But in the months after the [2006] Samarra [mosque] bombing, I had started to question whether our approach matched the reality on the ground."[66] The President concluded that he required a new strategy with radically new resources and policies.[67]

The situation in Afghanistan was no better. As President Bush put it,

The problem was crystallized by a series of color-coded maps I saw in November, 2006. The darker the shading, the more attacks had occurred in that part of Afghanistan. The 2004 map was lightly shaded. The 2005 map had darker areas in the southern and eastern parts of the country. By 2006, the entire southeastern quadrant was black. In just one year the number of remotely detonated bombs had doubled. The number of armed attacks had tripled. The number of suicide bombings had more than quadrupled.[68]

When the United States invaded Afghanistan in November 2001, 89% of those polled believed that the United States had not made a mistake sending troops to Afghanistan, and only 9% thought sending troops was a mistake. By December 2006, the numbers were 25 and 70%, respectively.[69] The United States and NATO strategy was failing, the Afghans had lost faith in their government, sanctuaries in Pakistan contributed to this worsening situation, and the legitimacy of the war in the eyes of the American public became a question.[70]

This synopsis illustrates that the conduct of war, *jus in bello*, is not limited to what happens on the battlefield. Such a narrow focus omits a crucial way in which senior political and military leaders can meet or fail to meet their wartime responsibilities. *Jus in bello* must include both the war-fighting and war-waging aspects of the conduct of war. When war-waging responsibilities are not adequately attended to, the cost is paid in lives as surely as failures and violations of the *jus in bello* war-fighting principles. These kinds of failures are neither an "unfortunate consequence of war," nor are they merely examples of understandable human fallibility. Rather, they are the result of a kind of failure that just war theory must have the tools to identify, criticize, and judge.

The standard for deciding upon war aims, strategy, policy, and military campaigns, then executing those decisions and adapting as the war unfolds is not perfection; no government or set of civil–military leaders could ever meet that standard. Every government will make mistakes. Every government's policy and strategy as well as their execution will be only partially effective and efficient. If, however, a government's senior civil and military leaders do not learn and adapt but continue to conduct a war for unattainable aims, using what are known to be inefficient and ineffective strategies and policies, or through what are known to be inefficient or ineffective organizations and management processes, those leaders should be morally blameworthy—even if not legally guilty—for the results of their actions, just as soldiers and their leaders ignoring the war convention should be held to account.

Soldiers and their leaders who observe the tactical *jus in bello* principles that Walzer presents mitigate part of war's nastiness. Applying these principles in combat is part of a soldier's and a leader's moral responsibility in war. Sufficient capacity at the strategic, war-waging level can also mitigate part of war's nastiness. Applying the appropriate war-waging principles is part of a senior political and military leader's moral responsibility in war. Just war theory, therefore, must identify appropriate principles for the strategic dimension of *jus in bello*. One might say that to be complete, just war theory needs both a tactical *jus in bello* and a separate-but-related strategic *jus in bello*.

FILLING THE GAP IN *JUS IN BELLO*

I suggest the following five principles to guide leaders, both military and civilian, with war-waging responsibilities.

> 1. *The Principle of Continuous Dialogue.* This principle recognizes the necessity for a robust civil–military dialogue prior to the initial decisions concerning war aims, and continued discussion of strategies, policies, and military campaigns throughout the conduct of war in order to adapt initial decisions to the dynamic nature of war. The President and Secretary of Defense are primarily responsible for setting the right conditions for this dialogue to take place, but the senior political and military leaders who participate in this regime are co-responsible for its conduct.

"Ideal" aims, strategies, policies, and campaigns are not the objective here. The goal is much more practical. What is best emerges from a reality-based civil–military dialogue. War is always complex, unpredictable, and fast-changing—especially so in an era of high-speed communications. Decisions and actions have a limited "shelf life" of utility. Hence, a robust, continuous dialogue, a *dialogue-and-execution regime*, is necessary not only before a war but also during the conduct of it.

The President and Secretary of Defense are legally positioned at the head of the U.S. chain of command. No President wants to be wrong when committing the nation to war. Nor does a President want to be wrong when it comes to waging a war once committed.[71] Recognizing this, the President and the Secretary of Defense should use their legal authority to gather the necessary participants in a proper war-waging dialogue-and-execution regime and to focus those participants on the problems they face together.

The President and the Secretary of Defense have the responsibility to ensure the set of senior political and military leaders focus on the right problems and make progress toward their resolution; have the information and analysis necessary when they need it; have the right forums to discuss, debate, and attain sufficient unity about their decisions; execute those decisions coherently; and adapt to emerging realities. The President and Secretary of Defense have the primary responsibility for setting the climate and convening the experts required for the dialogue-and-execution regime necessary to reach good war-waging decisions.

All participants, however, have the responsibility to contribute to the dialogue-and-execution regime necessary to wage war. Those involved in the lead up to a decision as well as the execution and adaptation are co-responsible for the integrity of the process and fidelity of the information. Participants are co-responsible for the quality of the dialogue and the resultant initial decisions, just as they are for the ongoing dialogue-and-execution regime needed during a war and the resultant adaptations.

Neither senior political nor military leaders have access to an "answer book." All are imperfect judges of which strategies and policies are likely to work. All are imperfect predictors, therefore, of the consequences of decisions and actions—at home, abroad, or on the battlefield. None can foresee enemy reactions or decisions. Whatever wisdom may be found in waging war emerges from the set of leaders executing a proper dialogue-and-execution regime, the process that ensures the President hears all relevant voices and is presented with all relevant information and options—however difficult such information and options may be. A process that is cut short, eliminating or subverting relevant voices and preventing relevant information to rise to the final authority's awareness, decreases the likelihood that the authority will be used well.

"Dysfunctional relationships," Richard Kohn says,

> between the topmost civilians and the most senior military officers—particularly lack of candor, consultation, coordination, and collaboration—can be disastrous for policy and decision making....[and] can cause the United States to undertake unnecessary wars, prosecute them unwisely, and pile up hundreds or thousands of dead and wounded Americans, not to speak of many times that number of enemies and innocent civilians.[72]

Speaking of the 2009 civil–military dialogue about Afghanistan, Secretary of Defense Robert Gates said, "On reflection, I believe all of us at the senior-most level did not serve the president well in this process."[73] This reflection reveals the multi-faceted nature of responsibility in this context. In it, the President is seen as responsible for making the final decision and also as the one who is served by a dialogue-and-execution regime in which a set of senior political and military leaders are co-responsible for its conduct and outcome.

2. *The Principle of Final Decision Authority.* This principle recognizes the essentiality of civil control of the military in democracies. At the same time, the principle recognizes that proper subordination and responsible exercise of final decision authority both require the specific kind of continuous civil–military dialogue-and-execution regime described in the first principle.

The final decision authority of the president extends not only to *jus ad bellum* matters, but also to war-waging *jus in bello* matters. War aims, strategies, and policies, as well as decisions about major operations and campaigns are political–military matters where the senior political leaders have final decision authority. Exercising this war-waging final decision authority irresponsibly risks unnecessarily prolonging a war, thereby wasting the lives of soldiers and resources and increasing risk to the political community as well as the lives of the innocent. Irresponsible use of final decision authority is morally blameworthy, even if not illegal.

Responsible exercise of final decision authority increases the likelihood of identifying war aims, strategies, policies, and campaigns with the highest probability of success and also increases the likelihood of adapting correctly as war unfolds. Senior civil and military subordinates are properly subordinate when they ensure a high-quality dialogue precedes any final decision. Those with "final decision authority" must demand that the dialogue leading to their decision is as complete, honest, and accurate as possible. Disagreement in the war-waging dialogue is not a sign of disrespect or disloyalty.

Civilian control of the military is completely consistent with the often rough and tumble dialogue-and-execution regime that waging war requires. Civilian control is also consistent with senior civil or military subordinates who, after a decision is made and executed, reengage in the dialogue if the results of that decision and action are found to be contrary to what was intended.

3. *The Principle of Managerial Competency.* This principle recognizes the necessity to use, by-pass, or change if necessary, civil and military bureaucracies to ensure governmental structures and processes work

to achieve war aims, execute strategies and policies, and support military operations. The principle also recognizes that the senior political and military leaders are responsible for managerial competency within their scope of authority.

Once a final decision is made, senior military and political leaders must make their respective bureaucracies work to support that decision. Senior political and military leaders who hold soldiers and leaders in combat responsible for proper tactical execution under high-risk conditions, but do not hold themselves accountable to execute their war-waging managerial responsibilities under much less risky conditions are at best duplicitous and at worse morally bankrupt. Making a bureaucracy work, especially making it do what it does not want to do—often anything new or fast—is especially hard.

Making bureaucracy work requires focused leadership and management. Among the many leadership and managerial tasks necessary to make a bureaucracy work, attention to at least three—compliance regimes, performance gap-and-adaptation regimes, and by-pass or change regimes—are among the more important when it comes to war-waging responsibilities.

Compliance regimes are those that involve setting and implementing monitoring mechanisms to enforce set standards. Conversations in compliance regimes are about whether individual or organizational behaviors meet standards, and if they do not, what behavioral changes are necessary to meet standards. There is no discussion about the standards themselves; they are already fixed. Compliance regimes are necessary to ensure contracting, acquisition, equipment, and financial accountability, and that personnel actions accord with law and regulation.

Performance gap-and-adaptation regimes are different. Performance gap-and-adaptation regimes are designed to identify the gap between what an organization wants to achieve and the reality the organization is actually facing. These regimes must stimulate a discussion about whether the ends are actually achievable. In a performance gap-and-adaptation conversation, the only fixed point is reality. Adaptation—of ends, ways, means, or all three—is based upon the fixed point of reality. A performance gap-and-adaptation regime is necessary in a dynamic environment like a war where initial assessments, decisions, and actions need constant reassessment. Corporate executives use performance gap-and-adaptation regimes[74]; so should senior political and military leaders who wage war.[75]

Substituting a compliance discussion where a performance gap-and-adaptation discussion is needed will inhibit an organization's success. For example, if war aims, strategies, or policies become "fixed standards" the resultant conversation will be compliance-oriented. The conversation will not include the viability of ends, ways, or means; it will only include a discussion of whether behaviors meet standards. Over time, a strictly compliance regime discussion can produce an "unreality."

Perhaps this is exhibited in President Bush's statement: "For two and a half years, I had supported the strategy of withdrawing our forces as the Iraqis stepped forward. But in the months after the [February, 2006] Samarra bombing, I had started to question whether our approach matched the reality on the ground."[76] Following his intuition, the President initiated a performance gap-and-adaptation discussion calling several outside government experts to Camp David to a two-day, top-level review because "nobody within the administration was prepared to directly challenge Rumsfeld or Casey in front of the President."[77] As the President began the review, General Casey seemed to have no doubts. With Prime Minister Maliki and his cabinet in office and Zarqawi dead, the general was convinced that his strategy was on track—and that it was time to begin withdrawing the next few brigades of American troops.[78] He was "executing the plan," which is a clear indication that the approach to monitoring the war in Iraq from 2004–2007 resembled a compliance regime more than a performance gap-and-adaptation regime.

The third important leadership and managerial task necessary to make a bureaucracy work is a *by-pass or change regime*. This involves identifying parts of a bureaucracy that do not perform as necessary, then either creating a way to by-pass or change them. Conversations relative to by-pass or change regimes are about the difference between the speed at which bureaucracies normally work and the speed necessary to support dynamic war efforts. The former is generally too slow for the latter. For example, the "routine" Pentagon process for buying new equipment is a multi-year, often decades-long process. In Iraq, because of the number of casualties caused by Improvised Explosive Devices, soldiers needed better protection much faster than the routine procedure would allow. Two by-pass mechanisms were put in place, one by Secretary Rumsfeld and another by Secretary Gates. The first delivered better countermeasures; the second delivered better vehicles. Neither of these fast-delivered innovations would have been possible using routine systems.

The point is that in addition to identifying adequate war aims, strategies, and policies, and in addition to directing which military campaigns or major operations take place, senior political and military leaders must translate initial decisions into action, then adapt as the dynamics of war create new realities. Simply put, senior political leaders must be more than "politically reliable," and senior military leaders must be more than "good warfighters." To execute their *jus in bello* war-waging responsibilities, all must be competent leaders and managers, individually and as a group.

4. *The Principle of War Legitimacy.* This principle recognizes that even justified wars can lose their legitimacy in the sense that an administration begins to lose or has lost the support of some significant portion of the population. Creating and maintaining legitimacy, in this sense, is a function of maintaining support of the population as one conducts a war which, in turn, rests upon the righteousness of the war (a *jus ad bellum* concern) and progress toward probable success (a war-waging *jus in bello* concern). In effect, legitimacy is tied directly to the competency of senior political and military leaders in executing their war-waging responsibilities.

When a war is perceived as just, its aims seen as achievable, and progress is being made toward achieving those aims, the casualties resulting from the war are usually viewed as "worth the cost" and the war usually viewed as legitimate. Much of the public formed its attitudes regarding the war in Iraq, for example, by weighing the costs and benefits. U.S. casualties stand as a cost of war, but they are usually a cost the public is willing to pay if it thinks the initial decision to launch the war was correct, and if it thinks the war will succeed.[79]

Fighting a war poorly erodes legitimacy; so does waging war poorly. In 2001, for example, only 9% of polled Americans thought the war in Afghanistan was a mistake; in 2013 that number was 44%.[80] The "righteousness" of this war had not changed, but the way it has been waged had led 74% of Americans to conclude the U.S. ought to either stick to the 2014 withdrawal date or accelerate withdrawal.[81] This illustrates how senior leaders who fail to develop sufficient leadership and managerial abilities with respect to their war-waging responsibilities gamble with a war's legitimacy.

5. *The Principle of Resignation.* This principle recognizes that senior political or military leader resignation is necessary and permissible under certain conditions. Senior political and military leaders remain moral agents, not "mere instruments" of a government. Nevertheless, this principle is limited by the necessity to retain civil control of the military in a democracy.

Resignation poses a dilemma. On one hand, the right to resignation is necessary. Resignation acknowledges that everyone, including senior political and military leaders, remain moral agents responsible for their conscience. Resignation is also a useful recuperative mechanism that helps large organizations know when there are significant problems in their operations. Finally, resignation is useful in a performance-oriented, dialogue-and-execution regime, for it provides a way to ensure no participants can merely be steamrolled into agreement. On the other hand, the right to resignation has a significant potential downside, especially applicable to the senior military leaders in a democracy: it can be or be perceived as a direct challenge to civil authority, civil primacy, and civil control of the military.

In the right circumstances, resignation can serve as a healthy and necessary organizational recuperative mechanism. As Albert O. Hirschman argues, departures of senior executives (what he calls "exit") or discussions and arguments at important meetings concerning whether their firm's policies and actions are having the desired effects (what he calls "voice") are ways that can help firms, organizations, and governments know that what they are doing isn't working and prompt them to do something about it.[82]

Hirschman recognizes, however, that while feedback through exit or voice is in the long-term interest of managers, their short-term interests lead them to entrench themselves and to enhance their freedom to act as they wish, unmolested as far as possible by either desertions or complaints.[83] In other words, some managers and leaders don't want feedback; they want silence and compliance—even in the face of evidence that what they are doing is not working. These managers and organizations impose discipline by simply shutting down both exit and voice. Such is the case with autocratic managers for whom compliance and obedience are more important than success or progress and the threat of punishment replaces leadership. It is also the case in totalitarian governments where neither citizens nor leaders can leave or complain.

Denial is another organizational response. This response is common for customers, members, or leaders who have invested a great deal and so have a considerable stake in the product, service, plan, or the organization in general.[84] In the case of senior leaders, this investment may have been a lifetime of service that included difficult sacrifices that, in turn, generated significant loyalty. In fact, Hirschman points out, the more loyal a person is to an organization, the more he or she has invested in the organization or a specific product, service, or activity within the organization, the greater the ability to deny reports of decline.[85]

Co-opting is a third common organizational response to criticism. In this case, the organization domesticates the dissenters.[86] The doubter is kept on and given an explicit role as "devil's advocate" or as a member of "the red team." In this way, the dissenter's conscience may be assuaged, but his or her effectiveness is reduced to a point where it is virtually ignored. Co-opting forces the dissenter to give up, a priori, his or her strongest weapon: the threat to resign under protest.[87]

Whether managers and organizations choose to shut down, deny, or co-opt criticism, the result is the same: it denies them needed recuperative mechanisms. When one or more of these approaches are employed, organizations are simply robbed of the ability to recognize and reverse deteriorating performance.[88]

General Harold K. Johnson, the Army's Chief of Staff from 1964 to 1968 during the Vietnam War, provides a good example. "When the President elected not to follow the advice of the Joint Chiefs of Staff, they had little choice but to go along or resign," says the historian and biographer Lewis Sorley.[89] Voice had failed, so at one point in his tenure, General Johnson concluded that he had to resign. He said,

> I remember the day I was ready to go over to the Oval Office and give my four stars to the President and tell him, 'You have refused to tell the country they cannot fight a war without mobilization; you have required me to send men into battle with little hope of their ultimate victory; and you have forced the military to violate almost every one of the principles of war in Vietnam. Therefore, I resign and will hold a press conference after I walk out of your door.[90]

The principles governing *jus in bello*'s tactical, war-fighting dimension mandate that soldiers and their military leaders retain their moral agency. "Soldiers," Walzer reminds us, "can never be transformed into mere instruments of war...Trained to obey 'without hesitation,' they remain nevertheless capable of hesitating...it is a mistake to treat soldiers [or their military leaders] as if they were automatons who make no judgments at all."[91] Senior political and military leaders, too, remain moral agents. As such, they remain responsible for the strategic, war-waging decisions and actions they take.

Leaving a position of significant responsibility is difficult. Co-option is very powerful. Any "final policy decision," Hirschman shows, "can always be made to look as some middle course between the two opposing points of view...hence [all] are made to feel that 'if it had not been for me, an even more sinister decision would have been taken.'"[92] The desire to remain close to power is also very strong. Hirschman suggests a variant to a famous dictum, "Power corrupts; and even a little influence in a country with huge power corrupts hugely."[93]

Deciding to resign should always be hard. This difficulty, however, does not eliminate a senior leader's responsibility to their conscience, to the larger institution and the nation they serve, to the innocent, or to soldiers that execute war-waging decisions. Loyalty sometimes requires criticism. To operate properly, and especially in war, the nation to which a senior leader is loyal needs to know when its war aims, strategies, policies, and military operations are failing. Without this feedback—whether expressed through voice, as should take priority in the case of senior officers, or exit, the choice of last resort—the nation diminishes its chances of correcting its performance.

With respect to senior military leaders, however, resignation or criticism must be exercised in a way that does not challenge civil control of the military: "candidly and privately," in the words of Secretary Gates—at least for senior military leaders.[94] Exit or voice options for senior civilian leaders are a bit different. Because their resignation or dissent does not threaten civil control of the military, senior civilian dissent can be more public.

Mass resignations of senior military officials like that considered by the Joint Chiefs during the Johnson Administration, or public resignations like General Johnson's would have been, are problematic because of the threat to civilian control. Public criticism of senior political leaders still in office, as Secretary Rumsfeld was subjected to by several retired general officers, is similarly problematic because this kind of criticism also challenges, directly or indirectly, civil control of the military. Resignation simply because "advice is ignored" is also problematic, but for different reasons. Here petulance seems more at play than morality or the desire to provide the nation an opportunity to wage war successfully.

Voice seems to have a recognized place with respect to senior political and military leaders, but not exit. Richard Kohn, for example, rejects resignation even if kept private. He writes, "Resignation—even the very hint of it, much less the threat or the act—is a direct assault on civilian authority. Civilian officials rightly interpret it as such. It inherently violates civilian control."[95] Kohn believes that all lawful orders, even if immoral, are to be followed. Kohn correctly points out that "even military officers at the very top of the chain of command…cannot know all of the larger national and international considerations involved, a calculation that belongs properly to the political leadership, elected and appointed. Nor is there historical evidence that military judgment has been superior to that of the politicians."[96] The scope of the president's responsibility is larger than the scope of a general's. That's why resignation over mere disagreement or the feeling of being ignored, disrespected, or treated badly is wrong. A conclusion to resign cannot be taken lightly.

Those were not the grounds for resignation that General Johnson cited, however. His was not a problem of not knowing "all of the larger national and international considerations," as Kohn puts it. Rather, his was a problem of what he did know: that the lives of soldiers were being wasted. His was a moral problem that involved recognizing first that the value of human life is such that, while under certain circumstances it can be used, it cannot be wasted, and second that he, his fellow Chiefs, the President, and other senior political leaders are co-responsible for the lives they use. The issue was not whether he believed that he must obey distasteful, seemingly foolish, or sometimes disastrous orders. He knew that he must, after all he fought the futile defense of the Philippine Islands following the 1941 Japanese invasion, was captured, and survived the Bataan Death march, Japanese hell ships, and the neglect, brutality, illness, and starvation of extended captivity until September 1945. His problem was that the strategies and policies in Vietnam had deteriorated to the point that, on its current course, the war could not be won and, therefore, the lives of soldiers and others were being wasted.

Neither good order and discipline, nor civilian control of the military, is at risk over the proper exercise of moral agency. If soldiers and leaders are to remain moral agents on the battlefield, they must be moral agents in the boardroom as well. Further, the correct exercise of moral agency in some circumstances might result in better organizational performance.

CONCLUSION

Conducting a war involves both fighting it and waging it. *Jus in bello* must, therefore, address both dimensions. This essay attempted to identify and resolve a deficiency in the traditional view exemplified by Walzer: restricting *jus in bello* to fighting. The five war-waging principles—plus the senior political and military leaders' three war-waging responsibilities from which the principles derive—more completely describe the ethics of the conduct of war. Adding the strategic, war-waging understanding to the traditionally recognized war-fighting principles and responsibilities results in a more complete account of the conduct of war's moral dimension. Surely, there is much more to be said about the ethics of waging war. I merely hope this chapter will stimulate more discussion about an important yet overlooked dimension of just war theory.

NOTES

1. Michael Walzer, *Just and Unjust Wars*, 5th ed. (New York: Basic Books, 2015).
2. Brian Orend, *The Morality of War* (Ontario: Broadview Press, 2006), 24.
3. Walzer, *Just and Unjust Wars*, 44. See also, Geoffrey S. Corn et al., *The Law of Armed Conflict: An Operational Approach* (New York: Wolters Kluwer, Law and Business, 2012), 107–413.
4. Walzer, *Just and Unjust Wars*, 45.
5. Corn et al., *The Law of Armed Conflict*, 133–38 and 143–45; Walzer, *Just and Unjust Wars*, 146, and 150–51; and Orend, *The Morality of War*, 112–15.
6. Walzer, *Just and Unjust Wars*, 153, 155; Corn et al., *The Law of Armed Conflict*, 152–52 and 161–86.
7. Walzer, *Just and Unjust Wars*, 129; Orend, *The Morality of War*, 118; Corn et al., *The Law of Armed Conflict*, 187–89 and 191.
8. Walzer, *Just and Unjust Wars*, 156; Orend, *The Morality of War*, 116.
9. Walzer, *Just and Unjust Wars*, 254. In Chapter 8 of this volume, Jeremy Waldron attempts to show that Walzer's discussion of the ethics of supreme emergencies does not assert a principle that permits violating the war convention.
10. Ibid., 136
11. Ibid., 42, 138, 140, and 144.
12. Ibid., 144.
13. Ibid., 43.
14. Ibid., 146.

15. I have argued that Walzer's view of the distinction between combatants and noncombatants is too absolute in James Dubik, "Human Rights, Command Responsibility, and Walzer's Just War Theory," *Philosophy and Public Affairs* 11, no. 4 (Fall 1982): 354–71. See also Henry Shue's chapter in this volume for a discussion of the practical value of the prohibition of attacks on noncombatants.

16. *Just and Unjust Wars*, 152.

17. Ibid., 287.

18. Ibid., 288.

19. Ibid., 34–47 and 127–59.

20. Ibid., 226–27 and 304.

21. Ibid., 306.

22. Ibid., 316. See also Michael Walzer, "Two Kinds of Military Responsibility," in *Arguing About War* (New York: Yale University Press, 2004), 23–32; and Corn et al., *The Law of Armed Conflict*, 526–69.

23. Walzer, *Just and Unjust Wars*, 319–22. See also Corn et al., *The Law of Armed Conflict*, 526–31 and 550–57.

24. Three examples from our current wars that demonstrate how laxity resulted in war crimes are described in: Jim Frederick, *Black Hearts: One Platoon's Descent into Madness in Iraq's Triangle of Death* (New York: Random House, 2010); Anna Mulrine, "Pentagon Had Red Flags About Command Climate in 'kill team' Stryker Brigade," *Christian Science Monitor*, October 28, 2010, https://www.csmonitor.com/USA/Military/2010/1028/Pentagon-had-red-flags-about-command-climate-in-kill-team-Stryker-brigade; and Charlie Savage and Elisabeth Bumiller, "Iraqi Massacre, a Light Sentence and a Question of Military Justice," *The New York Times*, January 27, 2012, https://www.nytimes.com/2012/01/28/us/an-iraqi-massacre-a-light-sentence-and-a-question-of-military-justice.html.

25. Walzer, *Just and Unjust Wars*, 321–22.

26. Ibid., 36, 40, 45, 306, and 311.

27. I present an extended argument concerning the durability of a soldier's right to life in "Human Rights, Command Responsibility, and Walzer's Just War Theory." I use the term "citizen-now-soldier" to highlight the fact that soldiers remain citizens. Political leaders retain responsibilities relative to these citizens while they are in uniform. Part of these responsibilities are executed using the military chain of command. Walzer himself acknowledges this fact. Another part is executed through the three war-waging responsibilities that I adduce later in this essay and fully in *Just War Reconsidered*.

28. Walzer, *Just and Unjust Wars*, 155; Walzer, "Two Kinds of Military Responsibility," 23–32.

29. Stanley McChrystal, *My Share of the Task* (New York: Portfolio, 2014), 185
30. Ibid., 186.
31. Walzer, "Two Kinds of Military Responsibility," 24.
32. Walzer, *Just and Unjust Wars*, 38–39.
33. Ibid., 292, 298, and 304.
34. Ibid., 292 and 302.
35. Ibid., 38–39.
36. Bernard Brodie, *War and Politics* (New York: Macmillan Publishing, 1973), 1–28; Karl von Clausewitz, *On War*, eds. Michael Howard and Peter Peret (Princeton: Princeton University Press, 1976), 75–88.
37. Walzer, *Just and Unjust Wars*, 316.
38. For brevity's sake, I will no longer use the longer term "citizens-now-soldiers." Whenever you read "soldiers," know they also remain citizens.
39. George W. Bush, *Decision Points* (New York: Crown Publishers, 2010), 184.
40. Text: President Bush Addresses the Nation, eMediaMillWorks, September 20, 2001, http://www.washingtonpost.com/wp-srv/nation/specials/attacked/transcripts/bushaddress_092001.html.
41. Bush, *Decision Points*, 184–91.
42. Sean Naylor, *Not a Good Day to Die: Chaos and Courage in the Mountains of Afghanistan, the Untold Story of Operation Anaconda* (New York: Berkley Books, 2005), 10–11, 13–14, 18–19, 20, 24, 43, 48, 53, 56, 87–88, 122–33, 135–37, 149–50, 154–57, 172–74, and 271–72.
43. Bush, *Decision Points*, 211.
44. Ibid., 220.
45. Ronald E. Neumann, *The Other War: Winning and Losing in Afghanistan* (Washington, DC: Potomac Books, 2009), xi–xii.
46. Dov S. Zakheim, *A Vulcan's Tale: How the Bush Administration Mismanaged the Reconstruction of Afghanistan* (Washington, DC: Brookings Institution Press, 2011), 61, Kindle.
47. Ibid., 96 and 126, Kindle.
48. Ibid., 1210–411, Kindle.
49. Ibid., 1912–36, Kindle.
50. Bruce Riedel is quoted from the forward he wrote to Ambassador Neumann's book: Neumann, *The Other War*, vii–x. See also Rajiv Chandrasekaran, *Little America: The War Within the War for Afghanistan* (New York: Alfred A. Knopf, 2012).
51. Ricardo S. Sanchez, *Wiser in Battle: A Soldier's Story* (New York: HarperCollins, 2008), 167–69.
52. Donald Rumsfeld, *Known and Unknown: A Memoir* (New York: Sentinel, 2012), 501.
53. Sanchez, *Wiser in Battle*, 382.

54. Michael R. Gordon and Bernard E. Trainor, *Cobra II: The Inside Story of the Invasion and Occupation of Iraq* (New York: Pantheon, 2006), 149.
55. Ibid., 152.
56. Ibid.
57. Ibid., 156.
58. L. Paul Bremer III, *My Year in Iraq: The Struggle to Build a Future of Hope* (New York: Threshold Editions, 2006), 5–13.
59. Rajiv Chandrasekaran, *Imperial Life in the Emerald City: Inside Iraq's Green Zone* (New York: Alfred A. Knopf, 2007), 16, 21, 64, 90–94, and 98–99.
60. Bush, *Decision Points*, 249–50, 257–61, and 268–69.
61. Jeffrey Record, *Dark Victory: America's Second War Against Iraq* (Annapolis: Naval Institute Press, 2004), 116 and 129.
62. Gordon and Trainor, *Cobra II*, 495.
63. For more complete accounts of this period, see: Ali A. Allawi, *The Occupation of Iraq: Winning the War, Losing the Peace* (New Haven: Yale University Press, 2007); Bremer, *My Year in Iraq*; Chandrasekaran, *Imperial Life in the Emerald City*; Gordon and Trainor, *Cobra II*; Record, *Dark Victory*; Thomas E. Ricks, *Fiasco: The American Military Adventure in Iraq* (New York: Penguin Press, 2006); and Sanchez, *Wiser in Battle*.
64. Gallup polling data: http://www.gallup.com/poll/1633/iraq.aspx.
65. Bush, *Decision Points*, 367.
66. Ibid., 363. The Askariya shrine at the Golden Mosque of Samarra is one of the holiest sites in Shia Islam. On February 22, 2006, two massive explosions destroyed the mosque. The attack was an enormous provocation designed to incite a war between Iraqi Shia and Sunnis.
67. Ibid., 371.
68. Ibid., 210–11.
69. Gallup polling data: http://www.gallup.com/poll/116233/afghanistan.aspx.
70. Bush, *Decision Points*, 211–17.
71. Ibid., 184.
72. Richard H. Kohn, "Building Trust: Civil-Military Behaviors for Effective National Security Decision-Making," in *American Civil-Military Relations: The Soldier and the State in a New Era*, eds. Suzanne Nielsen and Don Snider (Baltimore: Johns Hopkins University Press, 2009), 269.
73. Robert M. Gates, *Duty: Memoirs of a Secretary at War* (New York: Vintage, 2015), 384.
74. Two of the many good business books on this topic are: Larry Bossidy and Ram Charan, *Execution: The Discipline of Getting Things Done* (New York: Random House Business, 2002); Stephen P. Bradley and Richard L. Nolan, *Sense & Respond: Capturing Value in the Network Era* (Boston: Harvard Business School Press, 1998).

75. Gates, *Duty*, 362–385.
76. Bush, *Decision Points*, 363.
77. Michael R. Gordon and General Bernard E. Trainor, *The Endgame: The Inside Story of the Struggle for Iraq, from George W. Bush to Barack Obama* (New York: Vintage, 2013), 208.
78. Ibid.
79. Peter Feaver et al., "Success Matters: Casual Sensitivity and the War in Iraq," *International Security* 30, no. 3 (Winter 2005/06): 8.
80. February 14, 2014 Gallup poll available at: http://www.gallup.com/poll/116233/afghanistan.aspx.
81. Ibid.
82. Albert O. Hirschman, *Exit, Voice, and Loyalty: Responses to Decline in Firms, Organizations, and States* (Cambridge: Harvard University Press, 1979), 1–20.
83. Ibid., 92–93.
84. Ibid., 93.
85. Ibid., 94–96.
86. Ibid., 115.
87. Ibid., 115–16.
88. Ibid., 117.
89. Lewis Sorley, *Honorable Warrior: General Harold K. Johnson and the Ethics of Command* (Lawrence: University Press of Kansas, 1998), 268.
90. Ibid., 304.
91. Walzer, *Just and Unjust Wars*, 311.
92. Hirschman, *Exit, Voice, and Loyalty*, 116.
93. Ibid.
94. Gates, *Duty*, 370.
95. Kohn, "Building Trust," 282.
96. Ibid.

BIBLIOGRAPHY

Allawi, Ali A. *The Occupation of Iraq: Winning the War, Losing the Peace*. New Haven: Yale University Press, 2007.

Bossidy, Larry, and Ram Charan. *Execution: The Discipline of Getting Things Done*. New York: Random House Business, 2002.

Bradley, Stephen P., and Richard L. Nolan. *Sense & Respond: Capturing Value in the Network Era*. Boston: Harvard Business School Press, 1998.

Bremer, L. Paul III. *My Year in Iraq: The Struggle to Build a Future of Hope*. New York: Threshold Editions, 2006.

Brodie, Bernard. *War and Politics*. New York: Macmillan, 1973.

Bumiller, Elisabeth, and Charlie Savage. "Iraqi Massacre, a Light Sentence and a Question of Military Justice." *The New York Times*, January 27, 2012. https://www.nytimes.com/2012/01/28/us/an-iraqi-massacre-a-light-sentence-and-a-question-of-military-justice.html.

Bush, George W. *Decision Points*. New York: Crown Publishers, 2010.

Chandrasekaran, Rajiv. *Imperial Life in the Emerald City: Inside Iraq's Green Zone*. New York: Alfred A. Knopf, 2007.

———. *Little America: The War Within the War for Afghanistan*. New York: Alfred A. Knopf, 2012.

von Clausewitz, Karl. *On War*. Edited by Michael Howard and Peter Peret. Princeton: Princeton University Press, 1976.

Corn, Geoffrey S., Victor Hansen, Richard Jackson, M. Christopher Jenks, and Eric Talbot Jensen. *The Law of Armed Conflict: An Operational Approach*. New York: Wolters Kluwer, Law and Business, 2012.

Dubik, James M. "Human Rights, Command Responsibility, and Walzer's Just War Theory." *Philosophy and Public Affairs* 11, no. 4 (Fall 1982): 354–71.

———. *Just War Reconsidered: Strategy, Ethics, and Theory*. Lexington: University of Kentucky Press, 2016.

Feaver, Peter D., Christopher Gelpi, and Jason Reifler. "Success Matters: Casual Sensitivity and the War in Iraq." *International Security* 30, no. 3 (Winter 2005/06): 7–47.

Frederick, Jim. *Black Hearts: One Platoon's Descent into Madness in Iraq's Triangle of Death*. New York: Random House, 2010.

Gates, Robert M. *Duty: Memoirs of a Secretary at War*. New York: Vintage, 2015.

Gordon, Michael R., and Bernard E. Trainor. *Cobra II: The Inside Story of the Invasion and Occupation of Iraq*. New York: Pantheon, 2006.

———. *The Endgame: The Inside Story of the Struggle for Iraq, from George W. Bush to Barack Obama*. New York: Vintage, 2013.

Hirschman, Albert O. *Exit, Voice, and Loyalty: Responses to Decline in Firms, Organizations, and States*. Cambridge: Harvard University Press, 1979.

Kohn, Richard H. "Building Trust: Civil-Military Behaviors for Effective National Security Decision-Making." In *American Civil-Military Relations: The Soldier and the State in a New Era*, edited by Suzanne Nielsen and Don Snider, 264–89. Baltimore: Johns Hopkins University Press, 2009.

McChrystal, Stanley. *My Share of the Task*. New York: Portfolio, 2014.

Mulrine, Anna. "Pentagon Had Red Flags About Command Climate in 'kill team' Stryker Brigade." *Christian Science Monitor*, October 28, 2010. https://www.csmonitor.com/USA/Military/2010/1028/Pentagon-had-red-flags-about-command-climate-in-kill-team-Stryker-brigade.

Naylor, Sean. *Not a Good Day to Die: Chaos and Courage in the Mountains of Afghanistan, the Untold Story of Operation Anaconda*. New York: Berkley Books, 2005.

Neumann, Ronald E. *The Other War: Winning and Losing in Afghanistan*. Washington, DC: Potomac Books, 2009.

Orend, Brian. *The Morality of War*. Peterborough: Broadview Press, 2006.

Record, Jeffrey. *Dark Victory: America's Second War Against Iraq*. Annapolis: Naval Institute Press, 2004.

Ricks, Thomas E. *Fiasco: The American Military Adventure in Iraq*. New York: Penguin Press, 2006.

Rumsfeld, Donald. *Known and Unknown: A Memoir*. New York: Sentinel, 2012.

Sanchez, Ricardo S. *Wiser in Battle: A Soldier's Story*. New York: HarperCollins, 2008.

Sorley, Lewis. *Honorable Warrior: General Harold K. Johnson and the Ethics of Command*. Lawrence: University Press of Kansas, 1998.

Walzer, Michael. "Two Kinds of Military Responsibility." In *Arguing About War*, 23–32. New York: Yale University Press, 2004.

———. *Just and Unjust Wars*, 5th ed. New York: Basic Books, 2015.

Zakheim, Dov S. *A Vulcan's Tale: How the Bush Administration Mismanaged the Reconstruction of Afghanistan*. Washington, DC: Brookings Institution Press, 2011.

CHAPTER 8

Reflections on "Supreme Emergency"

Jeremy Waldron

Toward the end of *Just and Unjust Wars*,[1] Michael Walzer introduces a discussion that many have found alarming because it seems to compromise what is otherwise a firmly deontological view of the rules of armed conflict expressed in the rest of the book. I am talking about Chapter Sixteen, which is entitled "Supreme Emergency" and which canvasses the possibility that a society desperate to avoid military defeat when the stakes are very, very high, might understandably resort to methods of waging a war that are ordinarily forbidden.

BRITAIN 1939–42

Walzer's book is "a moral argument with historical illustrations." The illustration he provides for this discussion is the predicament of Britain in the early 1940s when Winston Churchill responded to the possibility of defeat at the hands of Nazi Germany by ordering the large-scale area bombing of German cities, a strategy calculated to bring death and terror to the ordinary men, women, and children living in those cities, leading

J. Waldron (✉)
New York University School of Law, New York, NY, USA
e-mail: jeremy.waldron@nyu.edu

© The Author(s) 2020
G. Parsons and M. A. Wilson (eds.), *Walzer and War*,
https://doi.org/10.1007/978-3-030-41657-7_8

157

hopefully to a collapse of civilian morale in Germany. Was this a crime—murder—as deliberate attacks on civilians in wartime must ordinarily be judged? Or was its wrongness offset, mitigated, excused, or at least made understandable by the supreme emergency Britain faced when it stood almost alone against Germany in 1940.

The history is complicated by the fact that Churchill used the phrase "supreme emergency" twice in relation to hard wartime choices, but actually neither of them referred to any decision about terror-bombing of cities. Churchill spoke of "supreme emergency" in a memo to Cabinet dated December 16, 1939.[2] This was before he became Prime Minister. As First Lord of the Admiralty, he proposed mining Norwegian territorial waters to force German vessels carrying iron ore from Sweden to "come onto the high seas," making themselves more vulnerable to attack.[3] He acknowledged that this would be a technical violation of international law, but he said

> We are fighting to re-establish the reign of law…. Our defeat would mean an age of barbaric violence…. We have a right, and are indeed bound in duty, to abrogate for a space some of the conventions of the very laws we seek to consolidate and reaffirm. Small nations must not tie our hands when we are fighting for their rights and freedom. The letter of the law must not *in supreme emergency* obstruct those who are charged with its protection and enforcement. It would not be right or rational that the aggressive Power should gain one set of advantages by tearing up all laws, and another set by sheltering behind the innate respect for law of its opponents.[4]

It is a little like Abraham Lincoln's question in response to Justice Taney's decision in *Ex parte Merryman*: "Are all the laws but one to go unexecuted and the government itself go to pieces lest that one be violated?"[5] And, in its dismissive reference to "small nations," it is uncomfortably like the Athenian attitude in the Melian dialogue: large states will exact what they can, small states will bear what they must.[6]

Walzer discusses this memo at length at the end of Chapter Fifteen of his book.[7] He makes it clear that Churchill did not then contemplate anything like the wholesale repudiation of central parts of the laws of war that forms the focus of the discussion in Chapter Sixteen. And he condemns Churchill's use of the language of "supreme emergency" in the memo as "rhetorical heightening" of a quite ordinary crisis in the course of military life.[8]

Churchill became Prime Minister on May 10, 1940 and he deployed the phrase "supreme emergency" a few days later when Britain was in a much more desperate situation. On May 19 it seemed the battle for France might be lost. And Britain did indeed face the probability then of catastrophic defeat. Churchill's broadcast speech on that day included the following passage:

> After this battle in France abates its force, there will come the battle for our Island—for all that Britain is, and all that Britain means. That will be the struggle. In that *supreme emergency* we shall not hesitate to take every step, even the most drastic, to call forth from our people the last ounce and the last inch of effort of which they are capable. The interests of property, the hours of labor, are nothing compared with the struggle of life and honor, for right and freedom, to which we have vowed ourselves.[9]

Notice that in this speech Churchill did *not* use "supreme emergency" to justify the infringement of what he called earlier in the same speech "the unwritten laws of war."[10] He certainly didn't use it to justify any proposal about bombing. The bombing of civilian areas—which is supposed to be the response to supreme emergency worth considering—did not begin in earnest until mid-1942, by which time the Battle of Britain had been over for more than eighteen months, the immediate threat of invasion had receded, Hitler had commenced his doomed invasion of the Soviet Union, and the United States had entered the war against Germany.[11] No, in the broadcast speech of May 19, 1940, Churchill used the idea of supreme emergency to justify the commandeering of life, labor, and property *within Britain*. On another occasion we might debate this also: i.e., the proposition that supreme emergency might justify a government in imposing extreme burdens upon—maybe as Hayek would say, "the enslavement of"[12]—its own population. But that is not the concern of Chapter Sixteen of *Just and Unjust Wars*.

Still, with some adjustments, one can entertain and work with a not-too-fanciful hypothetical version of the British illustration.[13] At a time when Britain and its dominions stood alone against Germany, defeat at the hands of Hitler's forces would indeed have been a national catastrophe of the highest order; Churchill's rhetoric of "a new dark age" was by no means an exaggeration.[14] And Britain's offensive options in mid-1940 were almost non-existent. One can imagine that a debate in the War Cabinet about the area bombing of German centers of civilian population might have commenced at that stage, in the spirit of "This is our last resort. If we bomb their cities, we can undermine their civilian morale. Until other offensive options present themselves, this is the only thing we can do." One can imagine the language of "supreme emergency" being used in this way. And so the question Walzer is putting to his readers is a valid one: how should we think about the burning of cities in order to kill and terrorize large numbers of their civilian inhabitants, night after night, for years if necessary—something absolutely forbidden by the laws of war—in this extremity, in the supreme emergency constituted by the prospect of otherwise unavoidable British defeat?

THE SCALE OF THE PROBLEM

It is very important to approach the question on this scale, which is why the original Norwegian example would not have been helpful in focusing Walzer's discussion. Because "supreme emergency" characterizes the fate of a whole community or civilization, any response to it of the sort that Walzer is contemplating is always going to involve a major change in tactics or strategy. It is never going to be about the shooting of this or that prisoner, the killing of this or that civilian, or the mining of this or that harbor. The closest Walzer comes to contemplating a singular event under these auspices is his discussion of the possibility that the nuclear incineration of one or two Japanese cities might have been considered a response to a supreme emergency faced by the United States. He considers that and rejects it.[15] I suppose there are philosophers who can concoct hypothetical cases involving the destruction of civilization unless this particular man is tortured or that particular hospital blown up, but such hypotheticals are far-fetched and corrupt. The advantage of Walzer's more-or-less real-life examples is that they demonstrate the scale on which these matters actually arise.

So, the discussion of supreme emergency in Chapter Sixteen contemplates a large-scale violation of the laws of war. Walzer sometimes phrases it as a breach (or "shattering") of "*the* war convention"[16]—that is, of the fundamental principle that demands discrimination between combatants and civilians as possible targets of armed operations.[17] The deaths of tens or hundreds of thousands of people are likely to be involved.[18] But more than just the alarming scale of the arithmetic, it is that we are tempted in circumstances of supreme emergency to take up a position in the realm of utilitarian arithmetic, which it is the whole point of the laws of war to keep us away from. Supreme emergency pushes us up against what are supposed to be "the final limits of war-making."[19] The response that Walzer's protagonist is contemplating is a game-changer, which is why (as we will see) the challenge of the Chapter Sixteen discussion is so important. Sometimes, in order to pose the choice starkly, Walzer talks of a *determinate* crime (these many thousands of civilians murdered) versus the *immeasurable* evil[20] that we are trying to avoid. But, let me repeat, the issue of scale is not just about the numbers. The shattering of the war convention that is being contemplated consists in the first place in the resort to such calculations. "My own action is determinate … only as to its direct consequences, while the rule that bars such acts is founded on a conception of rights that transcends all immediate considerations."[21]

If we accept that emergencies of this kind and on this scale may arise and measures of this kind and on this scale may be necessary or inevitable in response to them, then we may begin to wonder whether war—certainly war on the colossal scale of the Second World War—is the sort of thing that can be regulated at all. I don't mean that we should actually doubt that it is the sort of thing that can be governed by law, but in relation to certain circumstances we should at least be willing to ask. And I believe it would have been *unseemly* to finish a book like *Just and Unjust Wars* without considering the questions that are posed in this difficult late chapter.

Is the British Example Too Easy?

The British illustration has a number of special features that are useful for advancing Walzer's discussion. But they leave us with some questions. The war by the British, standing almost alone against Nazi Germany, was a just war and the stakes were staggeringly high and civilization-wide. As Churchill said in June 1940:

> The whole fury and might of the enemy must very soon be turned on us. Hitler knows that he will have to break us in this island or lose the war. If we can stand up to him, all Europe may be free and the life of the world may move forward into broad, sunlit uplands. But if we fail, then the whole world, including the United States, including all that we have known and cared for, will sink into the abyss of a new Dark Age, made more sinister, and perhaps more protracted, by the lights of perverted science.[22]

Everyone agrees that the Germans needed to be stopped—Walzer talks rightly of "evil objectified in the world … in a form so potent and apparent that there could never have been anything to do but fight against it"[23]—and it is not fanciful to insist that the Nazi onslaught needed to be stopped "by any means necessary." But is this case too easy?

A couple of possible complications need to be explored. First, what if the stakes are not the loss of a civilization, but simply the loss of a national political community? Walzer explores this at length—he invites us to consider what we should think if it was only *British* national survival that was at stake—and he reckons that community, rather than civilization, is key to whatever grip the supreme emergency discussion has on us. We will discuss this in the section entitled "Community or Civilization?"

Secondly, if "supreme emergency" refers to the likely destruction of a national community, then we have to ask whether this applies even to communities whose survival *we* do not relish, though their own members do. Does the application of the supreme emergency idea depend on a war's being just, so that it could not apply to both sides in a conflict like the Second World War? Or does it, like other aspects of *jus in bello* (on Walzer's otherwise plausible account) float free of *jus ad bellum*?[24] Is the lifting of *in bello* constraints in an emergency something that might work for our enemies as well as ourselves? Should we think of Adolf Hitler as facing a supreme emergency in 1944–45—the pending destruction of his "Thousand Year Reich"—just as Churchill faced a supreme emergency in 1940? We will discuss this in the section called "A Neutral Principle?"

As we will see, this is not just a question for Walzer to answer, as though one could go either way and his say-so binds us as to the terms of all subsequent discussion. We want to follow the logic of his argument. The normative implications of the supreme emergency idea have to be responsive to the underlying considerations. Why must extreme measures be contemplated, or why is it inevitable that they will be contemplated, in a supreme emergency? Unless we answer that, or unless we figure out the range of possible answers, we will not be able to tell who gets or who should get the benefit (such as it is) of Walzer's argument. That is the main thing I want to consider in this chapter, and this is the approach that I shall take.

A Proposal for a Legal Doctrine?

Let me elaborate that last point. When I accepted the invitation to contribute to this volume I thought I would criticize supreme emergency as a doctrinal proposal, reading Walzer in Chapter Sixteen as though he were presenting a form of "threshold deontology" (as it is sometimes called by moral philosophers),[25] an idea which, given the opportunity, I would like to contest.[26]

I was inclined to evaluate Chapter Sixteen by asking, in Richard Arneson's words, "Is Walzer's supreme emergency doctrine coherent and plausible? Should supreme emergency become a principle of just war theory?"[27] Like Arneson, I wanted to press questions about the discontinuities that the proposal seemed to involve: differences of degree among emergencies that seemed to trigger a qualitatively different approach to the laws of war.

But I took the precaution of rereading the chapter. I think now that Walzer's discussion of "supreme emergency" should not be approached as a normative proposal—to be evaluated and criticized by clever philosophers born in peacetime—but as a meditation on the whole enterprise of subjecting this terrible business of war to rules of restraint on the killing and mayhem that may legitimately be inflicted. I see the chapter on supreme emergency now as more reflective than argumentative. And I would like to pay tribute to it as such.

If we *were* contemplating a doctrine called "Supreme Emergency," presented as a legal proposal, i.e., as a proposed modification of the laws of war—I say we should not be considering it as such, but *if* we were—then Walzer would have to be pestered with a whole bunch of questions. There would be questions about the definition of "emergency" and "supreme"; about the standard of "imminence," and whether it needed to be insulated from extension to accommodate the measures contemplated[28]; about the meaning of "necessity" and the interplay between necessary and sufficient conditions[29] that would be required to prevent the use of Supreme Emergency as just a permission to lash out when one's situation was hopeless or as just to be seen as doing *something* even when something is never going to be enough; about whether the doctrine was to be understood as a justification (like the defense of necessity in criminal law) or as the basis of an excuse (like the defense of provocation); about whether we should understand it as a proposal for setting up a derogation mechanism from the laws of war, analogous to the mechanism embodied in Article 15 of the European Convention on Human Rights[30]; about whether such derogation might cover infringements of all kinds (including, for example, the use of forbidden weapons) or whether there might be certain acts (like torture, for example)[31] that remained prohibited even in the light of Supreme Emergency; and so on.

Walzer has a certain amount to say that is germane to these topics, though the derogation model, as far as I understand, is not one he has explored.[32] A possible reason for this is that, unlike the ECHR, the laws of war are already oriented to emergency conditions: they already address "time of war," which the ECHR regards in itself as a triggering condition for derogation. So, some would insist that since the laws of war are already designed to cope with the stress of emergency, an additional provision for derogation—over and above what "time of war" already involves—should not be added just because the emergency can be reckoned extreme. A suggestion of this kind raises issues connected to the debate about monism and dualism in the juridical mechanisms used in constitutional theory to address states of emergency.[33] Unfortunately, we cannot explore that here.

THE MORAL INTERPRETATION

If it is not treated as a legal proposal, how else might we regard the discussion in Chapter Sixteen of *Just and Unjust Wars*? I suppose it might be intended as a straightforward moral argument: the use of certain measures or tactics might be morally justified or permitted, or something one has a right or even an obligation to carry out, whatever the positive law says. Walzer uses all these terms: justifiability, permission, entitlement, and moral requirement. And naturally enough, many moral philosophers have evaluated Walzer's discussion in the light of moral theory.

It need not be regarded as a moral proposal for legal change (which would take us back to the section called "A Proposal for a Legal Doctrine?"). It might be seen instead in the light of what Jeff McMahan calls deep morality,[34] a basis for normative thinking about the laws of war which does not necessarily yield legal proposals. I have some general reservations about this kind of inquiry.[35] But I guess it may be warranted if the point of the discussion is guarded moral reflection, not changes in doctrine.

A moral assessment of supreme emergency would require us to pay attention to the issue of thresholds and discontinuities.[36] I don't mean in the sense of actually telling us (numerically or otherwise) where the thresholds ought to be set: deep moral reflection is not that sort of enterprise. But the very idea of there being differences of degree among emergencies that seem to trigger a qualitatively different approach to the laws of war bears critical attention. Is that how normativity could conceivably operate in this realm? Does supreme emergency as a moral idea make sense, even if its non-administrability is conceded?

And what does the impulse to take such an approach tell us about moral sensibility generally? Some see Walzer's argument as yet another example of weak-kneed deontology, "blinking" before a consequentialist onslaught spearheaded by rhetoric about the heavens falling. We start by saying there is an absolute duty not to target civilians; it remains murder even in the midst of war; civilians have a right not to be targeted; and that right should not have to yield to the exigencies of emergency calculations. That's the official position. But then—as I said in an article about torture—most so-called deontologists turn out to be moderates when the numbers get too high[37]:

> They are willing to abandon even cherished absolutes in the face of what Robert Nozick once called "catastrophic moral horror." For a culture supposedly committed to human rights, we have amazing difficulty in even conceiving—without some sort of squirm—moral absolutes. Academics in particular are so frightened of being branded "unrealistic" that we will fall over ourselves at the slightest provocation to opine that of course moral restraints must be abandoned when the stakes are high enough. Extreme circumstances can make moral absolutes look ridiculous, and those in our position cannot afford to be made to look ridiculous.[38]

So Darrell Cole condemns the Chapter Sixteen discussion for "the horrors that Walzer's consequentialism may countenance,"[39] and cites it as an instance of what G. E. M. Anscombe pointed to when she said that "modern moral philosophy…constructs formally beautiful theories of ethics, which always allow someone to commit dreadful acts in the name of doing something that is the 'morally right' thing to do."[40]

Admittedly this assessment is complicated by the issue of "dirty hands" that seems to be implicated in Walzer's discussion.[41] Despite some loose terminology, Walzer is emphatically not saying that it would have been, morally speaking, *alright* for Churchill to have ordered the bombing of cities and the deliberate killing of civilians during the crisis of the early 1940s. The decision never ceased to be a crime and Churchill and his colleagues (and, I guess, the British people in whose name these decisions were taken) had to bear "the burdens of criminality."[42] "[T]he destruction of the innocent, whatever its purposes, is a kind of blasphemy against our deepest moral commitments. This is true even in a supreme emergency, when we cannot do anything else."[43] The point about dirty hands is that Walzer wishes to maintain whatever tension exists here.[44] What Churchill and the others did in this supreme emergency was both justifiable and wrong. (And both terms—"justifiable" and "wrong" have something approaching their full-blooded sense; neither of them is ironic or in scare-quotes.) It was necessary, perhaps. But it was similar to some of what their worst enemies were doing.[45] And it was incumbent on Churchill and the others to "abhor the immoral acts to which [they were] driven."[46] Walzer is not sanitizing or "domesticating" these decisions; they are more "properly understood as participating in the darkness of political tragedy."[47]

This is heady stuff, and it is easy (and unhealthy) to get over-intrigued by the possibility that Churchill and the others made themselves mass murderers because (to adapt a saying of Machiavelli's) they loved their country more than the salvation of their own souls.[48] But instead of embracing a toxic form of amoralism, we may want to see the ambivalence of this verdict as embodying the uncertainties and paradoxes in any reflections that are elicited by the British illustration from the 1940s. We don't have a determinate conclusion here: what they did was both right and wrong, but they had to do it. A plurality of strident and all-things-considered normative judgments is precipitated out of our reflections and there is no escaping either from any one of them or from the tension between them. This is not conventional moral analysis. It is not trolley-ology or reflective equilibrium. It is not in any way business-as-usual for moral philosophy. It is not what Anscombe was crying out against, but nor is it bad faith: I don't accept that "Walzer appears to be attempting to hold onto an absolutist moral position without being willing to accept all of its consequences."[49] Instead we should say: when you explore the limits of what is possible in the normative regulation of human extremity, this is the sort of mess you come up with.

THE CIRCUMSTANCES
OF THE REGULATION OF ARMED CONFLICT

"Supreme Emergency" is not proposed in Chapter Sixteen of *Just and Unjust Wars* as a legal doctrine and I believe it is also not proposed (in any straightforward sense) as a moral idea. The tone of Walzer's writing is open-ended and paradoxical, rather than dogmatic. Conclusions are put forward, but they are put forward tentatively, "not without hesitation and worry"[50] and not without the gravest warning "to be careful" with them,[51] given the panic and hysteria that will inevitably accompany the circumstances in which such thoughts practically arise. I think we can make the best sense of the tensions and contradictions, the provocations and paradoxes that Walzer repeatedly mentions,[52] by asking what we should expect when we explore the limits of the application of normative analysis. Supreme emergencies, says Walzer, "put morality itself at risk."[53] Let me explain what I think he means by that.

There is a sense in Walzer's discussion that in certain circumstances, *the bottom drops out of our ability to argue our way legally or morally through a problem,* because the assumptions that normally underpin such arguments have been shaken or have otherwise evaporated. Some of that involves the chaos, horror, rage, and fear at the level of individuals that characterizes large-scale combat—the fog of war and the outer reaches of human endurance and the capacity for self-restraint. We may ask: what limits do these aspects of war impose on the good sense and practicability of legal and moral rules of various kinds?[54] That's one set of considerations to reflect upon—and they are very important.

Let me step back a bit. In political philosophy, the difficulties that might arise out of such extremities are sometimes discussed under the heading of "the circumstances of justice," by which is meant those aspects of the human condition, such as limited altruism and moderate scarcity which make justice as a virtue and a practice both possible and necessary.[55] It is thought, for example, that desperate scarcity undermines the talk of justice that is usually associated with distributive issues. David Hume said this about necessity

Suppose a society to fall into such want of all common necessaries, that the utmost frugality and industry cannot preserve the greater number from perishing, and the whole from extreme misery: It will readily, I believe, be admitted, that the strict laws of justice are suspended, in such a pressing emergence, and give place to the stronger motives of necessity and self-preservation. Is it any crime, after a shipwreck, to seize whatever means or instrument of safety one can lay hold of, without regard to former limitations of property?[56]

When the circumstances of justice fail in this way, the result is not a neat *alternative* set of moral prescriptions, but rather some radical uncertainty about whether we can think normatively at all. We don't say that the drowning man in a shipwreck who seizes a spar that another is clinging to, shaking him off it, is perfectly entitled or permitted to do that; we may feel an inclination in that direction, but really we do not know what to say. The bottom has dropped out of the conditions which usually make sense of our talk of entitlements, obligations, and permissibility.

Maybe it's a little like P. F. Strawson's concept of presupposition, as when we say "The present King of France is bald" lacks a truth-value—is neither true nor false—because since France is a republic one of the presuppositions of any talk about "the present King of France" is lacking.[57] Now "lacks a truth value" is a (relatively) tidy thing to say about a proposition, but practical discourse is not just propositional. It is prescriptive and its prescriptivity goes awry when its presuppositions fail. We don't know what to say—what prescriptions to issue—to the man who unseats another from the single available spar in a shipwreck. We blurt things out and we kind of contradict ourselves.

Similarly, we may think about something we might call the failure of the "circumstances" of laws of armed conflict.[58] Think of some of the things the regulation of war depends on: it depends on a shared sense that war will not continue forever, that it will yield to peace; that people have memories; that humans do have self-control; that people crave a decent self-image; that a fearful man does not just become an animal; and so on.

Now, at the individual level, Walzer believes we have discovered that law can and should make normative demands on combatants, even in the extremes of individual necessity. "From the standpoint of the combat soldier, war is a rapid succession of supreme emergencies: his life is constantly at risk. But we are very reluctant to allow soldiers to save themselves by killing innocent and helpless people."[59] At the individual level, necessity does not represent a failure of the circumstances of the laws of armed conflict. And self-restraint is not an impossibility.

> It is simply not the case that individuals will always strike out at [the] innocent ... rather than accept risks for themselves. We even say, very often, that it is their duty to accept risks (and perhaps to die); and here as in moral life generally, "ought" implies "can." We make the demand knowing that it is possible for people to live up to it.[60]

But Chapter Sixteen of *Just and Unjust Wars* reflects on a different set of considerations relevant for understanding the challenge of regulating and limiting warfare. This is the challenge posed by how high the *overall* stakes are in some conflicts, not just in terms of individual combatants' lives or well-being, not just in terms of this or that value, but of whole social schemes of value. That is what Walzer means by supreme emergency.

Philosophers sometimes make fun of moral absolutists by saying they believe "*Fiat justitia ruat caelum.*" But since no one really knows what "*ruat caelum*" means—is it supposed to be an astronomical concept?—it is easy enough for either side to say, from the comfort of the philosopher's armchair, that justice should or should not be done when the heavens are in danger of falling.[61] But the imminent destruction of a whole horizon of value—of the sort that a Nazi victory in the Second World War might have led to—is the closest we have come in real-world experience to the heavens really falling. "Nazism was an ultimate threat to everything decent in our lives, an ideology and a practice of domination so murderous, so degrading even to those who might survive, that the consequences of its final victory were literally beyond calculation, immeasurably awful."[62] And Walzer is exploring the possibility that when this sort of thing is in prospect, the conditions—the presuppositions—for sensible talk of normative constraints on war-making may have collapsed.

Not all wars pose this kind of supreme emergency. War is not always over ultimate values "where the victory of one side would be a human disaster for the other."[63] But the illustration from the Second World War—stylized though it is—shows that this possibility is not out of the question. And so we have to say something about it. By which I mean: it is incumbent on us, who for fifteen chapters have been reading about the regulation of war, to reflect finally on what might be at stake in a country's going to war—the stakes of victory and defeat—and to consider whether all our talk of rules, restraints, and conventions is practicable in that context. It is something—I mean *thinking about this* is something—that it would be indecent or unseemly not to do.

In more recent work, Michael Walzer has talked about "the triumph of just war theory."[64] Against all the odds, in a century of unprecedented carnage and savagery, a sense that there are norms and restraints on war-making has actually been upheld. Not perfectly, but systematically. And people accept that now in the military, in politics, and in the academy, whose realist predecessors did not accept it seventy years ago. However, we know some wars have been fought and some future wars will be fought in circumstances where everything seems to be at stake. If our present faith in the rules of war is justified, then they have to be able to operate in that very high stakes environment, and we need to have something to say about the prospect that they can't. That is the topic of Walzer's Chapter Sixteen.

It sounds like I am tilting toward an understanding of Walzer on supreme emergency that is based on *the psychological impossibility* of statesmen restraining themselves when their backs are to the wall and a proposed breach of the war convention is all that stands between their community and everything that they hold dear. In the section titled "What Choice Do I Have?", I will explore the tension between the "can't" and the "shouldn't" in Walzer's account of the shattering of the war convention in the circumstances he envisages. But before I do that, I want to say a word about two other dimensions of his account.

A Neutral Principle?

So far, our discussion has been mainly exegetical. But I now want to turn directly to consider how we should understand the very idea of "supreme emergency," and various possible responses to it, whether they are set out in Walzer's work or not.

I said in the section called "The Circumstances of the Regulation of Armed Conflict" that some wars are fought in circumstances where everything seems to be at stake. Seems? *Seems so to whom?* Are we thinking of a "detached observer" here—*us*, the readers, for example—who can objectively identify the values that are at stake? That's what the British illustration initially suggests: a Nazi victory would be immeasurably awful; as men and women of good will, "we are likely to find ourselves united in fear and abhorrence,"[65] so we must explore the implication of *that shared view* of a radical threat to "human values."

Or is the "seems" rather in the eye of the beholder? If it is thought that supreme emergency may take us beyond the realm of the circumstances of the regulation of combat, must we accept that the challenges and dilemmas Walzer is discussing might arise on either side (or both sides) of a given war? In any war, there may come a point where one side or the other or each of them at different times has to stare down the prospect of catastrophic defeat. Consider the American Civil War. In 1862 Abraham Lincoln had to face the prospect of the loss of the Union;

the Confederacy faced the loss of its distinctive way of life in 1865. We, as observers, may value the preservation of the Union more (much more) than the preservation of the Southern way of life (including, as it did, slavery) and so we may be less patient, less accepting of any designation of the possible loss of the latter as a supreme emergency for its members. We have less sympathy for it; the communal form at stake is one we do not regard as of great value. But its members did, and presumably some of the phenomenology of supreme emergency would come along with that *in extremis*.

This is like the debate about "neutral principles" in legal and political philosophy. In a 1974 article, Gerald Dworkin asked whether those in the civil rights movement who participated in civil disobedience would support or tolerate its use in defense of principles they disagreed with.[66] "[T]hose who defend the civil disobedience of Martin Luther King are asked to specify a relevant difference between his actions and those of George Wallace." Now, their response might be "that the laws that King broke were unjust while those Wallace violated were just" (though Wallace would not accept that).[67] That would be a non-neutral application of the principle of civil disobedience. A neutral application would involve trusting the principle's deployment even in the hands of one's ideological opponents.[68]

There will no doubt be limits on our willingness to generalize whatever argument about supreme emergency we accept. The Confederacy example will be at or near those limits for some people. The Nazi example will be well beyond them: do we really want to acknowledge the loss of the Third Reich and Germany's descent (yet again!) into defeat and shame as a supreme emergency for Hitler and his gang of murderers?

Then there are intermediate cases. It is not hard to sympathize with gallant England and the possible loss of that decent and long-established political community on the damp British Isles. But Britain also faced the loss of its world-wide empire in the Second World War, and American military and political leaders had much less sympathy with that dimension of Churchill's supreme emergency.

Or consider the following case, connected in several ways to the British example. In his book *Retribution: The Battle for Japan 1944–45*, while asking why Japan continued to fight despite no realistic prospect of victory, Max Hastings drew an analogy between the situation of Japan in 1944 and the desperate situation of the United Kingdom in June 1940:

Japan's options in late 1944, a Japanese might say, were not dissimilar to those of Britain in 1940. Winston Churchill's commitment to resist Nazi Germany after the fall of France was neither more nor less rational than that of Japan after losing the Marianas. Without allies, Britain possessed no better prospect of encompassing the defeat of Nazi Germany than did Japan of defeating the Americans. Britain's salvation was achieved overwhelmingly through the actions of her enemies in forcing the Soviet Union and the U.S. into the war, not by any military achievement of her own save that of defiance in the face of hopeless odds. ... If the cause of Japanese militarism seems to posterity immeasurably less admirable than that of British democracy, it engaged its adherents with equal devotion.[69]

Don't we have to consider that devotion as a possible basis of at least the phenomenology of extreme emergency, which might seem—subjectively at least—to have justified the Japanese in some of the more desperate measures they contemplated and took in 1945?

It is tempting to just sort through these possibilities, crediting some and discrediting others. But the question in an exploration of this kind should not be about which applications we are comfortable with—so that we adjust the principles we are manufacturing to match our considered judgments about particular cases in reflective equilibrium—but about where the various factors that Walzer invites us to consider actually lead us. Does the logic of his discussion invite us to understand the predicament of *anyone* who faces (what seems to him or her) a loss of the kind that Walzer talks about? Or are we to factor in our own best estimate of the *objective* value of what is at stake in the emergency.

Another question—disturbing in a somewhat similar way—asks about the relationship between the idea of a just war and what Walzer says about supreme emergency. Does a doctrine of supreme emergency operate independently of *jus ad bellum* (in the way that other doctrines concerning *jus in bello* are supposed to operate)? Indeed, what is the relation between just war and emergency defense of civilization or community? Suppose the collapse of Christian civilization would have been the upshot of the defeat of the unjust Crusaders in the twelfth or thirteenth centuries? Or suppose the end of the war that Nazi Germany waged in Europe had presaged the reduction (as was proposed by some among the allies) of the whole of Germany to deindustrialized pastureland. The loss of a civilization or the loss of a national community is still a loss even if the war that brought it about was waged unjustly.

Some of Walzer's critics and commentators seem to condition the whole possibility of a justified departure from the laws of war in response to supreme emergency on the proposition that the war in question is just. Zachary Calo tells us that "Walzer develops the concept of supreme emergency in the course of examining whether it is permissible to target civilian populations *during a just war*."[70] But I don't think Walzer ever says that, and it is a further question whether he would have been in a position to defend it if he had.

Maybe it would have been a good idea to give us in Chapter Sixteen some sort of illustration of supreme emergency for a community that we would not find appealing though its members surely do. Be that as it may, it is instructive for us to consider such cases, not in order to embarrass Walzer with questions about them, but to challenge ourselves concerning the viability on all sides of this overall normative enterprise.

COMMUNITY OR CIVILIZATION?

A connected set of questions concerns the *scale* and the *nature* of what is at stake in a supreme emergency. In the 1940s illustration, the prospect of British defeat raises the specter of (1) the "immeasurable evil" of Nazism over Western civilization[71] with "the abyss of a new Dark Age" and "an age of barbaric violence."[72] And on a more modest scale, it betokens (2) the subjugation and occupation of Great Britain or, at best, its diminishment by humiliating peace terms into an abjectly neutral facilitator of German dominance in Europe. Prospect (1) represents high civilizational stakes; prospect (2) is communal rather than civilizational—the loss or fatal humiliation of the British national community. Walzer uses language appropriate to both prospects. But he seems to opt—if "option" is the right word—for the *community* interpretation.

As I said before, I actually don't think we should be interested in an *option* on Walzer's part as between (1) and (2). For again, supreme emergency is not a doctrine he has proposed that stands in need of interpretation; it is an occasion for contemplation on where the limits of the laws-of-war enterprise are likely to be found. (1) and (2) are so bound up with one another in the 1940s illustration that it seems impossible or inappropriate to separate them. But I guess we can imagine a civilizational loss without a loss of any national community—for example, if after a German victory in the 1940s Britain, France, Holland, etc., were to become fascist independent states rather than liberal-democratic independent states. And we can imagine the loss of a national community without its necessarily representing the loss of a civilization: for example, the danger to Israel from its enemies from 1948 to 1973 might be seen in this light. As a matter of fact, either type of case might pose the prospect of the radical and thorough-going loss of a whole horizon of value that Walzer has in mind in his discussion.

More analysis may be appropriate, however, for a couple of reasons. (i) It is important because the civilizational aspect enables a move to resist the "supreme emergency" exception (if that is what it is) that the communal aspect does not enable. Also (ii) such analysis may be helpful as a continuation of our discussion in the section called "Community or Civilization?": a civilizational understanding seems more objective and detached; a communal one more open to what we called then a "neutral" application by either side in an armed conflict.

(i) With the stakes conceived as civilizational, it may be easier to make an internal case *against* the wrongdoing that supreme emergency seems to call for. What I mean is that the value of civilization may be present on both sides: there is the threat posed by the emergency; but also the proposed response to the emergency may itself compromise the fabric of the civilization it is our purpose to defend. "Our civilization and morality," as Walzer puts it, may already comprise "our collective abhorrence of murder, even when it [*murder*] seems, as it always does, to serve some purpose."[73] This will not be a trumping argument, but it is important nonetheless. "[T]he destruction of the innocent, whatever its purposes, is a kind of blasphemy against our deepest moral commitments. (This is true even in a supreme emergency, when we cannot do anything else.)"[74] It sponsors a way of resisting the practical response to supreme emergency: we resist (for example, we refuse to bomb civilian populations) because that *in itself* would begin the process of the loss of our civilization.

(ii) On the second point: when Walzer rescinds from the civilizational dimension of British defeat in the 1940s to the communal dimension, he seems to be asking us a neutral question: "Can soldiers and statesmen override the rights of innocent people for the sake of their own political community?"[75] It seems like this could apply to any set of statesmen in relation to any political community. And what he says about the importance to people of their national community in *Just and Unjust Wars*, but particularly in *Arguing About War*, could be applied as well to our enemies' political communities as to our own. I mean the Burkean stuff about "*ongoingness*",[76] about "political community as a contract between 'those who are living, those who are dead, and those who are yet to be born,'" and about trying "to carry on, and also to improve upon, a way of life handed down by our ancestors" to pass it on to "recognizable descendants, carrying on and improving upon our own way of life."[77] This commitment to continuity across generations seems morally neutral, by which I mean not that it fails to be valuable or important, but that it seems to apply indifferently so far as concerns the value-content of the shared way of life "developed by their ancestors, to be passed on to their children."[78] Whatever that shared way of life may be, Walzer seems to be saying, its loss will be a generational catastrophe for those who follow it. A threatened community faces the possibility of "moral as well as physical extinction,"[79] but the moral dimension here seems to refer to whatever the positive morality is of the community in question.

I don't mean to ignore the point that from the inside, i.e., from a non-detached point of view, the internal values of a given community will feel like universal values to their adherents. Nor do I mean to deny that even from a detached point of view, the survival of independent communities is objectively one of "the highest values of international society."[80] The situation with the values here is very complicated, and it is a virtue of Walzer's account that it drives home those complications to us.

At one point, Walzer says that "[s]upreme emergency is a communitarian doctrine."[81] I don't want to get into an argument about his philosophical claim that "communities, in emergencies, seem to have different and larger prerogatives" than individuals.[82] Walzer is surely right that attachment to community "is a feature of our lived reality, a source of our identity and self-understanding."[83] But the feature of modern communitarianism that seems most prominent here is the one that subordinates concern for universal values to the survival of community as such. We are not to judge communities as more or less worthy of survival, and a communitarian doctrine of supreme emergency will not be invested in any such discrimination.

I guess in principle we could take an analogous approach to civilizations. The loss of any civilization is a disaster whether we would judge the content of that civilization as good or bad. But in fact—as the Nazi example illustrates—a civilizational standard does seem to carry with it usually a substantive element of evaluation.

So, in exploring these possibilities—does supreme emergency involve potential loss of community or potential loss of civilization?—we are exploring how far a substantive evaluation of the form of life in question (undertaken from a detached and objective moral viewpoint) is entangled with the plethora of other conflicting judgments that supreme emergency evokes, such as "We have no choice but to do this" and "History will not forgive us if we fail to protect this way of life."

"WHAT CHOICE DO I HAVE?"

A lot of the best work in Chapter Sixteen of Walzer's book is his imagination of the phenomenology of this sort of emergency thinking. What was it like, what would it be like, to face such a supreme emergency and the prospect of communal or civilizational catastrophe that it brought with it? Objectively this involves exploring the facts of the situation, but also people's responses to those facts: it means exploring "regions of desperation and disaster."[84] In this section, I want to consider the phenomenological dimension, because this, if anything, will take us to the heart of the problem for normativity. What is it like for the bottom to seem to fall out of our sense of moral and legal restraint?

Of course, any such account is speculative, except to the extent we have memoirs or recordings of conversations at the time. And all such speculations are fallible and liable to refutation in light of better evidence. But by exploring the kinds of thoughts that must have permeated the consciousness and conversations of the participants, we can begin to articulate the stakes.

What we see in Walzer's account is movement back and forth between the phenomenology summed up in statements like "I can't help but do this," statements like "I have to do this," and statements like "I am required to do this."[85]

Let's begin with the locutions that suggest actual constraint—his talk, for example, of what one is "forced" to do.[86] Walzer asks his readers:

> Can soldiers and statesmen override the rights of innocent people for the sake of their own political community? ... *What choice do they have?* ... Faced with some ultimate horror, their options exhausted, *they will do what they must* to save their own people.[87]

It sounds almost like a causal prediction. It is like a sort of inevitability. It might even suggest that a civilization or community has some sort of automatic last-resort defense mechanism in the consciousness and likely behavior of its representatives. In some speculation about the phenomenology of the Hiroshima bombing, Walzer quotes this from Secretary of War Stimson's view of his own and others' state of mind faced with the "choice" about using a weapon of mass destruction: "No man, in our position and subject to our responsibilities, holding in his hand a weapon of such possibilities for ... saving those lives, could have failed to use it." And, though he disagrees with the Hiroshima decision, Walzer observes that in principle "[t]his is by no means an incomprehensible or, on the surface at least, an outrageous argument."[88]

On the other hand, in the passage from *Just and Unjust Wars* that I quoted a moment ago, Walzer writes that the idea of inevitability is not what he is trying to get at:

> That is not to say that their decision is inevitable (I have no way of knowing that), but the sense of obligation and of moral urgency they are likely to feel at such a time is so overwhelming that a different outcome is hard to imagine.[89]

I think he is trying to convey a sense of persons being "overwhelmed"[90] but of their being overwhelmed *with reasons* rather than causally overwhelmed by the circumstances themselves. It is a fine line. In philosophical discussions of coercion, we sometimes distinguish two kinds of threat: in one kind, a person is faced with a threat that simply alters the balance of costs and benefits relating to some action and calls for some sort of rational deliberation[91]; in a second kind, the threat induces a sort of panic or terror that makes rational deliberation very difficult, and to that extent has something more like a causal impact. An example I have used of the second type of coercion is that of a person who has been soaked with gasoline and threatened with fire if he does not yield the combination to a safe.[92] That's not exactly the situation we are imagining facing Churchill and his war cabinet: panic and terror as reasons drowning out all other possibilities. Even the option they had "no choice" but to select required deliberation and thought.

Sometimes Walzer uses the language of what we can be expected to bear or put up with. He talks of the prospect facing Churchill as "a loss of value greater than men and women are morally obliged to bear."[93] Connected with this, there is a sense that in some circumstances we are *morally* overwhelmed, and we say: what choice do I have? There is no option, nothing else to be done, in the face of the prospect of "evil objectified in the world ... in a form so potent and apparent that there could never have been anything to do but fight against it."[94]

Peter Winch uses a locution like this—necessity as being morally over-whelmed—in a commentary on the parable of the Good Samaritan.[95] According to Winch, the Samaritan in the parable evidently did not see his helping the man who had fallen among thieves as a matter of discretion, which he might deliberate about. He saw it as a necessity:

> The Samaritan responds to what he sees as a necessity generated by the presence of the injured man. What I mean by introducing this word ["necessity"] can be brought out by considering what someone in the Samaritan's position, and responding as he did, might say if urged by a companion to hurry on so as not to miss his important appointment. "But I can't just leave him here to die."[96]

Evidently the "can't" is not physical impossibility: the priest and the Levite in the parable experienced no difficulty in passing by on the other side after they saw the injured man's plight. But there is something like moral impossibility here, responsive to a necessity that rivets the attention of those who are sensitive to what might be at stake here.

The sensitivity that generates that thought might be regarded as moral sensitivity, but that in itself won't do because Walzer never wants to let go of the equally compelling moral sense—for the bombing case—that the action dictated by the necessity is also one that a good person "can't" perform. (It is after all the murder of thousands of people.) There are "can'ts" all over the place here. If there is a basis for experience of the "necessity" (in the normative sense we are exploring) of the bombing option, it comes perhaps from the role that is filled by those who are facing the decision. For Churchill and the others are not just moral agents (as we say) facing a dilemma, like a trolley problem that they have stumbled into. They are designated leaders, representatives of the community whose survival is at stake here, and their overwhelming sense that they *can't* just let Britain be defeated has to do with that status. They have a job to do, not for themselves, but for the community, and they are overwhelmed by that responsibility.[97]

We have canvassed a lot of possibilities here. But I have no patience with any question that requires Walzer to settle on just one of them as his "real" view. We are reflecting on what it means for what I called "the circumstances of the laws of war" to fail and for the normative bottom to drop out of our ordinary processes of legal and moral deliberations. In this situation, we may be tongue-tied or we may find our agency and our reasoning tossed back and forth amidst a plethora of prescriptions, none of them determinate, none of them easily reconcilable with any of the others, certainly not reconcilable in a neat theory. There is no settled answer here and I don't read Walzer as proposing one.

I do want to say that the more we emphasize the chaotic and conflicted character of the phenomenology here, we must expect to see it in response to threats to communities whose survival *we* do not cherish. It may be difficult for us to endorse that or empathize with it in some of the cases mentioned in the section I called "Community or Civilization?", but that doesn't make the phenomenology go away. And I believe there is enough hesitation in Walzer's own endorsement of the response to supreme emergency in the illustration he has chosen to leave room for recognition of important similarities in these other even more problematic instances.

A Dangerous Doctrine?

Many of Walzer's critics see his discussion of Supreme Emergency as a doctrinal proposal (in law or morality), and they criticize it as such. Some say that the very act of thinking all this through in Chapter Sixteen is dangerous. George Wright says that "it is important to see the supreme emergency principle as not only incomplete, logically questionable, and unnecessary, but as affirmatively dangerous as well."[98] I don't agree with either assessment. I think the Chapter Sixteen discussion, fraught as it is with uncertainty and hesitation, is indispensable as part of the good faith with which *Just and Unjust Wars* is written. It is indispensable *just as it is* in any mature meditation on the limits of the enterprise that is the subject of the book as a whole.

Above all, we need to remember the subject-matter. Regulating war is not like regulating traffic or securities trading. In the midst of our exultation over what Walzer calls "the triumph of just war theory," we must not forget that the theory is supposed to be oriented to practices of blood, terror, anger, and almost the highest stakes that human societies can conceive of. Is regulation of all that going to be possible? Sometimes, in extremity, who knows?

NOTES

1. Michael Walzer, *Just and Unjust Wars: A Moral Argument with Historical Illustrations*, 5th ed. (New York: Basic Books, 2015).
2. Ibid., 251.
3. I owe this background to Henry Shue, "Liberalism: The Impossibility of Justifying Weapons of Mass Destruction," in *Ethics and Weapons of Mass Destruction: Religious and Secular Perspectives*, eds. Sohail Hashmi and Steven Lee (Cambridge: Cambridge University Press, 2004), 139–40.
4. Winston Churchill, *The Second World War*, vol. 1: *The Gathering Storm* (London: Houghton Mifflin, 1948), 547, my emphasis.
5. *Ex parte Merryman* 17 F. Cas. 144 (C.C.D. Md. 1861). For Lincoln's response, see William Rehnquist, *All the Laws but One: Civil Liberties in Wartime* (New York: Alfred A. Knopf, 1998).
6. For Walzer's discussion of the Melian dialogue, see *Just and Unjust Wars*, 5–13.
7. Ibid., 245–50.
8. Ibid., 251.
9. Broadcast speech of May 19, 1940, my emphasis.
10. Ibid. Churchill said: "I am sure I speak for all when I say we are ready to face [the "hideous apparatus" of German aggression]; to endure it; and to retaliate against it—to any extent that the unwritten laws of war permit."
11. Walzer talks about "the terrible two years that followed the defeat of France, from the summer of 1940 to the summer of 1942, when Hitler's armies were everywhere triumphant" (*Just and Unjust Wars*, 255). But he acknowledges in the middle of the chapter that "the supreme emergency passed long before the British bombing reached its crescendo" (261).
12. F. A. Hayek, *The Road to Serfdom* (Chicago: University of Chicago Press, 1944).
13. Walzer talks explicitly about the stylizing of his illustrations: "[T]he cases are necessarily sketched in outline form. In order to make them exemplary, I have had to abridge their ambiguities" (*Just and Unjust Wars*, xxii). He stylizes what is at stake in the British example: "The danger [of German victory] was a general one. But suppose it had existed for Britain alone. Can a supreme emergency be constituted by a particular threat—by a threat of enslavement or extermination directed against a single nation?" (254). And necessarily he has to leave out other aspects of the strategic situation, such as that the direction of RAF resources to city-bombing Europe imperiled the protection of absolutely essential and vulnerable supply lines in the Atlantic. This is the argument of Jonathan Dimbleby, *The Battle of the Atlantic: How the Allies Won the War* (Oxford: Oxford University Press, 2016).
14. See the passage quoted in text accompanying footnote 15, *infra*, from Winston Churchill, broadcast speech of June 18, 1940.

15. *Just and Unjust Wars*, 263–68.
16. Ibid., 251 and 259, my emphasis.
17. One of Walzer's section headings is "Overriding the Rules of War." See *Just and Unjust Wars*, 255.
18. *Just and Unjust Wars*, 262: "To kill 278,966 civilians (the number is made up) in order to avoid the deaths of an unknown but probably larger number of civilians and soldiers is surely a fantastic, godlike, frightening, and horrendous act."
19. Michael Walzer, *Arguing About War* (New Haven: Yale University Press, 2000), 36.
20. *Just and Unjust Wars*, 259.
21. Ibid., 260.
22. Winston Churchill, broadcast speech of June 18, 1940.
23. *Just and Unjust Wars*, 253.
24. For general discussion of the independence of *ius in bello* from *ius ad bellum*, see *Just and Unjust Wars*, 34–47.
25. Threshold deontology is the view that side-constraints on action (like the rule against torture) apply absolutely up to a point; but when the stakes get to high the erstwhile has to yield to consequential pressure. And that is supposed to be a good thing. Robert D. Sloane, "The Cost of Conflation: Preserving the Dualism of Jus Ad Bellum and Jus in Bello in the Contemporary Law of War," *Yale Journal of International Law* 34, no. 1 (2009): 112 says that Walzer's view of supreme emergency bears a family resemblance to threshold deontology. For threshold deontology, see Michael Moore, *Placing Blame: A General Theory of the Criminal Law* (Oxford: Oxford University Press, 2010), 158; Eyal Zamir and Barak Medina, *Law, Economics, and Morality* (Oxford: Oxford University Press, 2010); and Larry Alexander, "Deontology at the Threshold," *San Diego Law Review* 37 (2000): 893.
26. See Jeremy Waldron, "Torture and Positive Law," in *Torture, Terror, and Trade-Offs: Philosophy for the White House* (Oxford: Oxford University Press, 2010), 217.
27. Richard Arneson, "Just Warfare Theory and Noncombatant Immunity," *Cornell International Law Journal* 39, no. 3 (2006): 687.
28. See, for instance, the stretching of the concept of "imminence" to make the use of drone-based targeted killing possible: Amos Guiora and Laurie Blank, "Targeted Killing's 'Flexibility' Doctrine that Enables US to Flout the Law of War," *The Guardian*, August 10, 2012.
29. See the discussion of necessary and sufficient conditions in Jeremy Waldron, "Security and Liberty: The Image of Balance," in *Torture, Terror, and Trade-Offs*, 44: "It is never enough for the government to show that reducing a given liberty is a necessary condition for combatting terrorism effectively. It may be a necessary condition, and yet—because

sufficient conditions are unavailable—the terrorist threat may continue unabated."

30. ECHR Article 15 (1): "In time of war or other public emergency threatening the life of the nation any High Contracting Party may take measures derogating from its obligations under this Convention to the extent strictly required by the exigencies of the situation, provided that such measures are not inconsistent with its other obligations under international law." See also Article 4 (1) of the International Covenant on Civil and Political Rights.

31. See ECHR, Article 15 (2) and ICCPR, Article 4 (2).

32. The closest he comes is a negative observation in *Arguing About War*, 34: "moral limits are never suspended—the way we might, for example, suspend habeas corpus in a time of civil war."

33. A dualist believes in the necessity of a separate legal regime to deal with states of emergency. A monist believes that, since constitutional rights have been designed with the vicissitudes of public life and its emergencies in mind, they should not be abandoned whenever an emergency arises. See Ian Zuckerman, "One Law for War and Peace? Judicial Review and Emergency Powers Between the Norm and the Exception," *Constellations* 13, no. 4 (December 2006). Zuckerman cites Benjamin Constant as a persuasive monist: "There are, no doubt, for political societies, moments of danger that human prudence can hardly conjure away. But it is not by means of violence, through the suppression of justice, that such dangers may be averted. It is on the contrary by adhering, more scrupulously than ever, to the established laws, to tutelary procedures, to preserving safeguards. ... Any moderate government, any government resting upon regularity and justice, is ruined by every interruption of justice, by every deviation from regularity." Benjamin Constant, "Spirit of Conquest and Usurpation and Their Relation to European Civilization," in *Constant: Political Writings*, ed. Biancamaria Fontana (Cambridge: Cambridge University Press, 1988), 136.

34. Jeff McMahan, "The Ethics of Killing in War," *Ethics* 114, no. 4 (July 2004): 730.

35. See the discussion in Jeremy Waldron, "Deep Morality and the Laws of War," in *Oxford Handbook of Ethics of War*, eds. Seth Lazar and Helen Frowe (Oxford: Oxford University Press, 2018), 80–95.

36. See, for example, the observation in Arneson, "Just Warfare Theory and Noncombatant Immunity," 687–88: "[T]he basic logic of [Walzer's] position supports killing innocent bystanders under far broader circumstances." Arneson elaborates the point in a footnote: "Any proposed definition of absolute catastrophe or supreme emergency would necessarily appear arbitrary. Wherever one draws the line that separates supreme emergency from a lesser problem, the question arises, why draw the line there

and not elsewhere? Walzer provides no answer. A further difficulty is that wherever one draws the line, one must justify the extraordinary difference in the permissibility status of a violation of noncombatant immunity that occurs just below the line compared to a similar violation that occurs just slightly above it."

37. *Arguing About War*, 35–40 seems like an example of this dialectic.
38. Waldron, *Torture, Terror, and Trade-Offs*, 217.
39. Darrell Cole, "Death Before Dishonor or Dishonor Before Death? Christian Just War, Terrorism, and Supreme Emergency," *Notre Dame Journal of Law, Ethics, and Public Policy* 16, no. 1 (2002): 90.
40. Ibid., 87.
41. See Michael Walzer, "Political Action: The Problem of Dirty Hands," in *Thinking Politically: Essays in Political Theory* (New Haven: Yale University Press, 2007), 278.
42. *Just and Unjust Wars*, 260.
43. Ibid., 262.
44. See, for instance, Richard Miller, "Review of *Just and Unjust Wars*," *Journal of Law and Religion* 16, no. 2 (2001): 1016.
45. *Arguing About War*, 49.
46. Ibid., 48.
47. This phrasing is from Zachary Calo, "Torture, Necessity, and Supreme Emergency: Law and Morality at the End of Law," *Valparaiso University Law Review* 43, no. 4 (2009): 1598.
48. See Max Weber, "Politics as a Vocation," in *From Max Weber: Essays in Sociology*, eds. H. H. Gerth and C. Wright Mills (New York: Oxford University Press, 1946), 126.
49. John Coverdale, "An Introduction to the Just War Tradition," *Pace International Law Review* 16, no. 2 (2004): 275–76.
50. *Just and Unjust Wars*, 254.
51. *Arguing About War*, 33.
52. Ibid., 33, 35, 45, and 50.
53. Ibid., 33.
54. I tried to say something about this in Waldron, "Deep Morality and the Laws of War," 86, when I spoke of the problem of "the reasonableness of the burdens that the laws and customs of armed conflict lay upon combatants. The laws of war (especially *ius in bello*) have to be administered not only in circumstances of moral disagreement, but in circumstances of panic, anger, and great danger. The moral burdens they impose have to be shouldered by those whose lives may be imminently at risk as a result of compliance. … What is true of danger is also true of anger. We impose certain absolute prohibitions that have to stand up against and curb the worst excesses of the anger that combat involves…. [A] delicate balance must be struck; for the most part, the laws of war must work around

the emotions like fear and anger that the circumstances of warfare impose rather than assuming they do not exist (just because morally they should not exist). Moreover, we must not assume that this is a balance that can be arrived at in the philosopher's armchair...."

55. The phrase is from John Rawls, *A Theory of Justice*, revised edition (Cambridge: Harvard University Press, 1999), 109–12; the description is from Jeremy Waldron, *Law and Disagreement* (Oxford: Oxford University Press, 1999), 102.

56. David Hume, "An Enquiry Concerning the Principles of Morals," in *Enquiries Concerning the Human Understanding and Concerning the Principles of Morals*, ed. L. A. Selby-Bigge (Oxford: Oxford University Press, 1902), 147 (Section III, 1). Hume, ibid., 148, applied this also to war: "The rage and violence of public war; what is it but a suspension of justice among the warring parties, who perceive, that this virtue is now no longer of any use or advantage to them?"

57. P. F. Strawson, "On Referring," *Mind* 59 (1950): 320.

58. For use of "the circumstances of..." formula in other contexts, e.g., the circumstances of politics or the circumstances of Dworkinian integrity, see Waldron, *Law and Disagreement*, 102, 159–60, and 189–92.

59. *Arguing About War*, 41.

60. *Just and Unjust Wars*, 252.

61. Much the same is true of philosophers' attachment (usually without explanation) to Robert Nozick's phrase "catastrophic moral horror." Can we say anything here about the connotations of "catastrophic"? Or, for that matter, about "moral horror"?

62. *Just and Unjust Wars*, 253.

63. Ibid.

64. See *Arguing About War*, 3.

65. *Just and Unjust Wars*, 253.

66. Gerald Dworkin, "Non-Neutral Principles," *Journal of Philosophy* 71, no. 14 (1974): 491.

67. Ibid., 491–92.

68. For the application of this logic to the case of targeted killing see Jeremy Waldron, "Justifying Targeted Killing with a Neutral Principle," in *Targeted Killings: Law and Morality in an Asymmetrical World*, eds. Claire Finkelstein, Jens Ohlin, and Andrew Altman (Oxford: Oxford University Press, 2012), 112–34.

69. Max Hastings, *Retribution: The Battle for Japan 1944–45* (New York: Knopf, 2008), 41.

70. Calo, "Torture, Necessity, and Supreme Emergency," 1599; my emphasis.

71. *Just and Unjust Wars*, 259.

72. Respectively, these phrases are from Churchill's broadcast speech of June 18, 1940 and his broadcast speech of May 19, 1940.

73. *Just and Unjust Wars*, 262.
74. Ibid.
75. Ibid., 254.
76. *Arguing About War*, 43.
77. Ibid., 42–43.
78. *Just and Unjust Wars*, 254.
79. *Arguing About War*, 43.
80. *Just and Unjust Wars*, 254.
81. *Arguing About War*, 54.
82. *Just and Unjust Wars*, 254.
83. *Arguing About War*, 49.
84. *Just and Unjust Wars*, 253.
85. Ibid., 259.
86. Ibid., 261.
87. Ibid., 254, my emphasis.
88. Ibid., 267. But Walzer goes on to say: "But it is not the same as the argument I suggested in the case of Britain in 1940. It does not have the form: if we don't do *x* (bomb cities), they will do *y* (win the war, establish tyrannical rule, slaughter their opponents). What Stimson argued is very different. Given the actual policy of the U.S. government, it amounts to this: 'if we don't do *x, we* will do *y.*'" Ibid.
89. Ibid., 254.
90. *Arguing About War*, 30.
91. I have in mind the old Jack Benny routine: "Your money or your life!" (Silence), "C'mon, I said 'Your money or your life'" "I'm thinking. I'm thinking!"
92. See the discussion in Waldron, "Terrorism and the Uses of Terror," in *Torture, Terror, and Trade-Offs*, 54–59.
93. *Arguing About War*, 47.
94. *Just and Unjust Wars*, 253.
95. Luke 10: 25–37.
96. Peter Winch, "Who Is My Neighbor?" in *Trying to Make Sense* (Oxford: Basil Blackwell, 1987), 157.
97. This view is clearest in "Emergency Ethics," in *Arguing About War*, 45. As an instance of necessity generated by role-morality, it is little like what Robert Cover referred to as "the judicial 'can't'" in the antebellum fugitive slave cases. (See Robert Cover, *Justice Accused: Antislavery and the Judicial Process* [New Haven: Yale University Press, 1975], 122.) Judges who were anti-slavery in their personal moral and political convictions maintained that, as judges, they were unable to rely on those convictions in the face of a legally compelling claim that a particular runaway slave had to be returned to his owner. In *Miller v. McQuerry*, 17 F. Cas. 332 (C.C.D. Ohio, 1853), p. 339. Justice John McLean wrote:

with the abstract principles of slavery, courts called to administer the law have nothing to do. It is for the people, who are sovereign, and their representatives, in making constitutions and in the enactment of laws, to consider the laws of nature, and the immutable principles of right. This is a field which judges can not explore... They look to the law, and to the law only. A disregard of this by the judicial powers, would undermine and overturn the social compact.

The judge's role allows him to do no other, even as his own deepest convictions cry out against it. (For the sincerity of Justice McLean's anti-slavery convictions, see his dissent in *Dred Scott v. Sandford* 60 U.S. 393 [1856] at 550.)

98. R. George Wright, "Combating Civilian Casualties: Rules and Balancing in the Developing Law of War," *Wake Forest Law Review* 38, no. 1 (2003): 163–64.

BIBLIOGRAPHY

Alexander, Larry. "Deontology at the Threshold." *San Diego Law Review* 37 (2000): 893–912.

Arneson, Richard. "Just Warfare Theory and Noncombatant Immunity." *Cornell International Law Journal* 39, no. 3 (2006): 663–88.

Blank, Laurie, and Amos Guiora. "Targeted Killing's 'Flexibility' Doctrine That Enables US to Flout the Law of War." *The Guardian*, August 10, 2012.

Calo, Zachary. "Torture, Necessity, and Supreme Emergency: Law and Morality at the End of Law." *Valparaiso University Law Review* 43, no. 4 (2009): 1591–1612.

Churchill, Winston. *The Second World War*, Vol. 1: *The Gathering Storm*. London: Houghton Mifflin, 1948.

Cole, Darrell. "Death Before Dishonor or Dishonor Before Death? Christian Just War, Terrorism, and Supreme Emergency." *Notre Dame Journal of Law, Ethics, and Public Policy* 16, no. 1 (2002): 81–99.

Constant, Benjamin. "Spirit of Conquest and Usurpation and Their Relation to European Civilization." In *Constant: Political Writings*, edited by Biancamaria Fontana, 44–169. Cambridge: Cambridge University Press, 1988.

Cover, Robert. *Justice Accused: Antislavery and the Judicial Process*. New Haven: Yale University Press, 1975.

Coverdale, John. "An Introduction to the Just War Tradition." *Pace International Law Review* 16, no. 2 (2004): 221–77.

Dimbleby, Jonathan. *The Battle of the Atlantic: How the Allies Won the War*. Oxford: Oxford University Press, 2016.

Dworkin, Gerald. "Non-Neutral Principles." *Journal of Philosophy* 71, no. 14 (1974): 491–506.

Hastings, Max. *Retribution: The Battle for Japan 1944–45*. New York: Knopf, 2008.

Hayek, F. A. *The Road to Serfdom*. Chicago: University of Chicago Press, 1944.

Hume, David. "An Enquiry Concerning the Principles of Morals." In *Enquiries Concerning the Human Understanding and Concerning the Principles of Morals*, edited by L. A. Selby-Bigge. Oxford: Oxford University Press, 1902.

McMahan, Jeff. "The Ethics of Killing in War." *Ethics* 114, no. 4 (July 2004): 693–733.

Medina, Barak, and Eyal Zamir. *Law, Economics, and Morality*. Oxford: Oxford University Press, 2010.

Miller, Richard. "Review of *Just and Unjust Wars*." *Journal of Law and Religion* 16, no. 2 (2001): 1013–17.

Moore, Michael. *Placing Blame: A General Theory of the Criminal Law*. Oxford: Oxford University Press, 2010.

Rawls, John. *A Theory of Justice*. Revised edition. Cambridge: Harvard University Press, 1999.

Rehnquist, William. *All the Laws but One: Civil Liberties in Wartime*. New York: Alfred A. Knopf, 1998.

Shue, Henry. "Liberalism: The Impossibility of Justifying Weapons of Mass Destruction." In *Ethics and Weapons of Mass Destruction: Religious and Secular Perspectives*, edited by Sohail Hashmi and Steven Lee, 139–62. Cambridge: Cambridge University Press, 2004.

Sloane, Robert D. "The Cost of Conflation: Preserving the Dualism of Jus Ad Bellum and Jus in Bello in the Contemporary Law of War." *Yale Journal of International Law* 34, no. 1 (2009): 48–112.

Strawson, P. F. "On Referring." *Mind* 59 (1950): 320–44.

Waldron, Jeremy. "Deep Morality and the Laws of War." In *Oxford Handbook of Ethics of War*, edited by Seth Lazar and Helen Frowe, 80–95. Oxford: Oxford University Press, 2018.

———. "Justifying Targeted Killing with a Neutral Principle." In *Targeted Killings: Law and Morality in an Asymmetrical World*, edited by Claire Finkelstein, Jens Ohlin, and Andrew Altman, 112–34. Oxford: Oxford University Press, 2012.

———. *Torture, Terror, and Trade-Offs: Philosophy for the White House*. Oxford: Oxford University Press, 2010.

Walzer, Michael. *Arguing About War*. New Haven: Yale University Press, 2000.

———. *Just and Unjust Wars: A Moral Argument with Historical Illustrations*. 5th ed. New York: Basic Books, 2015.

———. "Political Action: The Problem of Dirty Hands." In *Thinking Politically: Essays in Political Theory*, 278–95. New Haven: Yale University Press, 2007.

Weber, Max. "Politics as a Vocation." In *From Max Weber: Essays in Sociology*, edited by H. H. Gerth and C. Wright Mills. New York: Oxford University Press, 1946.

Winch, Peter. "Who Is My Neighbor?" In *Trying to Make Sense*. Oxford: Basil Blackwell, 1987.

Wright, R. George. "Combating Civilian Casualties: Rules and Balancing in the Developing Law of War." *Wake Forest Law Review* 38, no. 1 (2003): 129–72.

Zuckerman, Ian. "One Law for War and Peace? Judicial Review and Emergency Powers Between the Norm and the Exception." *Constellations* 13, no. 4 (December 2006): 522–45.

CHAPTER 9

Keeping Exceptions Exceptional in War: Could Any Revisionist Theory Guide Action?

Henry Shue

Introduction: The Triple Conjunction

Many philosophers routinely preface articles with the comment that they will be discussing morality, not law. Unlike them, I will be discussing law, but I will also not be discussing law instead of morality. I want to focus on law in light of morality, or on what I call morally justified law—law that a morally conscientious person can in fact obey in the world as it is. In this I follow my teacher Michael Walzer.[1] Such laws may, I think, be one instance of what Allen Buchanan, who also does not artificially separate morality and law, has recently called "directly action-guiding norms" as distinct from "objective justifications" in the form of abstract principles.[2]

International humanitarian law, or the laws of armed conflict (LOAC), is the police officer at a particularly treacherous intersection of three very different forces.[3] First, LOAC must function as law, as international law specifically, embodying the features of a unique kind of thin law that can effectively govern the behavior of parties that differ radically in culture, history, religion, power, and domestic political and legal system. Second,

H. Shue (✉)
University of Oxford, Oxford, UK
e-mail: henry.shue@politics.ox.ac.uk

© The Author(s) 2020
G. Parsons and M. A. Wilson (eds.), *Walzer and War*,
https://doi.org/10.1007/978-3-030-41657-7_9

LOAC must limit violent conflict by operating effectively in the midst of the conflict, constraining to the maximum extent possible all the parties participating in an extraordinary competition in death, wounds, and destruction. Third, LOAC must be morally justifiable, although it will not, cannot, and need not mirror or recapitulate all the requirements of morality, which is impossible in the midst of a contest in violence, most of which would in any other circumstances certainly be immoral.

In general, the specific requirements of morality need to vary according to the specific circumstances to which they are relevant. Morality in war, if possible at all, will certainly be unique because the circumstances of war are unique. But if moral considerations do not make the rules for the circumstances of war significantly different from the rules that would have been required by only the first two forces, law and war, morality is not being effective. The ultimate goal is to force the radically divergent functional necessities of these three realms—law, war, and morality—into some kind of overlap and thereby to come as close as possible to specifying all-things-considered rules for war. We must, as Walzer has consistently argued, attempt "the adaptation of ordinary law and morality to the peculiar circumstances of war."[4] Whether such a triple conjunction is possible is a distinctly open question. Here I will concentrate on how to combine the capacity to function inside conflicts with moral justification.

THE ALMOST IRRESISTIBLE TEMPTATION: INDEFINITE REFINEMENT

The human capacity to make exceptions to rules is extremely valuable—perhaps even, as William Talbott has tantalizingly argued, the engine of moral progress.[5] But we also confront kinds of situations in which it is important to inhibit or prohibit the making of exceptions. My thesis is that war is a situation for exceptionless rules, which means that fine qualifications and philosophical subtleties ought to be left aside. The type of rules needed is what David Luban has aptly labeled rules that are "usable off the shelf."[6] This chapter, then, will be a philosophical argument in favor of leashing philosophical argument in the specific circumstances of armed conflict. To do so we must overcome an almost irresistible temptation that arises in abstract methodologies like philosophy.

Here's the temptation. Suppose we have a rule that specifies the right actions in a certain kind of circumstance—call it "the first rule." But we can think of a second rule that could be derived from the first rule either by prohibiting one additional kind of action, which we think it might be better to discourage, or by permitting one additional kind of action, which we think it might be better to encourage. The second rule is in principle superior to the first rule—it is, as it were, more precisely targeted—because it more accurately zooms in on exactly the right actions for the circumstance in question. The second formulation sharpens the focus of the rule and in this respect is an improvement on the first rule. So, we infer, we ought to replace the first rule with the second rule in practice.

This inference is the mistake that is almost irresistibly tempting! The mistake is to assume that if we can think of a superior formulation, we ought to promote replacing the conceptually inferior first rule with the conceptually superior second rule in practice. At heart the mistake is to assume that what is superior in thought, or in conception, will automatically be superior in practice. But this assumption, which we could call the illusion of ever more precise conceptual targeting, is false. Why? Basically because it makes the methodological mistake of relying exclusively on logic, or conceptual rigor, and neglects epistemology, especially what information is accessible from a particular situation, and psychology, especially emotion and motivation. The tempting inference ignores the difference between the bright light of theory and the murky shadows of practice. Let's explore how the simple inference from better-in-thought to better-in-action can go wrong.

There is a difference between the second rule and the first rule. The second formulation either rules in something that the first formulation rules out or rules out something that the first formulation rules in. I will refer to the difference between the two rules as simply "the difference." At the conceptual level we can see "the difference"—that's how we know that the second formulation is a superior conception to the first. But for the second rule to be preferable in practice, it is necessary for the agents whose conduct is intended to be guided by the rule to accurately interpret "the difference" in the circumstances for which the rule is being proposed—to apply it correctly to the concrete case. If we have good reasons for believing that the judgments of these agents about "the difference" are likely to be either over-inclusive or under-inclusive, we should be cautious about authorizing them to make such judgments. If we morally authorize them to judge for themselves by telling them that they should follow the second rule, they may make more or worse mistakes by trying to discriminate about "the difference" than they would have made if they had routinely ignored the difference by abiding by the conceptually inferior first rule. It is an empirical issue when and where this tendency toward misapplication holds. One place is war.

Let me, now, concretely illustrate this tendency for conceptual refinement to be practically counter-productive during war. The fundamental rule for the conduct of war is: never target civilians. Let's call this the simple rule. Suppose a philosopher suggested that a superior formulation would ideally be a more complicated rule—we will call it the "complex rule"—that said something like the following: never target civilians except when they are morally responsible for the prosecution of an unjust war (and are therefore morally liable to be targeted to be killed). Agents who were expected to follow this more complex rule instead of the simple rule would be expected to see, in the circumstances in which they must apply it, the difference between civilians who are sufficiently morally responsible to be liable for targeting and civilians who are not thus liable.

The burden of proof for establishing that a person is morally liable to be killed when the person has no opportunity to defend herself against the claims against her—by, for example, pointing out that she is being mistaken for someone else or showing that she had entirely different motives from those being attributed to her—should be extremely high (impossibly high, I think, but that is a different argument). A judgment of liability to being killed by military action—without any kind of due process—would at the very least require a considerable quantity of highly reliable information about factors relevant to moral responsibility, like degrees of choice and intentions, known to be accurately ascribable to the specific individual in question. Any typical combatant—no matter how competent—is most unlikely to command an adequate supply of this kind of information about individual civilians in any adversary society. This is not a fault in the combatant, but a feature of the circumstances. It reflects, not cognitive impairment, but poverty of information.[7]

Consider soldiers assigned to find Saddam Hussein and high-ranking members of his regime in Iraq in 2003. They were given a so-called "playing card" for each individual, containing his photograph and specific details about him that had been gathered by multiple intelligence agencies over years; even so, soldiers were under orders, if possible, to capture, not kill, the individual in question so that due process could be provided before any killing. The availability of this level of information about individual adversaries during combat is very unusual, and even it was understood to be insufficient to establish liability to be killed—hence, the order to capture, not kill. By contrast, the average soldier in an ordinary conflict cannot possibly discriminate between civilians morally liable to be killed without process (if anyone were) and civilians who are not, for lack of even remotely adequate information of the relevant kinds about individual strangers.

Lack of evidence is not the only issue. Besides ignorance of detailed information about individuals, deeper issues arise about divergences in conceptions of justice that may underlie opposing views of the justice of the war held by individuals on the two sides of the conflict, as analyzed by Tamar Meisels in a recent study.[8] One may mistakenly believe certain civilians to be liable to be killed for the same reasons one mistakenly believes that one's own side is justified in fighting the war, if one is in fact mistaken about the war. This same error would, of course, infect one's killing of adversary combatants, but that is at least an irremovable element of war once one chooses to fight. One cannot fight a war without sometimes trying to kill adversary combatants. By contrast, intentionally executing supposedly liable civilians is completely avoidable. But I leave aside Meisels' important deeper problem about diverging conceptions of justice and restrict myself here to inadequacy of evidence.

Some philosophers who think the rules for combat ought to be more complex and morally subtle have come to be called revisionists. That makes my argument anti-revisionist. The leading revisionist, Jeff McMahan, and I have come to agree about the best rule to follow in war in the present, but we disagree about why and consequently about the prospects for change in rules in the future. McMahan writes:

> We must recognize that this is an area in which people tend to make bad judgments if they try to act in conformity with morality in conditions of significant moral uncertainty. The proper response to this is not to pretend that morality is other than it is, but to impose *laws* designed to motivate people to act in ways that are most likely to be morally right. In this case, the solution is to impose an *exceptionless* legal prohibition of intentional attacks on noncombatants, as well as a stringent proportionality restriction on the killing of noncombatants as a side effect of military action. At least at present, the laws of war must diverge from the morality of war [emphasis added].[9]

My main disagreement with McMahan is his suggestion that my position requires us "to pretend that morality is other than it is... at least at present." This issue has major implications for how theorists ought to analyze war, if they are interested in their work being action-guiding, and for the kind of contribution, if any, we theorists can actually ever make to limiting war. For now, McMahan and I both think that fighters should abide by the existing basic principle of LOAC: never target civilians. He understandably but, I think, groundlessly, hopes that this is a temporary compromise on what he considers a merely conventional law that has only an instrumental justification, namely that this is "at present" one good means for restraining the violence of war. But I think this is a fully justified law for circumstances of violent conflict and will remain a morally justified law of war until either war itself or human beings radically change in ways for which I see no prospect and can hardly imagine.

Some other revisionists reject McMahan's temporary compromise. Helen Frowe, for example, argues for the general principle, which she takes to be applicable both outside and inside war, "that those who are morally responsible for indirect unjust threats are liable to defensive killing" and then argues for the case of war "that if a non-combatant has a reasonable opportunity to avoid posing an unjust threat and intentionally fails to take that opportunity, she is liable to defensive killing."[10] So Frowe concludes that "we ought to reject the idea that the Principle of Non-Combatant Immunity picks out any morally significant feature of noncombatants, and with it the idea that it is always morally impermissible for just combatants to attack noncombatants on the unjust side of the war. This is in part because noncombatants knowingly turn themselves into threats by contributing to their country's war effort."[11]

We need to have a hard look at the epistemological demands presupposed by this kind of suggestion. I will focus sharply on the fundamental point that any revisionist position that, like Frowe's, wishes to treat some civilians as liable to attack and some as not liable to attack depends in practice on combatants being capable of competently following a complex general rule (whatever exactly that rule says).

It is important to appreciate the seriousness of the difficulties here. In the first systematic examination of how the American public actually thinks about some issues raised by revisionism, Scott Sagan and Benjamin Valentino have shown empirically that a randomly selected significant proportion of Americans are ready to accept the killing of civilians by combatants (not necessarily American combatants) who are said to be fighting a just war. For example, they inquired:

whether the influence of just cause on Americans' ethical assessments of soldiers' conduct during war extends to a willingness to overlook war crimes committed by soldiers in just wars. Although neither revisionists nor traditionalists advance this proposition, we wanted to explore how far the public might be willing to expand the license given to soldiers fighting for a just cause. We found that the public was much more inclined to judge the attack on the military base, including the systematic execution of 48 innocent civilians, as ethical when it was described as occurring during a just war.[12]

The proposition that combatants on the just side are allowed kinds of killing that combatants on the unjust side are not allowed is in fact widely appealing intuitively, at least in the United States, so one cannot defend the traditional approach to constraining war by mere appeals to hypotheticals and intuitions about the hypotheticals. Free-floating intuitions often favor outrageous practices. This is in harmony with Walzer's suspicion of "hypothetical and constructed cases (variations on the famous trolley car story, say)."[13] Consequently, I turn now to arguments that go beyond appeals to intuition by taking seriously the realities of the circumstances of war and the functional requirements of international law as well as the demands of morality.

ERRONEOUS EXCEPTIONS

In the abstract, a simple rule saying "never target civilians" is over-inclusive about those whom it protects compared to a complex rule saying "never target any civilians except those who are morally liable to be killed," assuming for the sake of argument, as some revisionists do, that there can be civilians who could be morally liable to be killed without any procedure designed to filter out mistaken judgments about identity, motivation, and liability. If one assumes that there are civilians liable to be killed by military action, the simple rule is less precise and in this respect inferior to the complex rule with its exception for the civilians who are liable to be killed by the opposing military. A wide variety of difficulties arise here,[14] but the one I want to focus on now is this: even if the complex rule with the exception for civilians liable to death were superior in theory, it would be inferior in practice. Why?

In sum, this is because in practice the attempt to discriminate between liable and non-liable civilians, as required by the complex rule, instead of simply between combatants and civilians, as required by the simple rule, is likely to lead to both *more* errors and *worse* errors—in practice, it will lead to quantitatively and qualitatively inferior decisions. Space is not available to explore this fully, but the following are some partial indications of why the mistakes are likely to be more numerous and more serious.

Trying to follow the more subtle complex rule will lead to *more* errors because, while it can be hard enough sometimes to tell a combatant from a civilian, especially if the adversary is treacherously disguising combatants as civilians, it is harder still to judge the extent of the moral liability of individual strangers and decide whether any specific individual is liable to death without any kind of due process, unless the bar for liability is set outrageously low, and the judgment is made irresponsibly on meager evidence, or liability is assigned collectively simply on the basis of which side a person is on. Indeed, it is usually impossible for the average combatant to obtain the information required for an accurate assessment of moral responsibility, which is required for a judgment of moral liability, of any civilian she is at all likely to encounter in circumstances of hostility. The general poverty of information during group conflict about the factors relevant to moral responsibility in the cases of specific individuals will lead to many errors.

More importantly, the errors resulting from any attempt to make the more difficult discrimination required by the complex rule will be morally *more serious* errors. Showing this requires a more elaborate argument. Continue to grant for the sake of the argument the revisionist proposition that some civilians can be morally liable to be killed by military action and compare the errors likely on the simple rule and on the complex rule. The exceptionless simple rule, never target civilians, provides over-inclusive protection—it protects too many people: some number of civilians liable to be killed (by revisionist standards, assumed for the sake of argument) will not in fact be killed because of compliance with the simple rule. How morally serious are the mistakes from following the simple rule?

That someone is liable to be killed does not mean, for revisionists, that justice requires that she be killed—that would be true only if she deserved to be killed. So, these mistakes will not be failures in justice. Her being liable to be killed would mean only that she has no right not to be killed if killing her will significantly advance the defensive effort against the assault for which she bears some moral responsibility.[15] So if some such civilians are in error not killed because the simple rule is followed, what are lost are some opportunities to advance one's military effort. This is not insignificant, but normally the same military advantage that could have been gained by one measure can equally well be gained by one or more other measures. Ordinarily there are many ways to skin the military cat.

It is worth noting that any civilian whose contribution to the military effort was of decisive significance might be considered a direct participant in the military effort and accordingly be no longer entitled to claim the status of a "civilian." In that case, targeting such persons, who formerly held the status of "civilian" but had now become "combatants" under LOAC because of their direct participation in the military effort, would not depend on any exception for liable civilians built into a complex rule and would be permitted by the exceptionless simple rule. I think this is correct, but I will not press on this claim because the criteria of "direct participation" are contentious.[16]

If I do not rely on the claim that those in question are now only former civilians who have become combatants through direct participation, I have to grant that the cost of sticking to the exceptionless simple rule is that some military advantage is lost compared to what could be gained militarily by following the complex rule and attacking these (assumedly) liable civilians whom it would be advantageous to attack. The loss would, however, be exclusively in military advantage. Because of the difference between liability and desert, there is no loss at all in justice, as we have already seen.

But in order to compare the two rules fully, we need next to compare that loss of military advantage from abiding by the simple rule with the costs of trying to abide by the complex rule that depends on correctly applying the difference (as understood by the revisionist) between morally liable and morally non-liable civilians. I have already suggested that this is likely to lead to a significant *quantity* of errors of judgment because of the epistemological, or informational, poverty of war—the inadequacy of the information about specific individuals for judging individual liability. How important is the *quality* of these errors? What kind of errors are they morally?

Murderous Errors

Compared to the exceptionless simple rule, never target civilians, a second more nuanced rule along the lines of "never target civilians, except for specially liable ones," will lead to not only more errors, but worse errors.

An error in judgment about who is morally liable to be killed while trying to follow the complex rule can go in either of two opposite directions, so qualitatively the errors will be of two kinds. If civilians who are liable are judged to be non-liable, the losses will be of exactly the same kind as the losses from following the simple exceptionless rule: potential military advantage not actually gained. The issue between the simple and complex rules in this direction is: which would cost more in military advantage? It is not possible to provide a general answer because it would depend on the empirical situation in the particular war, especially the number and military importance of morally liable civilians, which would presumably vary from one war to another. Following the simple rule would result in failing to capitalize on all such cases, however, so following the complex rule seems highly likely to miss fewer. But if the total number were small, or if the military significance of the instances were only moderate, the difference in favor of the second rule might not be especially large. This comparison seems fairly indeterminate, although perhaps in favor of the complex rule.

Errors in the other direction, however, are an entirely different matter morally. Attempts to correct the (assumed) over-inclusiveness of the protection provided by the simple rule through following the complex rule may provide protection for civilians that is under-inclusive: it may not protect enough people, and civilians who are not morally liable to be killed may in error be judged to be liable and attacked. If civilians who are not morally liable to be killed are in error judged to be liable and attacked (or intentionally permitted to be killed by discounting their deaths in proportionality calculations), what will occur is murder. People with an uncompromised right to life will be intentionally killed wrongfully. The fact that the complex rule invites errors that are murderous counts heavily against it, especially if, as I have already contended, the errors are likely to be numerous as well as murderous. Any wish for indeterminate gains in military advantage would not even begin to justify a systematic risk of multiple murders. Nor, certainly, would any philosophical desire to make war morally "neater" than it is possible for it to be by introducing more complex and subtle rules. In order greatly to reduce the chances of multiple murders, then, we ought in practice to stick with the simple, exceptionless rule. As Walzer maintains, "in the circumstances of war, we cannot make these distinctions.... Individual attentiveness isn't possible."[17]

Dynamic Error and Reflexive Response

The challenges for the complex revisionist rule branch into two directions. First is the above concern about the static numbers of errors. To the extent that it is difficult to select out of a crowd of strangers the individuals with the most moral liability to be harmed by military action, there is no particular reason to believe that attempts to single out the morally liable will succeed especially often—the "error rate" may well be quite high, given how little most combatants are at all likely to know about the morally relevant features—like motives and reasons—of most of the individual civilians in the opposing society. Second, and more important still, is a dynamic effect: authorization to attempt to pick and choose morally liable individuals from among the civilians risks progressively muddying up one of the few relatively bright lines in warfare: the line between combatants and civilians. This is one place where it is crucial to consider human psychology and sociology, and not to rely purely on conceptual points.

So far, my argument has primarily been intended to show negatively that even if an alternative rule is superior in the abstract, it by no means follows that it yields superior results in practice. Now I want to argue positively that an embedded, exceptionless rule can, precisely because it is already entrenched in practice across many cultures and widely accepted as a governing norm, have strong advantages over a modified rule that is superior in its formulation. These advantages will be lost if the embedded rule is abandoned or undermined by moralistic criticism.

Obviously, it is not true that the line between combatants and civilians is now universally respected, or even approximately so. But even the terrorists who violate it as a matter of policy for the shock value of killing civilians are relying precisely on the fact that many people believe the distinction ought to be observed and so will be shocked by the violations.[18] The effectiveness of this kind of terrorism is parasitic on people believing in the norm it violates. So too the counter-terrorists who think that a looser interpretation of proportionality that allows the collateral killing of so-called "associated civilians" may intimidate other civilians from assisting the terrorists. The centuries-old distinction between combatants and civilians is widely understood in some fashion, although naturally different people interpret it somewhat differently, and some people, including both terrorists and counter-terrorists, exploit it in order to cause outrage rather than respecting it. Nevertheless, two simple facts have major importance:

in diverse cultures all across the planet many people already believe that the distinction between combatants and civilians marks a morally important line, and this belief has deep roots in virtually every religious tradition and every culture, firmly and deeply rooted in that culture's history and literature.

Taken by itself, this could be interpreted as a deeply conservative argument, with strong reactionary potential. Virtually every culture and religion also contain deeply entrenched norms about, for example, the treatment of women, most of which treat women as weaker, less valuable, and generally inferior. However, we do not, I hope, simply resign ourselves to these ancient embedded norms—instead we work to overthrow them, despite knowing that this revolution is the work of decades, if not centuries. So, any argument that amounts to "let sleeping dogs lie" generally in the realm of principles and norms is truly reactionary and should be rejected out of hand.

But, needless to say, war is a very, very special case. Consider both a political/sociological feature and a psychological/motivational feature. First, many norms function internally to a group and can be changed in one society, culture, nation, or religion at a time even if the ultimate goal is a global revolution in thought. Initially any modified principle needs to function within only one group at a time, although obviously that group may contain diverse subgroups some of which resist the change. Often the various subgroups will, however, share a single robust domestic legal system within which differences about the proposed modifications about how people are to be treated can be gradually worked out.

But the rules for the conduct of war need to function successfully in precisely the circumstances of violent conflict between radically divergent groups who share only the thinnest of legal systems—international law, which does not yet contain particularly effective mechanisms for reaching and enforcing uniform interpretations of rules. Sunni and Shia, Catholic and Protestant, Israeli and Palestinian, Chinese and Japanese, Indians and Pakistanis, Iranians and Saudis, government and rebels, Fascists and anti-Fascists—all these groups who disagree with each other so deeply and strongly need a shared rule to limit the violence when they enter into violent conflict with each other. Should the Pakistanis be encouraged to attack not only Indian combatants but also "morally liable" Indian civilians? Should the Saudis go after not only Iranian combatants but also "morally liable" Iranian civilians? I do not think so.

The distinction between combatants and civilians is already under pressure in some of these cases, in which each side considers the other to be profoundly evil. It is essential that both sides share the same limit because if one side adopts a more permissive limit, the other will certainly follow in order not to be at a relative disadvantage. In these specific circumstances, it seems far more likely that a limit on the killing can be kept stable if the limit is familiar, traditional, and simple and therefore relatively clear. "Fighters may target other fighters, but they may not target any non-fighters" is about as clear as it gets, although even so there are gray cases about degree of direct participation in the fighting. But the gray cases and the potential for a slide into a free-for-all would be vastly magnified if any "conceptual refinement" distinguishing one kind of civilian from another kind of civilian were introduced. This is an especially slippery slope.

Second, the psychological and motivational considerations are if anything stronger than the political and sociological ones. In what kind of context are rules for the conduct of war supposed to function? The context of the threat of death, sometimes the threat of defeat for one's most cherished ideals, and the horror and sometimes thrill of killing and wounding fellow human beings. One may be exhausted, highly stressed, panicked, angry, disoriented, or several of the preceding. This is not a state in which to acquire and carefully process the kinds of information relevant to an individual's relative degree of moral liability, even if authoritative detailed information about individuals were somehow available, which is unlikely in any case. Individuals in such situations need to respond *reflexively, not reflectively.* They need to have simple rules—rules of a kind that can be printed on one small card—drilled into them repeatedly so that their compliance with these few rules becomes second nature to them and is as nearly automatic as is humanly possible. This is not a circumstance for subtle distinctions, but for Luban's "off-the-shelf" rules. It is a time for bright lines: never target a civilian.

Genuine Exceptions: Objection and Response

Philosophical critics can naturally make up hypothetical examples in which a particular civilian is indispensable to the other side to such a degree that the failure to kill him would constitute a great loss. For example, he has just discovered how to make the atomic bomb before anyone else did and will provide the secret to Hitler if not killed. But such hypotheticals tend to be fantastic: there was no one secret to the bomb, no one person alone figured out what to do, etc. So, we can switch the hypothetical to the lab full of civilian scientists who collectively have figured out all the aspects of building the bomb.

The primary point here is that these civilians are not going to be encountered somewhere near the battlefield by the ordinary combatant for whom we are choosing the general rule. So, there is no need for the general rule for all combatants to take such possibilities into account. Perhaps it is acceptable to attack a group of scientists about to complete a new type of weapon of mass destruction, and an exception ought to be made for this rare case. But an exception like this is better construed as a genuine exception, that is, it is not a kind of case for the sake of which our general rule needs to be modified, but a special case in which commanders would be justified in violating the original unmodified rule in spite of the fact that the exceptionless rule is still the best rule generally. The best rule remains the best rule, but it ought not to be followed here. Such genuine exceptions call for special decision procedures and decision-makers who are not in the thick of the fray, not a blanket authorization for any combatant who thinks an exception should be made simply to go right ahead on his own and make it.

The critic may now respond that acknowledging the possibility of what I am calling genuine exceptions is logically equivalent to a more narrowly drawn second rule that provides for killing, not all seriously liable civilians, but exclusively civilians who are seriously liable precisely because they have developed a new kind of weapon of mass destruction. Nevertheless, it is valuable in practice to maintain a distinction between (a) a rule modified to incorporate an exception and (b) a rule to which an ad hoc exception can be made in rare circumstances but only through a special process. The distinction is valuable because the modified rule with the exception built-in authorizes all agents following the rule to make their own judgments about when a particular case satisfies the requirements of the built-in exception. By contrast, the special process can stipulate that an authority makes the rare ad hoc exception only at some higher level or with some special process and ideally with exceptionally extensive information.

For example, in killing done by US remotely piloted aircraft (RPA), or drones, it is reportedly the case that if the number of expected civilian casualties will be N or fewer, the regular team that operates the RPA can make the decision whether that many casualties would be excessive

in proportion to the military advantage of the killing under consideration; but if the number of expected civilian casualties is greater than N,
this decision about proportionality must be made at a higher level. It is
built into the rule that casualties up to N are permitted if they are not
excessive compared to the expected military value of the death of the
targeted individual, but that casualties above N require that a genuine
exception to the normal calculation of proportionality be made. Whether
this makes any practical difference depends on whether the higher-level
decision itself is merely reflexive or genuinely reflective, but the special
arrangement at least creates a possibility for especially cautious decision
procedures, requiring perhaps a higher level of proof than normal of the
value of the target to be required at the higher level of command.[19]

MERELY PRAGMATIC, NOT PRINCIPLED?

I have raised similar doubts about the dangers outside academia of revisionist theoretic approaches to the morality of war for several years, and
my position is sometimes characterized as—and criticized as—being a
purely pragmatic argument, not a principled argument. I now want to
characterize the basic nature of this argument more clearly than I have so
far succeeded in doing.[20]

I am not claiming, as I would need to do if I were trying to satisfy
revisionist standards, that if combatants follow the rule "never target civilians," they will kill or wound only morally liable individuals—far from it. I
recognize that in reality some of the combatants that their adversaries kill
may be less morally responsible for wrongful war than some of the civilians the adversaries do not kill. I may be correct, a critic may then say, that
sticking with the entrenched distinction between combatants and civilians
will prevent one kind of murder, namely the killing of non-liable civilians
while in pursuit of liable civilians. But compliance with the entrenched
distinction permits a different kind of murder, the killing of non-liable
combatants—combatants who are not liable to be attacked because they
are not morally responsible for wrongful war. The rule provides exceptionless protection for civilians, but all combatants, liable and non-liable,
are one giant exception to protection.

I acknowledge to a far greater extent than many revisionists that in a
typical war many—probably most—combatants on both sides die wrongfully, for either of two reasons. They may not be morally responsible for
wrongful war because their war is not wrongful but justified—they are

fighting on what many philosophers simplistically call the "just side" and not violating the rules for the conduct of war. Or combatants may not be morally responsible for wrongful war because although they are fighting for a side that is not justified—the philosophers' "unjust side"—they are not morally responsible for doing so, because, for example, they have been deceived by their government through impenetrable lies and persuasive propaganda that make the war sound justified, and they are not violating the rules for the conduct of war. So the objector is correct that when war is fought according to my, and Walzer's, recommendation—abiding by the traditional distinction between combatants and civilians—many people who are not morally liable to harm will be attacked, killed, or wounded, specifically combatants. Indeed, I emphasize above all else that in all wars many individuals are wounded or killed wrongfully. This is the immense, intractable moral horror of war.[21]

But, the critic can continue, while that may be, what makes it better to fight in accord with the conventional distinction between combatants and civilians instead of refining it by, for example, distinguishing between civilians morally liable to be harmed and non-liable civilians or finding some way to protect non-liable combatants? Don't I need to show at the very least that fewer non-liable persons overall will be harmed if war is conducted in accord with the traditional exceptionless rule than if it is conducted in accord with either the modified rule with an exception for morally liable civilians or some other rule that somehow exempts non-liable combatants from threat? I have contended that fewer non-liable civilians will be killed. But don't I need to show that fewer non-liable persons altogether, civilians and combatants, are likely to be killed? Then at least I could claim that the exceptionless rule does better at protecting the right to life than the modified rule—that the exceptionless rule produces better total numbers, better protects the right to life of all and only individuals who have not forfeited that right.

But I have not shown any such thing. Seth Lazar, by contrast, has a recent plausible argument that, other things being equal, a civilian is less likely to be morally liable to harm than a combatant.[22] This might make it better, in overall numbers, to focus, as I do, on not harming non-liable civilians. But I am not invoking that claim, because I am not persuaded that Lazar is correct—I think that many combatants on both sides die as wrongfully as non-liable civilians. Accordingly, I have no confidence that the entrenched rule protects most of the non-liable persons, many of whom are combatants. Then in what respect is it better to abide by the exceptionless rule to never target civilians? It is better, in a phrase, primarily because it is possible to implement and save some lives, while the allegedly morally superior complex alternatives do not seem workable. This is a modest claim, which has nothing to do with minimizing suffering overall.[23]

The exceptionless rule is not, of course, a kind of barrier that will always hold, but a kind of barrier that ordinary human beings in the extraordinary circumstances of war can reasonably be expected to maintain much of the time. The exceptionless rule is somewhat like Dutch dikes. Dutch dikes do not hold back all the sea-water—in times of stress, they allow some water from the North Sea to by-pass the dikes and collect in specially designated, often specially constructed, holding areas. Surely, someone will object, better dikes would contain all the sea-water. But through centuries of trial-and-error the Dutch have learned that dikes intended to block all the water cannot hold—that is to ask more than is possible. The dikes are, in turn, like trees that do not break because they bend. And dikes that allow some sea-water to pass but channel it into specific places will hold and will provide as much safety as it is humanly possible to provide in the prevailing circumstances.

The exceptionless rule about civilians is like the Dutch dikes in that it may seem rough-and-ready, not polished, but it can generally hold in the stressful circumstances of war, although of course it does not always hold. The exceptionless rule protecting civilians admittedly does nothing to stop the countless wrongful deaths of combatants—all those lives flow right past the rule to a much greater extent than the sea-water flows past the dikes. For the dikes, trying to hold back all the sea-water is what would erode them by asking more than what is possible; for the rule, trying to allow discrete exceptions among either civilians or combatants with insufficient information about individuals is what would erode it by asking more than is possible. Ill-grounded and inconsistent exceptions—sometimes too many, sometimes too few—are liable to wear away the rule.

The proposed improved rule, which requires attempting to distinguish between liable and non-liable civilians, is impossible for soldiers to follow in the circumstances of war, for all the reasons I have already spelled out, including its demand for far more information about the morally relevant features of individuals than could possibly be available and for the superhuman steeliness of nerve that would allow subtle and careful moral reasoning amidst the smoke, noise, danger, and stress of battle. The same would be even more abundantly true of any attempt to be selective about combatant deaths.

The familiar rule exceptionlessly protecting civilians is better as a practical guide simply because it is possible for ordinary fighters to follow it in the disorienting circumstances of battle. The conceptually more refined rule is inferior as a practical guide because it is impossible to follow accurately in the circumstances of battle. It is impossible to implement during combat because its informational and psychological requirements are superhuman. One cannot judge the relative moral responsibility of individual members of a group of strangers accurately and quickly even in peacetime, and it is worse than pointless to try during battle. Numerous murderous mistakes are likely to be made if, in accord with the refined rule, attempts are generally made to target civilians selectively; and if permission is granted to all fighters to try to implement selectively the prohibition on attacking civilians, the general prohibition is likely to erode under the pressure of frequent inconsistent exceptions. The exceptionless rule, if followed, avoids the intentional killing of all civilians. At the cost of protecting some civilians who are not entitled to protection, it protects all the other civilians too. The worst cost of course is that it does nothing to protect combatants who ought not to die, but no one has suggested a feasible way to do that other than avoiding war. The most plausible alternative may be a requirement to capture rather than kill, but that does not seem workable to me.[24]

Rousseau assumed in the *Social Contract* that the laws of civil society must be designed for mortals, not for angels. The laws of war must similarly be designed for ordinary humans in confusing circumstances. Rawls understood that principles of justice must be able to withstand the strains of commitment. Rules of war must similarly be able to withstand the strains of combat.

Does this mean, as McMahan insists, that rules for war like "never target civilians" and "always choose the objective with the least expected civilian losses" are merely instrumentally useful conventions, morally inferior to some more sophisticated and differentiated rules that might have replaced them? No, it means that such laws, compared to more ambitious and sophisticated principles, are ones that can produce relatively few mistakes in moral judgment—relatively few wrongs—by angry and frightened mortals wielding awesomely powerful weapons, which makes them morally justified rules for war. Or as fully justified morally as any rule that it is possible for humans to implement. But the best practically possible rule cannot change the fact that when wars start, the wrongful killing begins and continues until the war ends.

Exceptions Out of Necessity? Never

War is by far the worst and most destructive means of settling disputes. War is to be avoided at almost any cost. The only possible justification for the resort to war is the prevention of an evil so great that it is worse than the evil of war, and the evil of war is sufficiently great that few other evils exceed it. I believe that the Rwandan genocide in 1994, for example, was a greater evil than the relatively small war it would have taken at that time to stop it, and this is the case even if one ignores "Africa's World War,"[25] the still-continuing war in Eastern Congo that has flowed out of the unchecked Rwandan genocide in 1994 and has now killed more than 6 million people.

The best way to avoid harming people who are not morally liable to be harmed is not to resort to warfare unless it has become as clear as humanly possible both that the resort to war is necessary, in the sense that there is no less destructive means than war that is likely to be effective in preventing the evil in question, and that the great evils that it is always reasonable to expect to result from the war will be less than the evils that it is reasonable to expect in the absence of war. War must be, in short, both necessary and proportional, which are two independent standards, neither reducible to the other.[26]

It is absolutely essential to understand that military necessity is not, and could not be, a logically sufficient condition for justifying specific choices of conduct in war. Necessity in the conduct of war means that an action may be taken *only if* it is necessary militarily. Military necessity is only logically necessary for justifying conduct in war. If military necessity was logically sufficient, as in the now almost universally denounced doctrine of *Kreigsraison*,[27] no other limits, such as distinction or proportionality, could possibly apply. So, the principle for the conduct of war is definitely not: one may do whatever it is necessary to do in order to succeed. The principle is: one may do something only if it is necessary to do it in order to succeed.

This implies another important point about exceptions: military necessity is never an adequate ground for making an exception to any provision of international law. To ground an exception in military necessity would be to act as if necessity were sufficient to justify an action, entitling one to override a limitation. But military necessity is never sufficient. International lawyer Françoise Hampson has put the point crisply: "There can be no appeal to military necessity outside the rules."[28] This is of course because the balance between military considerations and humanitarian considerations is already built into the rules; military necessity had its due in the formulation of the rules—it is not allowed to count twice, once in shaping the compromises that underlie the rules and then again in grounding exceptions to the compromises. Even Francis Lieber, the tough Prussian who wrote the code of war for Abraham Lincoln, said in the famous paragraph 14 of the Lieber Code: "Military necessity... consists in the necessity of those measures which are indispensable for securing the ends of the war, and which are lawful according to the modern law and usages of war."

Military necessity is a powerful restraint. Its application to civilians is generally recognized. For example, the *First Additional Protocol of 1977*, Art. 57 (3), says: "when a choice is possible between several military objectives for obtaining a similar military advantage, the objective to be selected shall be that the attack on which may be expected to cause *the least* danger to civilian lives and to civilian objects." The civilian losses must be the minimum that are compatible with attaining a given military advantage, because any damage in excess of the minimum is unnecessary. Art. 57 (3) follows from the principle of necessity when military necessity is correctly construed as logically necessary.[29] Civilian losses that are not necessary are not permitted. They are excessive. Rightly understood, military necessity is a basis for restraint, not a reason for making exceptions. To treat military necessity as a sufficient reason for not abiding by a law of war is to lapse back into *Kriegsraison*.

But surely, some philosopher will say, we need not be so crude as to say that military necessity may never override existing international humanitarian law. What if, for example, the cost in force protection from choosing the military objective with the least civilian damage would be excessive? Combatants could be authorized to override the requirement of minimum civilian losses when the costs in force protection—the costs to themselves—are above some very high threshold, especially, McMahan has suggested, when the costs would instead be borne by civilians who are expected beneficiaries of the military effort that creates the costs.[30]

This would make the rule say, in effect: for the same amount of military advantage, always choose the military objective with the least expected civilian losses, except when the risks to you of doing so would be excessive and the risks would alternatively be borne by expected beneficiaries. In the abstract this may seem to be an improved, more finely tuned rule.

But in circumstances in which such a calculation leads to reduced risks to oneself the temptation to keep reaching that conclusion would be strong. The proposed exception would authorize a process of detached balancing that in the abstract could be perfectly reasonable, but that would need to be carried out in circumstances of danger in which to juggle the conflicting considerations conscientiously would require super-human efforts—efforts that, I would think, would be beyond the capacity of many ordinary mortals. To authorize in place of an exceptionless rule detached balancing in a threatening situation in which detachment would be possible only for those with steel backbones and laser minds seems more likely to produce decisions unreasonably favoring combatants over civilians than to eliminate cases of unreasonably favoring civilians over combatants. If so, the exceptionless rule will once again produce fewer bad decisions and save the lives that can be saved amidst all the killing that is war.[31]

My reasoning here provides further support for what I believe is Walzer's greatest contribution to just war theory: his more robust conception of "due care" as a right of every civilian:

> there are obligations that go with [soldiers'] war rights, and the first of these is the obligation to attend to the rights of civilians—more precisely, of those civilians whose lives they themselves endanger. The principle of double effect, then, stands in need of correction.... The third of the con-ditions...can be restated: 3. The intention of the actor is good, that is, he aims narrowly at the acceptable effect; the evil effect is not one of his ends, nor is it a means to his ends, and, aware of the evil involved, he seeks to minimize it, *accepting costs to himself.* [emphasis added][32]

With quiet eloquence Walzer immediately adds: "simply not to intend the death of civilians is too easy." The soldier's mission is not to find some objective balance between their risks and his risks. His mission is to put his finger firmly on their side of the scales. This means risking to some reasonable degree his life to protect theirs, as good soldiers do.[33]

And as LOAC requires them to do. In the very same year that the first edition of *Just and Unjust Wars* was published, the First Additional Pro-tocol of 1977, the most important statement of LOAC since the Geneva Conventions, introduced in Article 57 the concept of "constant care" as a precaution in attack. An exploration of the precise relation of Walzer's moral concept of due care and the First Protocol's legal concept of "constant care" would obviously require at least a separate essay, but in general they are strongly complementary. This is a remarkable convergence that is possible only for thinkers who keep a firm grip simultaneously on law, morality, and war. Indeed, the strong Walzerian concept of due care and the strong Protocol concept of constant care provide an intersection as close to an ideal triple conjunction as perhaps one can hope to see.

Acknowledgements   Earlier versions of this chapter were presented at the Peace Palace in The Hague and at the U.S. Military Academy at West Point. For helpful comments I am grateful to Toni Erskine, Seamus Miller, and especially the editors of this volume.

Notes

1. Michael Walzer, *Just and Unjust Wars: A Moral Argument with Historical Illustrations*, 5th ed. (New York: Basic Books, 2015 [1977]). See especially "Postscript: A Defense of Just War Theory," 335–46.
2. Allen Buchanan, "A Richer *Jus ad Bellum*," in *The Oxford Handbook of Ethics of War*, eds. Seth Lazar and Helen Frowe (New York: Oxford University Press, 2018), 167–84.
3. Henry Shue, "Laws of War, Morality, and International Politics: Compliance, Stringency, and Limits," in Shue, *Fighting Hurt: Rule and Exception in Torture and War* (Oxford: Oxford University Press, 2016), 469–93; reprinted from *Leiden Journal of International Law* 26, no. 2 (2013): 271–92.
4. Walzer, *Just and Unjust Wars*, 5th ed., 338.
5. William J. Talbott, *Human Rights and Human Well-Being* (New York: Oxford University Press, 2010), 103–29.
6. David Luban, "Just War Theory and the Laws of War as Nonidentical Twins," *Ethics & International Affairs* 31 (2017): 433–40, at 439.
7. On cognitive impairment, see the chapter by Judith Lichtenberg.
8. Tamar Meisels, *Contemporary Just War: Theory and Practice* (London: Routledge, 2018), 11–29.
9. Jeff McMahan, "The Just Distribution of Harm Between Combatants and Noncombatants," *Philosophy & Public Affairs* 38 (2010): 357–58.
10. Helen Frowe, *Defensive Killing* (Oxford: Oxford University Press, 2014), 162.
11. Ibid., 187.

12. Scott D. Sagan and Benjamin A. Valentino, "Just Wars and Unjust Soldiers: American Public Opinion on the Moral Equality of Combatants," *Ethics and International Affairs* 33 (2019): 411–44.

13. Walzer, *Just and Unjust Wars*, 5th ed., 343–44.

14. See Shue, *Fighting Hurt*, 401–68.

15. Jeff McMahan, "The Morality of War and the Law of War," in *Just and Unjust Warriors: The Moral and Legal Status of Soldiers*, eds. David Rodin and Henry Shue (Oxford: Oxford University Press, 2008), 19–43, at 22.

16. See, for example, International Committee of the Red Cross, "Interpretive Guidance on the Notion of Direct Participation in Hostilities Under International Humanitarian Law," *Reports and Documents* 90 (2008): 872.

17. Walzer, *Just and Unjust Wars*, 5th ed., 342–43.

18. This is not the only motive for terrorism, of course.

19. Whether the killing of so-called 'high-value' targets has much military value in fact is an empirical question that is far from settled—see Keith Patrick Dear, "Beheading the Hydra? Does Killing Terrorist or Insurgent Leaders Work?" *Defence Studies* 13, no. 3: 293–337.

20. An earlier attempt to explain the argument is in Janina Dill and Henry Shue, "Limiting the Killing in War: Military Necessity and the St. Petersburg Assumption," in Shue, *Fighting Hurt*: 447–68; reprinted from *Ethics & International Affairs* 26 (2012): 311–33.

21. See, for example, Bao Ninh, *The Sorrow of War* (London: Vintage, 1998).

22. Seth Lazar, *Sparing Civilians* (Oxford: Oxford University Press, 2015), 74–100.

23. Thus, Seth Lazar is quite wrong to claim: "Shue's argument includes two important propositions. First, that the morally best laws for war should aim to minimize the suffering that war causes. Second, these laws exhaust the morality of war"—Seth Lazar, "The Morality and Law of War," in *Routledge Companion to the Philosophy of Law*, ed. Andrei Marmor (New York: Routledge, 2012), 364–79, at 373. I have never endorsed either of the propositions Lazar attributes to me. The proposition that my argument turns on is that workable constraints are superior to unworkable ones.

24. Imaginative and provocative proposals about how to make war less murderous for the adversary's combatants (liable or non-liable) are in Gabriella Blum, "The Dispensable Lives of Soldiers," *Journal of Legal Analysis* 2 (2010): 115–71; Jens David Ohlin, "The Basic Structure of *Jus in Bello*," in *Cambridge Handbook of the Just War*, ed. Larry May (New York: Cambridge University Press, 2018), 234–54.

25. Gérard Prunier, *Africa's World War: Congo, The Rwandan Genocide, and the Making of a Continental Catastrophe* (New York: Oxford University Press, 2009).

26. Henry Shue, "Last Resort and Proportionality," in *Fighting Hurt*: 380–98; reprinted from Seth Lazar and Helen Frowe, eds., *The Oxford Handbook of Ethics of War* (Oxford: Oxford University Press, 2017), 260–76.
27. See Isabel V. Hull, *Absolute Destruction: Military Culture and the Practices of War in Imperial Germany* (Ithaca: Cornell University Press, 2005), 122–30 and 324–33.
28. Françoise Hampson, "The Principle of Proportionality in the Law of Armed Conflict," in *The Geneva Conventions Under Assault*, eds. Sarah Perrigo and Jim Whitman (London: Pluto Press, 2010), 43.
29. For much more thorough (and sceptical) consideration of Article 57, see Janina Dill, "Do Attackers Have a Legal Duty of Care? Limits to the 'Individualization of War'," *International Theory* 11 (2019): 1–25.
30. McMahan, "Just Distribution of Harm."
31. Walzer's greatest mistake is his overly permissive concept of supreme emergency, which, I believe, is an exception that ran out of control and threatens to undermine his concept of due care, which I embrace next in the text. I have already explained why I think Walzer's exception is too broad in "Supreme Moral Emergency: Shrinking the Walzerian Exception," in Shue, *Fighting Hurt*: 247–71.
32. Walzer, *Just and Unjust Wars*, 5th ed., 155–56 [1st edition, 155]. The 5th edition is the first in which the pagination of the main text sometimes differs slightly from the 1st edition.
33. I have taken a few halting steps toward spelling out further how much risk is reasonable in Shue, "Force Protection, Military Advantage, and 'Constant Care' for Civilians: The 1991 Bombing of Iraq," in Shue, *Fighting Hurt*: 330–47, at 337–42; reprinted from Evangelista and Shue, *The American Way of Bombing*: 145–57, at 152–57.

BIBLIOGRAPHY

Blum, Gabriella. "The Dispensable Lives of Soldiers." *Journal of Legal Analysis* 2 (2010): 115–71.

Buchanan, Allen. "A Richer *Jus ad Bellum*." In *The Oxford Handbook of Ethics of War*, edited by Seth Lazar and Helen Frowe, 167–84. New York: Oxford University Press, 2018.

Dear, Keith Patrick. "Beheading the Hydra? Does Killing Terrorist or Insurgent Leaders Work?" *Defence Studies* 13 (2013): 293–337.

Dill, Janina. "Do Attackers Have a Legal Duty of Care? Limits to the 'Individualization of War'." *International Theory* 11 (2019): 1–25.

Dill, Janina, and Henry Shue. "Limiting the Killing in War: Military Necessity and the St. Petersburg Assumption." In Henry Shue, *Fighting Hurt: Rule and Exception in Torture and War*, 447–68. Oxford: Oxford University Press, 2016; reprinted from *Ethics & International Affairs* 26 (2012): 311–33.

Frowe, Helen. *Defensive Killing*. Oxford: Oxford University Press, 2014.

Hampson, Françoise. "The Principle of Proportionality in the Law of Armed Conflict." In *The Geneva Conventions Under Assault*, edited by Sarah Perrigo and Jim Whitman, 42–73. London: Pluto Press, 2010.

Hull, Isabel V. *Absolute Destruction: Military Culture and the Practices of War in Imperial Germany*. Ithaca: Cornell University Press, 2005.

Lazar, Seth. "The Morality and Law of War." In *Routledge Companion to the Philosophy of Law*, edited by Andrei Marmor, 364–79. New York: Routledge, 2012.

———. *Sparing Civilians*. Oxford: Oxford University Press, 2015.

Lichtenberg, Judith. "Autonomy, Obedience, and Manifest Illegality." Chapter 10, this volume.

Luban, David. "Just War Theory and the Laws of War as Nonidentical Twins." *Ethics & International Affairs* 31 (2017): 433–40, at 439.

McMahan, Jeff. "The Just Distribution of Harm Between Combatants and Noncombatants." *Philosophy & Public Affairs* 38 (2010): 342–79.

———. "The Morality of War and the Law of War." In *Just and Unjust Warriors: The Moral and Legal Status of Soldiers*, edited by David Rodin and Henry Shue, 19–43. Oxford: Oxford University Press, 2008.

Meisels, Tamar. *Contemporary Just War: Theory and Practice*, 11–29. London: Routledge, 2018.

Ninh, Bao. *The Sorrow of War*. London: Vintage, 1998.

Ohlin, Jens David. "The Basic Structure of *Jus in Bello*." In *Cambridge Handbook of the Just War*, edited by Larry May, 234–54. New York: Cambridge University Press, 2018.

Prunier, Gérard. *Africa's World War: Congo, The Rwandan Genocide, and the Making of a Continental Catastrophe*. New York: Oxford University Press, 2009.

Sagan, Scott D., and Benjamin A. Valentino. "Just Wars and Unjust Soldiers: American Public Opinion on the Moral Equality of Combatants." *Ethics and International Affairs* 33 (2019): 411–44.

Shue, Henry. *Fighting Hurt: Rule and Exception in Torture and War*. Oxford: Oxford University Press, 2016.

———. "Force Protection, Military Advantage, and 'Constant Care' for Civilians: The 1991 Bombing of Iraq." In Shue, *Fighting Hurt*: 330–47; reprinted from Matthew Evangelista and Henry Shue, *The American Way of Bombing: Changing Ethical and Legal Norms, from Flying Fortresses to Drones*, 145–57.

———. "Last Resort and Proportionality." In *Fighting Hurt*: 380–98; reprinted from Seth Lazar and Helen Frowe, eds., *The Oxford Handbook of Ethics of War*, 260–76. Oxford: Oxford University Press, 2017.

————. "Laws of War, Morality, and International Politics: Compliance, Stringency, and Limits." In Henry Shue, *Fighting Hurt*: 469–93; reprinted from *Leiden Journal of International Law* 26, no. 2 (2013): 271–92.

————. "Supreme Moral Emergency: Shrinking the Walzerian Exception." In Henry Shue, *Fighting Hurt*: 247–71.

Talbott, William J. *Human Rights and Human Well-Being*. New York: Oxford University Press, 2010.

Walzer, Michael. *Just and Unjust Wars: A Moral Argument with Historical Illustrations*. 5th ed. New York: Basic Books, 2015 [1977].

CHAPTER 10

Autonomy, Obedience, and Manifest Illegality

Judith Lichtenberg

I

Everyone occasionally faces hard moral choices. But soldiers in wartime, and particularly those in combat, confront them on a regular basis. At least two features, both pretty obvious, burden the soldier more than the rest of us. First, the soldier's job is often to kill people, and to risk being killed. Second, soldiers must often make decisions in a moment, under circumstances of chaos, confusion, and fear, with little chance for reflection or deliberation. The moral dilemmas most people face are rarely life-and-death and often allow time to think.

Still, one aspect of the soldier's dilemma simply underlines a predicament facing all human beings who live under government (that is, these days, everyone). Here is Robert Paul Wolff's statement of the dilemma:

> The defining mark of the state is authority, the right to rule. The primary obligation of man is autonomy, the refusal to be ruled. It would seem, then, that there can be no resolution of the conflict between the autonomy of the individual and the putative authority of the state. Insofar as a man fulfills his obligation to make himself the author of his decisions, he will resist the state's claim to have authority over him.[1]

J. Lichtenberg (✉)
Georgetown University, Washington, DC, USA

© The Author(s) 2020
G. Parsons and M. A. Wilson (eds.), *Walzer and War*,
https://doi.org/10.1007/978-3-030-41657-7_10

The dilemma is particularly pointed with respect to military institutions, which require a high degree of discipline and obedience. As Field Marshal Maurice Comte de Saxe put it in the eighteenth century, military discipline is "the soul of all armies"; without it "they are no better than so many contemptible heaps of rabble, which are more dangerous to the very state that maintains them, than even its declared enemies."[2]

Wolff's formulation of the problem may seem too simple. After all, we do not, and could not, make up our own minds about everything. An enormous proportion of what people know, or have to assume for practical purposes, is second- or third- or fourth-hand. We know very little directly, and so to decide what to do we must continually make judgments (implicitly or explicitly) about which sources of information to trust.

So on the one hand military institutions require strict discipline and obedience in order to function well, and therefore soldiers must generally obey their superior officers. On the other hand, soldiers receive extensive training about acceptable and unacceptable ways of carrying out their mission, in addition to the moral knowledge and education every person is assumed to have. Soldiers are forbidden to follow illegal orders. Moreover, it is hard to disagree with Wolff that people can never cede their autonomy; they can never become wholly instruments of others' wills, but must decide for themselves what to do.

The conflict between these two moral imperatives is sharpened by the traditional (now called traditionalist) understanding of just war theory, which Michael Walzer made near-common sense with the publication in 1977 of his classic *Just and Unjust Wars*.[3] According to the traditionalist view, just war theory divides into two parts: *jus ad bellum*, which concerns the conditions under which it is just to wage war; and *jus in bello*, which concerns the legitimate rules of engagement within war. The two parts are, as Walzer says, "logically independent": "it is perfectly possible for a just war to be fought unjustly and for an unjust war to be fought in strict accordance with the rules."[4]

Over the last several decades the traditionalist understanding of just war theory has come under severe challenge. Among other things, revisionist critics question the two-part separation, arguing against traditionalists that soldiers are responsible for evaluating the justice or injustice of their cause and not simply their conduct within war. The revisionists' challenges bring to the fore questions about soldiers' responsibility for their conduct in war.

II

So how do we weigh these conflicting moral imperatives between the need for military discipline and the demand for human autonomy? To make progress in resolving this dilemma I will focus a good part of my discussion on the My Lai massacre, an infamous event of the American war in Vietnam.

The killings occurred shortly after the Tet offensive, on March 16, 1968 in Quang Ngai province, thought by the U.S. military to be an enemy stronghold.[5] Two days earlier, a sergeant from Charlie Company had been killed by a booby trap; several others were injured.[6] After the sergeant's funeral Captain Ernest Medina, the commanding officer of Charlie Company, gave his men a pep-talk and discussed the mission with them. Later, some remembered that he had ordered them to kill everyone in My Lai; others shared Medina's recollection that he had not said this— that he had been vague, "as if to leave the interpretation of his orders…up to the feelings and conscience of the individual soldier."[7]

The next day Lieutenant William Calley, a 24-year-old platoon leader under Medina's command who was not much respected by his soldiers, led his men into My Lai. He ordered two privates who were guarding villagers to "take care of them," and shortly thereafter ordered the soldiers to shoot the villagers. He also commanded his soldiers to kill men, women, and children in a drainage ditch; witnesses reported between 75 and 150 Vietnamese killed, none of them armed.[8] An army photographer, Ronald Haeberle, said he saw about thirty soldiers kill about a hundred civilians.[9] Some of Calley's men refused his orders, but many obeyed. Altogether somewhere between 347 and 504 unarmed Vietnamese women, children, and old men were killed and 20 women and girls were raped.[10]

After an extensive cover-up over the next year and a half, the Army decided to prosecute 25 officers and enlisted men. In the end only a few were tried and only Calley was found guilty. Most of the enlisted men escaped prosecution, perhaps because of lack of specific evidence, or because they had left the military and were therefore immune to prosecution by court-martial. Medina was acquitted of all charges after the jury deliberated for 57 minutes. Calley, who claimed Medina had ordered him to make sure everyone in the village was killed, was sentenced to hard labor for life in 1971, after the jury deliberated for 13 days. After spending one weekend in the stockade, however, President Nixon put him under house arrest and pledged to review the decision. In November 1974 he was paroled.[11] He has lived in Georgia ever since.

What does the law say about these soldiers' liability? As Paola Gaeta explains, "Under national legal systems, soldiers are duty bound to obey the orders of their superiors and cannot dispute their legality." But this is problematic—if not downright paradoxical—when soldiers are ordered to perform crimes. In that case "the duty of military obedience clashes with the supremacy of the rule of law, which prohibits the commission of criminal offenses."[12] Gaeta goes on to say that national courts have always denied the defense of superior orders in cases of war crimes on grounds that the illegality of the order was manifest or should have been known by subordinates.[13] Some acts, in other words, are such that their unlawfulness is manifest on its face.

In 1958, an Israeli court offered a vivid metaphor to explain the meaning of a manifestly illegal order:

> The mark of an order which is 'manifestly illegal' flies like a black flag over orders given as a warning sign, saying 'forbidden.' It is not formal illegality, hidden or half-hidden, not illegality evident only to the eyes of legal experts which is important here, but a violation of the law which is glaring and obvious, a certain and necessary illegality, which appears on the face of the order itself, a clear criminal character of the order... Illegality which strikes the eye and shakes the heart, if the eye is not blind and the heart is not deaf or corrupt...[14]

The German Military Penal Code asserts that "illegality is manifest when it is contrary 'to what every man's conscience would tell him anyhow.'"[15] So the question is whether a reasonable person would "recognize the wrongfulness of the act or order." When the soldier knows or should have known that the act is a violation of law, he is released from his duty to obey the command to do it; indeed, he has a duty *not* to obey. At the same time, he "must resolve all genuine doubts about wrongfulness in favor of obedience."[16]

It's obvious that manifest illegality cannot be separated from manifest immorality. It implies a natural law rather than a positivist conception of law: "what every man's conscience would tell him anyhow." "Anyhow" suggests that a person's conscience would so tell him irrespective of what he's learned in the military.

The judge in the Calley trial instructed the jury:

> Summary execution of detainees or prisoners is forbidden by law. …Thus, if you find that Lieutenant Calley received an order directing him to kill unresisting Vietnamese within his control or within the control of his troops, that order would be an illegal order.[17]

But Calley's acts would be excused, and would impose no criminal liability, unless the superior's order was "one which a man of ordinary sense and understanding would, under the circumstances, know to be unlawful, or if the order in question is actually known to the accused to be unlawful…"[18]

On appeal, Calley's lawyers objected to the judge's standard: whether "a man of ordinary sense and understanding" would conclude the order was illegal. They argued that the test should be whether "the order is so palpably or manifestly illegal that a person of 'the commonest understanding' would be aware of its illegality." The appellate judge explained that Calley's lawyers thought the trial judge's stricter standard would confront soldiers "who are not persons of ordinary sense and understanding with the dilemma of choosing between the penalty of death for disobedience of an order in time of war on the one hand, and the equally serious punishment for obedience on the other."[19] Perhaps, they suggested, Calley was a person of only the commonest understanding. To make sense of this suggestion, we must suppose that "commonest" means "lowest" rather than "most common," for the latter would be no different from the standard that was used: a person of "ordinary sense and understanding." In the chaotic conditions of combat, Calley's lawyers argued, it's unfair to expect a soldier to make a legal judgment on a question about which there may be considerable disagreement.

But the appellate panel upheld Calley's conviction 2-1, arguing that "there is no disagreement as to the illegality of the order to kill in this case. For 100 years, it has been a settled rule of American law that even in war the summary killing of an enemy, who has submitted to, and is under, effective physical control, is murder."[20] As Walzer puts it, when we require soldiers to refuse such orders, this "is best understood as an appeal up the chain of command over a superior officer to the superiors of that superior officer" rather than "a denial of or a rebellion against the military hierarchy."[21]

Did the military court rule correctly in Calley's case? And what about the enlisted soldiers under Calley who killed civilians pursuant to his orders? None were tried or convicted. What should have happened to them?

III

Philosophers John Doris and Dominic Murphy defend one approach. They believe that soldiers like those in My Lai are "typically cognitively degraded," and "when individuals are cognitively degraded they are not morally responsible for their behavior."[22] They should be excused because they find themselves in these circumstances "through no fault of their own." Doris and Murphy distinguish the kind of cognitive degradation typical of soldiers from chronic conditions suffered by the seriously mentally ill. Combat, they say, often induces in "quite normal subjects transient cognitive impairments that enable morally reprehensible behavior" but does not turn those subjects into [as they put it] "lifelong brutes."[23]

Doris and Murphy espouse situationism, a theory of human psychology arguing that "differences in situations account for much more of the observed variation in human behavior than do differences in personality."[24] Situationism helps to explain why soldiers who kill in combat don't become lifelong brutes.

Situationists are right that even small differences in the features of situations can produce dramatic differences in people's behavior; there's a great deal of evidence for this conclusion. Here is one famous example (out of many I could have chosen): in a 1972 experiment, subjects who have just emerged from a phone booth encounter a woman (a confederate of the experimenter) who has dropped a sheaf of papers on the ground. Will the subject stop to help her pick up the papers? Subjects who have just found a dime in the coin return of the public phone are much more likely to help than those who didn't find a dime: of those who found a dime, 14 people helped and two didn't; of those who did not find a dime, one helped and 24 didn't.[25]

Radical situationists hold to a kind of near-determinism that says that no one is responsible for their behavior: situations are all, human character almost nothing. But this is a dangerous misstep that we need not and should not take even if we are convinced, as I am, that there's a lot of truth in the situationist thesis. There are a variety of reasons why we should resist falling headlong into this kind of determinism. Here are a few.

First, it can be and has been persuasively argued that in our everyday lives we are incapable of acting as if determinism were true.[26] We treat people as if their behavior is at least partly subject to their own wills, and it is hard to imagine social life and institutions as we know them without such an assumption. We might think that this is not only pragmatically necessary, but that it's essential to human dignity to think of oneself, and others, mostly as responsible agents who make choices.

Relatedly, holding people responsible is among the causal factors that influence how they act.[27] If people knew they would never be held responsible for their behavior and never be subject to punishment, they would be more likely to behave badly. We might put this by saying that holding people responsible must be considered part of the situation that situationism needs to take into account. After extensive discussions with Vietnam War veterans, the psychologist Robert J. Lifton says he "was struck by the emphasis that the men…placed upon responsibility and volition."[28] Considering Lifton's findings, the philosopher Cheyney Ryan suggests that "claiming responsibility for them could be essential to reclaiming psychic health in so far as it led to a re-establishment of personal agency."[29]

Thus, despite the powerful influence of circumstances on behavior, their influence is not irresistible (unless we understand "circumstances" so broadly as to become meaningless). As Walzer notes in *Just and Unjust Wars*, although some soldiers at My Lai readily joined in the murders,

> there were a few who refused to fire their guns and others who had to be ordered to fire two or three times before they could bring themselves to do so. Others simply ran away; one man shot himself in the foot so as to escape the scene; a junior officer tried heroically to stop the massacre… Many of his fellows, we know, were sick and guilt-ridden in the days that followed.[30]

Walzer emphatically rejects one philosopher's claim about soldiers that "war…in some respects makes psychopaths of them all."[31]

Analogously, in the classic version of the Milgram experiments (one of the *ur*-texts for situationists) about a third of subjects did not shock the learner, even though two thirds did.[32] And in many of the variations of the experiments done by Milgram and others, the results were very different. For example, "when subjects were free to choose the shock levels to administer to the victim, only 3 percent delivered the maximum shock."[33]

Moreover, although in the standard version subjects complied with the experimenter's order, they did so not indifferently but in anguish—suffering in the way Walzer tells us many soldiers were after My Lai.

IV

So it's a serious mistake to say flatly that the soldiers in My Lai were not morally responsible for what they did. As Walzer puts it, "Soldiers can never be transformed into mere instruments of war."[34] But we should not go to the other extreme and neglect the enormous pressures soldiers in combat face. In many cases their culpability is mitigated—their behavior, while never justified, is partially or sometimes even wholly excused. Walzer's typically nuanced discussion reminds us of the terrible dilemmas soldiers may face and that we may face in judging them.

In the criminal law, excuses fall into two main headings—ignorance and duress—and these serve equally in the case of war.[35]

Consider first ignorance. Walzer argues that "ignorance is the common lot of the common soldier, and it makes an easy defense, especially when calculations of usefulness and proportionality are called for." The ordinary soldier is not "bound to seek out information; the moral life of a combat soldier is not a research assignment."[36] Yet the concept of manifest illegality discussed earlier implies that ignorance will rarely serve as an excuse for committing war crimes: every human being of normal capacities is expected to understand that killing noncombatants is not permissible, and soldiers are specially instructed in these matters. And Walzer does not disagree: "the soldiers in the Vietnamese village could hardly have doubted the innocence of the people they were ordered to kill."[37] A research assignment was not necessary.

But there are several factors that might serve as part of an ignorance excuse.

First, it seems plausible that a soldier's intelligence, level of education, and rank in the military stand as rough proxies for his epistemic situation and therefore his degree of culpability. So, for example, other things being equal officers are more culpable than enlisted men and can less plausibly plead ignorance.[38]

Second, it's not necessarily true that every war crime is manifestly illegal; there can be ambiguous cases. For example, because in asymmetric warfare it can be difficult to tell combatants from noncombatants, a sol-dier who knows it is forbidden to target noncombatants may still sincerely (or less sincerely) claim he believed a particular person was a combatant.

Third, because of the sometimes extreme division of labor within mili-tary organizations, soldiers can participate in obvious war crimes without knowing it. For instance, one could participate in launching missiles from a battleship but not know what the missiles are firing at.[39] If Walzer is right that the ordinary soldier is not "bound to seek out information," ignorance in this case would be an excuse.

Finally—this is a bit more speculative—it might be argued that the sheer size of the targeted group bears on the question of knowledge and ignorance: the larger the group, the more clear the criminal nature of the killing is. A massacre of hundreds, as at My Lai, or thousands, as in Srebrenica, may wear its immorality on its face more clearly than does the killing of a small number of people.

To consider duress, take the case of Dražen Erdemović, a young ethnic Croat living in Bosnia–Herzegovina who became a soldier in the Yugoslav National Army in 1990. In 1994, he resisted the order to slaughter civil-ians at Srebrenica, but when faced with the threat of death when he refused to comply, he obeyed the order. After the war ended, Erdemović told a journalist he wanted to go to the Hague to tell his story. Arrested by Yugoslav authorities and transferred to the Hague, he was sentenced to ten years in prison by the trial court at the Hague Tribunal. The Appeals Tribunal upheld his sentence, citing the traditional common law rule dis-allowing duress as a defense to murder.[40]

Clearly, Erdemović experienced duress of the harshest kind: kill or be killed. And afterwards he came forward to confess, with sorrow, what he had done. Moreover, no lives would have been saved had he refused to act; indeed one more—his own—would have been lost.[41] So despite the horrifying acts he committed, we might think him less culpable than someone confronting less stark choices.

Other factors are also relevant to judging the degree of duress a soldier experiences. Soldiers under totalitarian regimes experience more duress than those under liberal democratic governments; this is a spectrum with many places in between. Drafted soldiers have better excuses than volun-teers; almost by definition they act under duress.

It is sometimes said that in the common law duress never excuses homicide. But this may be more a claim about terminology than any-thing else. Duress is among the mitigating circumstances judges and juries consider that reduce a defendant's punishment. Whatever we call it, and whether it plays a role during the trial or only in the penalty phase, such mitigating factors as duress function as excuses—factors that reduce culpability. That such considerations enter into judgments of a person's culpability reflects our views about the sacrifices it is reasonable to expect ordinary people to make and the pressures to which we may expect them to succumb.

The other side of the coin is that if a soldier has no reason to think disobeying an order will cause him grief, he has less excuse not to disobey it. Walzer asserts that "At My Lai, those men who refused to fire never suffered for their refusal and apparently did not expect to suffer; and that suggests that we must blame the others for their obedience."[42] He does not give a reference for this claim, and its truth or falsity might make some difference to our judgment of those soldiers.

V

A central paradox is this: on the one hand, we must impress on soldiers that certain conduct, such as targeting civilians, is forbidden; on the other hand, many soldiers who cross the line are not fully culpable.

A useful distinction in explaining this paradox goes back at least to Jeremy Bentham:

> A law confining itself to the creation of an offence, and a law commanding a punishment to be administered in case of the commission of such an offence, are two distinct laws, not parts (as they seem to have been generally accounted hitherto) of one and the same law. The acts they command are altogether different; the persons they are addressed to are altogether different. Instance, *Let no man steal;* and, *Let the judge cause whoever is convicted of stealing to be hanged.*[43]

Some rules are addressed to the public and some to officials—and the acts they command, as Bentham says, are "altogether different." We want to impress on soldiers and others the impermissibility and wrongness of certain acts, but that is compatible with appreciating the forces that lead them to commit such acts and to reduce their culpability accordingly.

The trouble is that if individuals come to know that the consequences of rule-breaking are less dire than one might expect, that will likely influence their behavior. (Thus the saying "It's easier to get forgiveness than permission.") Ideally this does not happen. Meir Dan-Cohen calls this ideal state "acoustic separation": when those subject to the conduct rule do not know the decision rule and vice versa. But "in the real world," as Dan-Cohen notes, "the public and officialdom are not in fact locked in acoustically sealed chambers, and consequently each group may 'hear' the normative messages the law transmits to the other group."[44] The classic examples come from the criminal law, including the defense of duress, and illustrate exactly the problem before us here. Knowledge of the defense of duress may influence people's conduct.

The solution, selective transmission—i.e., partial acoustic separation—can be difficult to achieve, because military personnel are supposed to be acutely aware of the rules under which they operate and the consequences of ignoring these rules. That would make them more culpable, other things being equal, than civilians. But against this we must weigh the duress soldiers may endure in addition to the constraints of military discipline—"the soul of all armies."

No definitive resolution of this dilemma is possible. Walzer's particularist approach seems more promising: gather as much information as you can about the agent and the circumstances, then rely on judgments gleaned from experience as well as legal and philosophical insight to draw the best conclusions you can.

NOTES

1. Robert Paul Wolff, *In Defense of Anarchism* (New York: Harper & Row, 1970), 18.
2. Field-Marshal Count de Saxe, *The Art of War: Reveries and Memoirs* (London: J. Davis, 1811), Chapter 8, 48. Originally published posthumously in 1757.
3. *Just and Unjust Wars: A Moral Argument with Historical Illustrations*, 3rd ed. (New York: Basic Books, 2000). Seth Lazar uses this language in "War," *Stanford Encyclopedia of Philosophy*, https://plato.stanford.edu/entries/war/#WalzHisCrit. Lazar provides a comprehensive discussion of the debate. Jeff McMahan is the best known and most prolific revisionist.
4. Ibid., 21.
5. Michael Walzer discusses the My Lai massacre incisively in *Just and Unjust Wars*, 309–16. For a timeline, see My Lai Timeline, Charlie Company and the Massacre, PBS, American Experience, http://www.pbs.org/wgbh/americanexperience/features/my-lai-

charlie-company-and-massacre/. February had been calamitous for Charlie Company. Two platoons had stumbled on a minefield; three soldiers were killed and a dozen more injured.

6. According to the timeline, on March 14, 1968, "In one of the first documented instances of outright aggression, frustrated and angry members of Charlie Company" shot and killed a woman civilian working in a field while they were passing through a village returning to camp after the soldier's death.

7. Seymour Hersh, *My Lai 4: A Report on the Massacre and Its Aftermath* (New York: Vintage, 1970), 40. Hersh broke the story in an article for the *Cleveland Plain Dealer* on November 20, 1969 and wrote about it again at length in a two-part article for *The New Yorker* in 1972. See also Christopher J. Levesque, "The Truth Behind My Lai," *New York Times*, March 18, 2018, https://www.nytimes.com/2018/03/16/opinion/the-truth-behind-my-lai.html.

8. Levesque, "The Truth Behind My Lai," and My Lai Timeline, 9 a.m.

9. Douglas Linder, "The My Lai Massacre and Courts-Martial: An Account," https://www.famous-trials.com/mylaicourts/1656-myl-intro.

10. Levesque, "The Truth Behind My Lai."

11. Linder, "The My Lai Massacre and Courts-Martial." In 2009, Calley apologized for his role in the massacre. "There is not a day that goes by that I do not feel remorse for what happened that day in My Lai," he said. When asked if he broke the law, he replied: "If you are asking why I did not stand up to them when I was given the orders, I will have to say that I was a second lieutenant getting orders from my commander and I followed them—foolishly, I guess." NBC News, "Calley Apologizes for Role in My Lai Massacre," August 21, 2009, http://www.nbcnews.com/id/32514139/ns/us_news-military/t/calley-apologizes-role-my-lai-massacre#.XOb3CC-ZOu4.

12. Paola Gaeta, "The Defense of Superior Orders: The Statute of the International Criminal Court Versus Customary International Law," *European Journal of International Law* 10 (1999): 173.

13. But other commentators argue that "under Article 33 of the ICC Statute, orders to commit genocide and crimes against humanity are deemed to be manifestly unlawful, whereas the same is not expressly applicable to orders to commit war crimes. It could thus be inferred that the ICC does allow for a defense of superior orders in situations where war crimes have been committed. To so allow such a defense is arguably understandable, given the complexity of modern-day asymmetrical warfare, with myriad parties involved, the blurring of the distinction between combatants and civilians, and the conduct of hostilities and control of weapons from distant operation centers rather than in the field of combat" (Jamie Allan Williamson,

"Some Considerations on Command Responsibility and Criminal Liability," *International Review of the Red Cross* 90 (2008): 316–17.

14. The opinion was given in the Kfar-Kassem trial. "On October 29, 1956, on the eve of the Sinai Campaign, the Israeli army ordered all Israeli Arab villages near the Jordanian border placed under a wartime curfew… Any Arab on the streets was to be shot. The order was given to the Israeli border police at 3:30 before most of the Arabs from the villages could be notified. Many of them were at work at the time. Villagers began to arrive from work to their homes in Kfar Kassem and Israeli troops opened fire on them. A total of 47 Israeli Arabs were killed. The news of the killings was censored and the general Israeli public did not learn what happened until several weeks later when Prime Minister David Ben Gurion announced the findings of a secret inquiry. Eleven border policemen were eventually charged with crimes and eight were convicted. Those who were imprisoned had their terms reduced; no one served more than three and a half years in jail. The brigade commander received a symbolic penalty—a fine of 10 *prutot* …," District Military Court in the Kfar-Kassem trial; "The Suez-Sinai Campaign: Incident at Kfar-Kassem," October 29, 1956, Jewish Virtual Library, http://www.jewishvirtuallibrary.org/incident-at-kfar-kassem-october-1956.

15. German Military Code, cited in David J. Luban, Julie R. O'Sullivan, David P. Stewart, and Neha Jain, *International and Transnational Criminal Law*, 3rd ed. (Austin, TX: Aspen, 2019), 911.

16. Ibid.

17. *U.S. v. Calley*, 22 U.S.C.M.A. 534 (U.S. Ct. Mil. App. 1973), in Linder, "The My Lai Massacre, Decision of U.S. Court of Military Appeals in Calley Case," https://www.famous-trials.com/mylaicourts/1634-myluscma.

18. Ibid.

19. Ibid.

20. Ibid.

21. Michael Walzer, *Arguing About War* (New Haven: Yale University Press, 2004), 27.

22. John Doris and Dominic Murphy, "From My Lai to Abu Ghraib: The Moral Psychology of Atrocity," *Midwest Studies in Philosophy* 31 (2007): 26.

23. Ibid., 31.

24. David Luban, "Integrity: Its Causes and Cures," *Fordham Law Review* 72 (2003–4): 294.

25. A. M. Isen and P. F. Levin, "Effect of Feeling Good on Helping: Cookies and Kindness," *Journal of Personality and Social Psychology* 21 (1972). The result was explained in terms of mood: finding a dime (not worth much

even in 1972) apparently elevated a person's mood and so increased the chances she would help others.

26. See, e.g., P. F. Strawson, "Freedom and Resentment," *Proceedings of the British Academy* 48 (1962), reprinted in P. F. Strawson, *Freedom and Resentment and Other Essays* (London: Routledge, 2008).

27. See, e.g., Kathleen D. Vohs and Roy Baumeister, "Addiction and Free Will," *Addiction Research Theory* 17 (2009): 231–35, https://doi.org/10.1080/16066350802567103, arguing that when people believe in free will they are more likely to take responsibility for their actions and behave in ways better for themselves and others.

28. Robert J. Lifton, *Home from the War: Learning from Vietnam Veterans* (Boston: Beacon Press, 1992), 267; quoted in Cheyney Ryan, "Moral Equality, Victimhood, and the Sovereignty Symmetry Problem," in *Just and Unjust Warriors: The Moral and Legal Status of Soldiers*, eds. David Rodin and Henry Shue (Oxford: Oxford University Press, 2008), 140.

29. Ryan, "Moral Equality, Victimhood, and the Sovereignty Symmetry Problem."

30. Walzer, *Just and Unjust Wars*, 310.

31. Ibid., 307.

32. Stanley Milgram, *Obedience to Authority* (New York: Harper, 1975) and Results of the Milgram Experiment, https://www.mtholyoke.edu/~apkokot/results.htm.

33. John Doris, *Lack of Character: Personality and Moral Behavior* (Cambridge University Press, 2005), 46, citing Milgram, *Obedience to Authority*, p. 61; and A. G. Miller, *The Obedience Experiments: A Case Study of Controversy in Social Science* (New York: Praeger, 1986), 210.

34. Walzer, *Just and Unjust Wars*, 311.

35. See Walzer, *Just and Unjust Wars*, 312–16; Judith Lichtenberg, "How to Judge Soldiers Whose Cause Is Unjust," in *Just and Unjust Warriors: The Moral and Legal Status of Soldiers*, eds. David Rodin and Henry Shue (Oxford: Oxford University Press, 2008), 118–24.

36. Walzer, *Just and Unjust Wars*, 312.

37. Ibid., 313.

38. Linder reports that "the soldiers of Charlie Company, like most combat soldiers in Viet Nam, scored low on military exams. Few combat soldiers had education beyond high school." Linder, "The My Lai Massacre and Courts-Martial."

39. Thanks to Graham Parsons for this insight. Of course, sometimes ignorance is culpable.

40. The following paragraphs draw from Lichtenberg, "How to Judge Soldiers Whose Cause Is Unjust," 119–22. For an account of the case and an excellent analysis, see Rosa Ehrenreich Brooks, "Law in the Heart of

Darkness: Atrocity and Duress," *Virginia Journal of International Law* 43 (2003).

41. A point made by Brooks, "Law in the Heart of Darkness," 874. For a similar defense of the excuse of duress when the soldier is threatened with execution, see Walzer, *Just and Unjust Wars*, 313–14.

42. Walzer, *Just and Unjust Wars*, 315.

43. Jeremy Bentham, *An Introduction to the Principles of Morals and Legislation*, XVII: Of the Limits of the Penal Branch of Jurisprudence, https://www.econlib.org/library/Bentham/bnthPML.html?chapter_num=19#book-reader. Originally published 1789.

44. Meir Dan-Cohen, "Decision Rules and Conduct Rules: On Acoustic Separation in Criminal Law," *Harvard Law Review* 97 (1984): 625, 631.

Bibliography

Bentham, Jeremy. *An Introduction to the Principles of Morals and Legislation*. XVII.50: Of the Limits of the Penal Branch of Jurisprudence. https://www.econlib.org/library/Bentham/bnthPML.html?chapter_num=19#book-reader.

Brooks, Rosa Ehrenreich. "Law in the Heart of Darkness: Atrocity and Duress." *Virginia Journal of International Law* 43 (2003): 861–88.

Dan-Cohen, Meir. "Decision Rules and Conduct Rules: On Acoustic Separation in Criminal Law." *Harvard Law Review* 97 (1984): 625, 631.

Doris, John. *Lack of Character: Personality and Moral Behavior*. Cambridge: Cambridge University Press, 2005.

Doris, John, and Dominic Murphy. "From My Lai to Abu Ghraib: The Moral Psychology of Atrocity." *Midwest Studies in Philosophy* 31 (2007): 25–55.

Gaeta, Paola. "The Defense of Superior Orders: The Statute of the International Criminal Court Versus Customary International Law." *European Journal of International Law* 10 (1999): 172–91.

Hersh, Seymour. *My Lai 4: A Report on the Massacre and Its Aftermath*. New York: Vintage, 1970.

Isen, A. M., and P. F. Levin. "Effect of Feeling Good on Helping: Cookies and Kindness." *Journal of Personality and Social Psychology* 21 (1972): 384–88.

Levesque, Christopher J. "The Truth Behind My Lai." *New York Times*, March 18, 2018. https://www.nytimes.com/2018/03/16/opinion/the-truth-behind-my-lai.html.

Lichtenberg, Judith. "How to Judge Soldiers Whose Cause Is Unjust." In *Just and Unjust Warriors: The Moral and Legal Status of Soldiers*, edited by David Rodin and Henry Shue. Oxford: Oxford University Press, 2008.

Lifton, Robert J. *Home from the War: Learning from Vietnam Veterans*. Boston: Beacon Press, 1992.

Linder, Douglas. "The My Lai Massacre and Courts-Martial: An Account." https://www.famous-trials.com/mylaicourts/1656-myl-intro.

Luban, David. "Integrity: Its Causes and Cures." *Fordham Law Review* 72 (2003–4): 279–310.

Luban, David J., Julie R. O'Sullivan, David P. Stewart, and Neha Jain, *International and Transnational Criminal Law*. 3rd ed. Austin, TX: Aspen, 2019.

Milgram, Stanley. *Obedience to Authority*. New York: Harper, 1975.

Milgram Experiment, Results. https://www.mtholyoke.edu/~apkokot/results.htm.

My Lai Timeline, Charlie Company and the Massacre, PBS, American Experience. http://www.pbs.org/wgbh/americanexperience/features/my-lai-charlie-company-and-massacre/.

NBC News, "Calley Apologizes for Role in My Lai Massacre." August 21, 2009. http://www.nbcnews.com/id/32514139/ns/us_news-military/t/calley-apologizes-role-my-lai-massacre#.XOb3CC-ZOu4.

Ryan, Cheyney. "Moral Equality, Victimhood, and the Sovereignty Symmetry Problem." In *Just and Unjust Warriors: The Moral and Legal Status of Soldiers*, edited by David Rodin and Henry Shue. Oxford: Oxford University Press, 2008.

de Saxe, Field-Marshal Count Maurice. *The Art of War: Reveries and Memoirs*. London: J. Davis, 1811. Originally published 1757.

Strawson, P. F. "Freedom and Resentment." *Proceedings of the British Academy* 48 (1962), reprinted in Strawson, *Freedom and Resentment and Other Essays*. London: Routledge, 2008.

"The Suez-Sinai Campaign: Incident at Kfar-Kassem," October 29, 1956, Jewish Virtual Library. http://www.jewishvirtuallibrary.org/incident-at-kfar-kassem-october-1956.

U.S. v. Calley, 22 U.S.C.M.A. 534 (U.S. Ct. Mil. App. 1973). https://www.famous-trials.com/mylaicourts/1634-myl-uscma.

Vohs, Kathleen D., and Roy Baumeister. "Addiction and Free Will." *Addiction Research Theory* 17 (2009): 231–35. https://doi.org/10.1080/16066350802567103.

Walzer, Michael. *Arguing About War*. New Haven: Yale University Press, 2004.

———. *Just and Unjust Wars: A Moral Argument with Historical Illustrations*. 3rd ed. New York: Basic Books, 2000.

Williamson, Jamie Allan. "Some Considerations on Command Responsibility and Criminal Liability." *International Review of the Red Cross* 90 (2008): 303–17.

Wolff, Robert Paul. *In Defense of Anarchism*. New York: Harper & Row, 1970.

CHAPTER 11

Walzer's Soldiers: Gender and the Rights of Combatants

Graham Parsons

Discrimination in War

On March 3, 1943, the Battle of the Bismarck Sea took place off the northeastern shore of New Guinea. That morning Allied planes surprised a convoy of Japanese ships transporting the entire Fifty-First division, roughly 7000 men. Having intercepted and decoded Japanese communications about the troop movement, the Allies were aware of the significance of the transport. Planes attacked the convoy at low altitude in order

The views expressed in this chapter are the author's and do not represent the views of the United States Military Academy, the United States Army, or the Department of Defense. This publication was funded by the European Union's Programme FP/2007-2013, Grant Agreement N°[340956 - IOW]. The content of this publication represents only the views of the author and is his sole responsibility. The European Commission does not accept any responsibility for use that may be made of the information it contains.

G. Parsons (✉)
Department of English and Philosophy, United States Military Academy, West Point, NY, USA
e-mail: graham.parsons@westpoint.edu

G. Parsons and M. A. Wilson (eds.), *Walzer and War*,
https://doi.org/10.1007/978-3-030-41657-7_11

231

to inflict maximum damage, using mainly .50 caliber machine guns and bombs. As bombs struck the ships, the Japanese soldiers tried to escape into the sea. In the process they were mowed down by the machine guns. Those who made it into the water climbed onto lifeboats or clung to debris. Still, planes continued to strafe these helpless men for the next several hours. As one account describes it, "the water was whipped into a bloody froth, the blood mixing with chunks of flesh and the oil from the sunken ships. There was no respite for the survivors, who now floated defenseless, naked and exposed to machine gun fire. The grisly business continued into the night. When nothing was seen to move in the water, the strafing runs ended."[1] Almost 3000 Japanese soldiers were killed in the battle. There appears to have been no effort to rescue, to capture, or to solicit the surrender of Japanese forces even when they were floating in the open ocean. Allied forces operated on the policy that any Japanese combatant who is not presently offering to surrender may be attacked without hesitation. Reportedly, "some allied pilots and crews became sick and vomited at the low-level sight of the carnage their bullets and cannon shot were causing."[2]

One need not be a pacifist to find this incident troubling. Like the nauseated Allied airmen, many of us find this battle more than a little repellant. But, in fact, this operation did not unambiguously violate any law of war or even the traditional ethics of war. Despite our repugnance, when we turn to conventional military ethics and law we find few resources for mounting a criticism of this action. According to conventional views, combatants as such are fair game. It is believed to be the responsibility of combatants to declare their intention to surrender in order to avoid being attacked. Until then, they are, in Michael Walzer's words, "subject to attack at any time."[3]

The traditional view of discrimination in war divides human communities at war into two relevant groups—combatants and noncombatants—and demands radically different treatment of them. On one hand, noncombatants are never to be deliberately attacked. They can, in certain circumstances, be subjected to the risk of unintentional harm, or collateral damage, but cannot be intentionally killed or maimed.

On the other hand, the traditional view permits nearly unrestricted attacks on combatants. Regardless of how they came to be combatants (e.g., whether they volunteered or were conscripted), regardless of the justice of their cause (e.g., whether they are fighting in a colonial conquest or are defending others from aggression), and regardless of their current activity (e.g., whether they are asleep, retreating, or even on leave), those "fighting in war" are legitimate targets of deliberate attack. There are elaborate restrictions on the treatment of captured or surrendered combatants and there are some restrictions on the sort of weapons that may be used against them, but other than that combatants as such are legitimate targets. As Gabriella Blum concludes, "The striking feature of the mainstream literature is its general acceptance (albeit at times with some moral discomfort) of the near-absolute license to kill all combatants and of the law's view of combatants as nothing more than instruments of war."[4]

There is a small body of literature critical of the traditional permissiveness of the treatment of combatants.[5] I wish to add my voice to this literature. Unlike the other critics of the permission, however, I will try to show the role that gender has played in legitimating the traditional view. The idea that combatants in war, no matter which side they are on, are legitimate targets of deliberate attack is based, in part, on a sometimes implicit, sometimes explicit appeal to gender norms, in particular the norms of masculinity.

To be specific, the traditional idea of combatant non-immunity presupposes that there are some members of our political communities who by nature are sacrificial instruments of war. This assumption originates in a gendered division of social labor wherein men *as men* are primarily responsible for self-sacrificial military service and largely exempt from other social responsibilities. This gendered presumption underpins three important claims that arguments for combatant non-immunity rely on. It underpins, first, the view that combatants as such are liable to attack; second, the idea that the individuals who occupy the office of military servicemember can be reduced to their office; and, third, the view that there is a stark separation between the military and other basic institutions of civil society. While I believe these assumptions are evident in the thinking of many just war theorists, I will focus on the work of Michael Walzer who is the preeminent contemporary advocate of traditional just war thought.

One way these assumptions can be discovered in the theory of discrimination is by recognizing another assumption that often goes unquestioned. This assumption is that the word "combatant" is synonymous with "soldier" and the word "noncombatant" is synonymous with "civilian." Again and again in traditional just war theory, when its protagonists analyze the rights of combatants they speak only of the status of soldiers, and when they analyze the rights of noncombatants they speak only of the status of civilians. This is a highly presumptuous move.

Soldiers and civilians are much more specific things than combatants and noncombatants. The existence of soldiers and civilians presupposes not only the existence of states but the existence of states of a certain kind. To speak of soldiers and civilians is, according to conventional understanding, to speak of highly organized political communities, wherein soldiers are separated from the civilian world and given the singular social task of preparing for and engaging in war when ordered to by their political authority. In contrast, civilians are not so related to war and are engaged in the full spectrum of social activities that compose a robust human community, such as reproduction and child-rearing, the creation of cultural products, entrepreneurial activity, paid labor, and political activism. In short, soldiers and civilians exist in relation to each other. Soldiers live to protect civilians and civilians live nonmilitary lives in a civil society.

That the traditional theory of discrimination is based on the presumption of communities with a clear civilian-military divide is important because when traditional just war theorists defend the civilian-military divide they appeal very clearly to gender. It turns out that the duty to be a soldier, i.e., to be bound to fight in war to protect one's family and community when ordered to by one's political sovereign, is traditionally based on the view that men are by nature primarily responsible for self-sacrificial military service and largely exempt from other social responsibilities. This view of men, I will argue, is also what grounds the traditional view of combatant non-immunity in war. In this way, the presumed equivalence of the combatant/noncombatant distinction with the soldier/civilian distinction reveals the gendered origins of the theory of discrimination and the largely unrestricted permission to attack combatants.

Gender, Public War, and Sacrifice

It is not an accident that the office of military servicemember has, until quite recently, been reserved for men exclusively. Indeed, the exclusion of women from the military is nearly a universal, cross-cultural phenomenon.[6] Historically, the presence of women in combat units is extremely rare. In fact, often when women are allowed in the ranks it is in a noncombat role, such as the nurses of the Army Women's Corps. And, when women have been allowed to participate in combat, it is often because they are believed to be men, such as Deborah Samson, known as Robert Shirtliff in the American Revolution.[7] This being said, we should not succumb to the illusion that women are or have been passive in war. Even when they are excluded from combat women have often been enthusiastic supporters of war, acting as advocates, nurturing wounded, providing comfort, food, and clothing, and aggressively raising future fighters. Still, the business of fighting, of life-risking combat, has historically been seen as a males-only occupation.

The gender exclusivity of military service is due in large part to the central place that war sacrifice has in notions of masculinity.[8] Military service and the burdens it entails are central to the notion of manliness. On this view, a good man is not only physically strong but also knowledgeable in the arts of violence. Importantly, a good man also uses this capacity to protect others, thereby putting his body in harm's way for the sake of others. Facing fire without fear, or at least without debilitating fear, is a reliable way to affirm one's manhood. The self-sacrificial warrior is what Jean Bethke Elshtain calls, "the exemplary male identity."[9]

This view of masculinity is often assumed to have a basis in nature. It is believed that men are naturally endowed with the characteristics of a sacrificial warrior. For a man to fail to show these characteristics is a failure to reflect masculine virtues or even to possess the essence of his biological sex. As General George Patton once said, "a real man will never let his fear of death overpower his honor, his sense of duty to his country, and his innate manhood."[10] But this naturalist assumption is false. There is no evidence of the existence of innate warrior inclinations in men as a group. In fact, men and boys need to be socially conditioned to accept this identity beginning in their first years.

Boys are encouraged from a very early age that toughness and courage are the highest virtues of manhood. Preparing oneself for battle, physically and mentally, is one of their most important tasks. They often play with toys that simulate fighting and war, or play sports that prize physical, often injurious, competition. They are discouraged from showing feelings of empathy, fear, and sadness. As Joshua Goldstein says,

> Cultures produce male warriors by toughening up boys from an early age...Although boys on average are more prone to more rough-and-tumble play, they are not innately "tougher" than girls. They do not have fewer emotions or attachments, or feel less pain. It is obvious from the huge effort that most cultures make to mold "tough" boys that this is not an easy or natural task. When we raise boys within contemporary gender norms, especially when we push boys to toughen up, we pass along authorized forms of masculinity suited to the war system.[11]

Gender norms like these can influence how we think and act in many ways. Often they cause us to apply principles, rules, or laws in biased ways. But they can also bias the very principles, rules, or laws themselves. Our very standards can be grounded in gender bias. This has certainly happened in many cases. Our standards of marriage and divorce, paternity and reproductive rights, and the difference between the public and the private have been shaped by gender.[12] To overcome this form of bias we cannot simply apply the same old standards in a neutral way; we cannot simply "add women and stir." We must rethink the standards themselves and purge them, if possible, of gendered assumptions.

I want to show how traditional just war theory utilizes warrior masculinity to legitimate the duties of military service and, in turn, the idea that soldiers as such are disposable in war. The appeal to gender is subtle in traditional just war theory. Nevertheless, the appeal is clear. When traditional military ethicists attempt to explain how it is that a political subject can be bound to engage in life-risking battle upon command they appeal to the virtues of masculinity. In the end, then, the theory of public war is based on the idea that it is good for men—as men—to risk their lives in war for the sake of their communities. Any man who is unwilling or unable to risk his life in war is thought to be morally deficient.

Early modern military ethicists struggled more than their premodern predecessors to justify the duties of military service because in the early modern period the rights of individuals began to form the foundations of political justice. In the early modern period, the primary purpose of political society came to be seen as the protection of the equal natural rights or interests of individuals or, more accurately, men. Because the obligation to risk one's life for the sake of the community seems to imply that the community is more important than the individual, it was more of a challenge for theorists during this period to justify the obligations of military service. As Hegel describes the problem, "It is a grave miscalculation if the state, when it requires this sacrifice [military service], is simply equated with civil society, and if its ultimate end is seen merely as the security of the life and property of individuals. For this security cannot be achieved by the sacrifice of what is supposed to be secured—on the contrary."[13] As a result of this problem, early modern theorists worked hard to justify military service, offering substantive discussions of the basis of the obligations of soldiers. In most cases, they appeal to masculine virtues to justify the duties of military service. In this way, early modern contract theorists understand society as composed of naturally free and equal men who act in the service of their private rights or interests *and* men who are naturally bound to risk their lives in combat for the sake of their families and communities.

Hugo Grotius describes individual rights as prior to political society and political society as designed to protect those rights.[14] However, for Grotius, the duty to face danger in combat is based in natural virtue, not a social contract made by equal persons in a state of nature. He says, "some Acts of Virtue may by a human law be commanded, though under the evident Hazard of Death. As for a Soldier not to quit his Post...."[15] The relevant virtue for Grotius here is charity.[16] While charity is not immediately associated with masculinity, in an early work Grotius appeals more clearly to gender. Grotius praises risking one's life for the state as an expression of the virtue fortitude, one of the two virtues "most beneficial [to others], both in private and in public life."[17] Fortitude is a masculine virtue for Grotius. In the same passage, he quotes approvingly a passage from Tyrtaeus: "It is a glorious and manly thing,/To risk one's life in battle with the foe,/Defending loved ones, wife and native land."[18]

Thomas Hobbes struggles mightily to justify the obligations of soldiers. In his discussion of the problem, he clearly presupposes warrior masculinity as natural. He excuses women and feminine men from the duty to serve in war upon command. He says, "And there is allowance to be made for natural timorousness, not only to women (of whom no such dangerous duty is expected), but also to men of feminine courage."[19] The basis of the exception here is a character deficiency in women and some men. Feminine people are timorous; they have inadequate courage. In particular, they lack the moral character that would enable them to put their lives on the line in war upon command. This sort of feminine character is to be expected of women but not of men. This deficiency in men must be rare enough that not only can we burden men with the political obligation to serve in war, but also that we can be confident that the commonwealth will have a sufficient pool of soldiers to rely on in the event of war. Hobbes also asserts this gender division when he defends his claim that the succession of the throne should go to the monarch's male over his female offspring. This is because, according to Hobbes, "men are naturally fitter than women, for actions of labor and danger."[20]

Samuel von Pufendorf also describes political society as a contract made by its members so as to protect the equal rights they have by nature. Still, Pufendorf appeals directly to the virtue of bravery to ground the duty to risk one's life in war. According to him, it would simply be cowardly for a man to refuse to engage in combat out of fear of injury or death. In fact, Pufendorf claims that a good man will praise his commander for ordering him to risk his life. As he says, a soldier "is bound to defend the Post his Commander appoints him to, tho' perhaps he foresees he must in all probability lose his Life in it...And no man of Bravery or Spirit will ever complain that he is commanded upon such a Duty, but will rather commend his General's Judgment and Conduct in it."[21] Bravery and spirit are central to masculinity. In this way, then, gender norms form the foundation of Pufendorf's theory of public war.

Emer Vattel too asserts that political society is a voluntary association of its members so as to protect their equal natural rights. Yet he also appeals to the same gender division in his discussion of the duties of military service. As he says, "Every man capable of carrying arms should take them up at the first order of him who has the power of making war...Although there be some women who are equal to men in strength and courage, yet such instances are not usual; and rules must necessarily be general, and derived from the ordinary course of things."[22] For Vattel, only men have the political obligation to participate in military service because men, by nature, are inclined to have the moral character suited to "supporting the fatigues of war." In particular, men tend to have the courage to risk their lives in battle upon command. For a man to fail to do this is a peculiar kind of moral failure.

We can see in each of these cases, the theory of public war grounds the obligations of military service by appeal to norms of masculinity. It turns out that the gender norms endorsed by many cultures, which encourage boys and men to find honor in self-sacrificial service in war, are also at work in our traditional theories of military ethics. Gender bias has therefore infected the standards we use to evaluate military conduct. According to traditional military ethics, states have the right to use the male members of their society as instruments in war because men as men ought to be instruments of war for their communities and families. On this view, the duty to serve in war upon command is independent of any particular war, any particular enlistment contract, or the civil rights afforded to the members of any particular political society. Those who are bound by the duties of the office of soldier are so bound because of their nature. In this sense, those who occupy the office are reducible to it; their duties as soldiers are inseparable from who they are.

If traditional just war theorists presuppose this view of gender and military service, it is relatively easy for them to conclude that all combatants in public war are legitimate targets of attack. Their theories presuppose that political communities have members who are naturally bound to fight in war and for whom risking their life in battle is honorable. Simply put, they believe that political communities contain within them individuals who are expendable in war. Just as it is appropriate for the young men in one's own community to face fire in war, it is also appropriate to subject the young men in the enemy community to fire. Therefore, there is nothing objectionable to treating all combatants as legitimate targets. Assuming the combatants are performing their natural role, they are reducible to the status of soldier, a self-sacrificial instrument of war. They may be killed because that is what they are for.

Walzer's Soldiers

Michael Walzer endorses roughly the same political duties of soldiers and the theory of discrimination in war advocated by the traditional theorists. He holds that political subjects are bound to serve as soldiers in war and that combatants as such are legitimate targets in war. However, Walzer certainly does not endorse the gendered division of labor that the early modern just war theorists do. He does more than even most of his contemporaries to avoid gendered assumptions and in explicitly using gender-inclusive language, including frequently referring to the duties of military service as the duties of "men and women." In this sense, then, we might think of Walzer's goal here as simply to "add women and stir." That is to say, he embraces the traditional political and ethical duties of the office of the soldier while allowing women an equal opportunity to occupy it. Moreover, when he attempts to justify the traditional duties of military service, he does not appeal to the virtues of masculinity or any other gender norms directly. Ostensibly, he offers us a gender-neutral version of traditional military ethics.

This is not an easy task, however. The political obligation to fight for one's community upon command and the right to attack combatants as such in war are hard to justify. As the early modern theorists discovered, this is especially true when working within a broadly liberal-individualist framework. In at least one passage, Michael Walzer recognizes the problem:

> States exist to defend the rights of their members, but it is a difficulty in the theory of war that the collective defense of rights renders them individually problematic. The immediate problem is that the soldiers who do the fighting, though they can rarely be said to have chosen to fight, lose the rights they are supposedly defending. They gain war rights as combatants and potential prisoners, but they can now be attacked and killed at will by their enemies...'Soldiers are made to be killed,' as Napoleon once said; that is why war is hell.[23]

As we have seen, the appeal to natural masculinity helped solve this problem in traditional just war theory. If he is not going to do the same, how is Walzer going to solve this problem?

The Argument from Material Non-Innocence

One of Walzer's arguments is most conspicuous and has received the most comment. According to this argument, combatants in war are liable to attack because they are currently threatening their enemies, rightly or wrongly. According to this view, in as much as they are engaged in fighting, combatants are thereby liable to attack by their opponents. It is by becoming combatants, i.e., those engaged in or directly contributing to combat, that they lose their right not to be attacked. Combatants are liable to attack because, "simply by fighting, whatever their private hopes and intentions, they have lost their title to life and liberty, and they have lost it even though, unlike aggressor states, they have committed no crime."[24]

Noncombatants by contrast are not threatening their enemies and are therefore not liable to attack. The relevant distinguishing feature of noncombatants is innocence. According to Walzer, "innocent [is] a term of art which means that they have done nothing, and are doing nothing that entails the loss of their rights."[25] However, "innocence" here is used in a nonmoral sense. The innocent, according to this view, are those who are simply not threatening others. The non-innocent, then, are those threatening others. Their reasons for threatening others are irrelevant. To threaten others simply is to give up one's innocence.

This view produces a valid defense of all the aspects of the traditional principle of discrimination. If true, it would follow that the combatants on all sides of a war—regardless of their military usefulness, their particular role in combat operations, the strategic importance of attacking them, how they came to be combatants, or what their understanding is of the war—are liable to be attacked. According to this argument, combatants as such are legitimate targets.

That being said, the argument from material non-innocence has significant weaknesses. First, it seems unconvincing as a theory of justified violence. As Walzer himself admits, this view of liability to attack does not apply to other areas of social life. It is simply wrong to assert that one's liability to attack is independent of the morality of one's actions. Certainly, a person who attacks me on the street to take my wallet is liable to defensive attack. However, if I were to engage in defensive violence against this assailant I do not in turn become liable to attack because I now constitute a threat to her or him. I surely maintain my right not to be attacked even when I use violence to protect myself in situations like this. But the view of liability to attack presupposed by the argument from material non-innocence would seem to entail that by defending oneself against unjust violence, people become liable to attack. There is good reason to be skeptical of this.[26]

But there is another problem for the argument from material non-innocence. The argument runs into trouble when we try to reconcile it with the theory of public war and the view that soldiers are obligated to serve in war upon command.[27] Walzer, like traditional just war theorists, is a proponent of the theory of public war. According to him, soldiers are obligated to threaten their enemies when ordered to by their executive. As he summarizes, from the perspective of those who do the fighting, war is "morally as well as physically coercive."[28] But according to the argument from material non-innocence, combatants lose their right not to be attacked by threatening their enemies. The problem with this position is that it seems to over-determine the soldier's liability to attack in war. If one is obligated to engage in combat despite its life-risking character, it seems that one has already lost one's right not to be killed. Whether or not engaging in war makes one liable to be killed, so long as engaging is war is dangerous then the obligation to fight in war upon command is tantamount to the obligation to risk one's life upon command. In that case the soldier's social and political standing makes his life expendable. But to be subordinated in such a way is already to have one's right to not be killed undermined. Regarding soldiers then it seems that asserting that they lose their rights not to be harmed only because they have threatened others is redundant. They have already been rendered dispensable in war when they were bound to fight upon command. For this reason, the theory of public war embraced by traditional just war theory seems to make the argument from material non-innocence only indirectly relevant. If we want to figure out what is really rendering combatants liable to attack, we need to figure out why they are bound to fight upon command in the first place.

The Communitarian Argument

I have noted the tension between the sacrificial obligations of soldiers and a basic liberal vision of political society as designed to protect the rights of its members to life and liberty. As we have seen, this tension was handled by traditional just war theorists by asserting that it is a part of natural virtue for men to fight in war in service of their families, communities, and political sovereigns.

How does Walzer resolve the tension? In a number of places, Walzer leans heavily on the communitarian strands in this thought to ground the duties of military service and arguably abandons the ostensibly liberal framework he employs in *Just and Unjust Wars*. It should be recalled that Walzer is a famous protagonist in the communitarian critique of liberalism that began to flourish in the 1980s.[29] His rejection of liberalism was made most clear in *Spheres of Justice*, published in 1983, the book of his that immediately followed *Just and Unjust Wars*. In *Spheres*, Walzer abandons universalism in the theory of justice and embraces a radical pluralism. Instead of grounding justice in the universal rights of individuals, he holds that justice is grounded in the shared understandings of communities with a common way of life. Justice is relative to each particular view of the good embraced by each distinctive community and its culture, institutions, and language.[30] Interestingly, in the preface to *Spheres*, Walzer distinguishes the approach to distributive justice he takes in that work from the rights-based approach to the justice of war he takes in *Just and Unjust Wars*.

But perhaps we should not distinguish the two approaches, at least not so starkly. What if we attempted to use the communitarian theory of *Spheres* to solve the problem of the obligations of military service? In point of fact, there are many passages in Walzer's corpus where he defends the obligation to serve in war in communitarian terms. To cite just one example, in an early essay, "The Obligation to Die for the State," Walzer describes a non-liberal basis for the obligation to risk one's life in war upon command. According to this argument, it is the identity of individuals with the common life that they share with their fellows which makes death a potentially worthy price to pay to protect the community:

> When the State is in danger, its citizens rush to its defense, forgetful of all personal danger. They die willingly for the sake of the state, not because the state protects their lives—which would be, as Hegel argued, absurd—but because the state is their common life. So long as the state survives, something of the citizen lives on, even after the natural man is dead. The state, or rather, the common life of the citizens, generates these "moral goods" for which...men can in fact be obligated to die.[31]

On this approach, we must prioritize the shared meanings of our common lives over our rights as abstract individuals. We must treat justice as a theory of the good embodied in our particular community rather than a theory of liberal rights. Taking this approach does seem to effectively solve the problem of the ground for the duties of military service. On this view, there is no tension between the status of combatants and the rights of human beings in general. For we have abandoned the view that the status of soldiers must be reconciled with their rights as human beings. Instead, all we need to show is that the status of soldiers is grounded in the shared meaning of membership and communal protection in a particular community. It appears that this is not difficult to do.

One of the obvious concerns with this approach, however, is that it risks turning individuals into mere instruments of the state without any protections against harms or domination by political authorities. If our lives and liberties can be taken away by the state for the purposes of war, then it is difficult to see any limit on the power of the state over us. Of course, Walzer never does (and never would) endorse the complete reduction of the individual to servant of the state. As he argues in *Spheres*, the provision of national security and the burdens it places on citizens operate in their own sphere whereas other goods such as security and welfare operate in other autonomous spheres. Modern societies have developed distinct shared understandings of goods and, internal to those understandings, ideas about how they should be distributed. The various things we value as a community have relative significance and meaning to us that determines who ought to have access to them and to what extent. Thus, national security, the honors (and burdens) of military service, as well as personal security, welfare, and recognition are all things we are committed to providing to our co-citizens in ways that follow from how we have come to understand what they mean. As long as these various goods are allowed to be distributed in the ways that follow from the understandings internal to each good, then distributive justice is achieved.

In other words, justice is the maintenance of the autonomy of each sphere pertaining to each good. Injustice occurs when the understanding of appropriate distribution in one sphere is applied to, or "invades," another. For instance, if we distribute medical care to people who can afford to pay for it at prices that are determined by firms operating to maximize profit, we are allowing the standards of distribution appropriate for commodities in markets to be applied to a good that is not a commodity. The standards of distribution for markets has come to dominate another sphere that ought to maintain its autonomy. This domination of one sphere over others is the important form of injustice for Walzer. Hence, the provision of the good of national security and its attendant burdens is a sphere of justice that ought to exist alongside the other spheres we expect to exist in a modern society, including personal security, welfare, and liberty. In this way, Walzer's theory justifies the burdens of military service while offering philosophical resources that limit the power of the state over its citizens.

But this pluralistic autonomy of spheres is hard to comprehend when considering individual military service members. The sphere of military service prioritizes the community over all other goods. Soldiers are expected to fight and die upon command. The understanding of this good (an example of what Walzer calls a "negative good") is self-sacrificial. It asks everything of its participants. For those who are demanded (either through enlistment or conscription) to do it, this good is dominant over others. Personal security, welfare, liberty, along with all other things are "invaded" by the demands of military service. Even if we restrict the distribution of this good to certain members of our community so that we can preserve the other spheres for the other members, those on whose shoulders the burden falls are dominated by this one sphere. Walzer argues that military service requires self-sacrificial labor[32] and that this labor must be forced, at least once the enlistment contract has been completed.[33] Because of the severity of these burdens as well as the fact that it is socially necessary that it be performed, Walzer argues that conscription ought to be how the burdens of national security are distributed.[34] This may randomize the distribution of this burden, but it still does not solve the extent to which the conscripted (or enlisted) are dominated by this sphere.

There is another problem for this approach to justifying the obligation to fight and die in war. Because it makes justice relative to the shared understandings of goods that particular groups of people have developed, it provides few tools for perceiving and criticizing the gendered character of that understanding. As I have argued, military service is tied to notions of manliness and traditionally has been expected only of men as men. Another way of putting this is to say that our shared understanding of this good entails a gendered distribution of its burdens. If our shared understandings are all there are to justice, then this gendered distribution will go unchallenged and perhaps even unnoticed. As feminist critics of communitarianism have argued, theories of justice such as these leave gender invisible and provide insufficient critical distance between gender and justice.[35]

In *Spheres*, Walzer strongly rejects gendered distributions like the traditional exclusivity of military service. Understandings that attribute burdens to a certain subgroup based upon claims about the natural suitability of that subgroup to shoulder those burdens, he calls "ideologies." He seems deeply suspicious of ideologies in general. Indeed, in Chapter 7, he explicitly rejects the notion that negative goods like military service can be distributed to some subgroup only. However, immediately after this assertion, Walzer comes very close to claiming that military service should be restricted only to men due to their nature. As he says,

> Soldiering is a special kind of hard work. In many societies, in fact, it is not conceived to be hard work at all. It is the normal occupation of young men, their social function, into which they are not so much drafted as ritually initiated, and where they find the rewards of camaraderie, excitement, and glory...Young men are energetic, combative, eager to show off; fighting for them is or can be a form of play...John Ruskin had a wonderfully romantic account of "consensual war," which aristocratic young men fight in much the same spirit as they might play football. Only the risks are greater, the excitement at a higher pitch, the contest more "beautiful"...We might attempt a more down-to-earth romanticism: young men are soldiers in the same way that the French socialist writer Fourier thought children should be garbagemen. In both cases, passion is harnessed to social function. Children like to play in the dirt, Fourier thought, and so they are more ready than anyone else to collect and dispose of garbage...[But] it is hardly an accurate description of what garbagemen do to say that they *play* with the garbage. Similarly, the account of war as the natural activity of young men or the sport of aristocrats fits only a small number of

wars, or it fits only certain sorts of engagements in war; and it doesn't fit modern warfare at all. Mostly soldiers have little opportunity for play; nor would their officers by happy with their playfulness. What soldiers do is, in the strictest sense, hard work. [emphasis in original][36]

This passage is remarkable because Walzer rejects the proposals of Ruskin and Fourier only on the grounds that they are misunderstanding the hardness of soldiering. He does not directly attack them for making false assertions about men (and women), for claiming that men are naturally disposed to combat (whereas women are not). Nor does he explicitly reject the notion that soldiering is the natural social function of men. Rather, Walzer is concerned to point out that soldiering should not be treated as a casual activity that does not require discipline, training, focus, and sacrifice. If this is all that is wrong with these accounts of the distribution of the burden of military service, then Walzer has left standing the gendered nature of the distribution clearly asserted in these accounts. Perhaps we should not be surprised then to see him, in the following paragraph, describe the purpose of conscription as "to universalize or randomize the risks of war over a given generation of *young men*" [my emphasis].

If in these passages Walzer is implying that military service is for men as men, I am inclined to conclude that it is not a considered opinion he would assert in other contexts. The view seems to fly in the face of other settled positions he takes in *Spheres* and elsewhere, especially his grounding of military service in communal membership, his rejection of ideologies, and his defense of universal conscription. Still, it is revealing that the gendered assumptions about military service can so easily slip into the discussion. Not only does it corroborate my view that military service has been and continues to be gendered in our shared understandings, but it also suggests the limitations of communitarian theories of justice in addressing such gendered understandings. The worry is that simply resting our critical standards on our shared understandings will enable gender inequalities to go unquestioned in precisely this way.

The Argument from the Purpose of the Military

Walzer appears to offer a different argument in defense of combatant non-immunity than either of the above in a more recent essay, "Terrorism and Just War."[37] Here, Walzer again defends the traditional view of discrimination in war. He asserts, "once the fighting has begun, it is entirely legitimate to kill soldiers at random, as they come into range, so to speak, and it is legitimate to try to terrorize the ones who never come within range."[38] According to Walzer, this is because of "the meaning of membership in an army and in civilian society." Soldiers have a singular purpose—to fight their nations' wars. They are isolated from the rest of the community, trained and conditioned to pose a unified threat against any of their state's enemies. As Walzer describes it,

> The army is an organized, disciplined, trained, and highly purposeful collective, and all its members contribute to the achievement of its ends. Even soldiers who don't carry weapons have been taught how to use them, and they are tightly connected, by way of the services they provide, to the actual users. It doesn't matter whether they are volunteers or conscripts; their individual moral preferences are not at issue; they have been mobilized for a singular purpose, and what they do advances that purpose. For its sake, they are isolated from the general public, housed in camps and bases, all their needs provided for by the state. In time of war they pose a unified threat.[39]

Noncombatants, on the other hand, are not members of a military. Civilians differ from soldiers in two relevant respects. First, on the individual level, civilians are a diffuse set with myriad roles and purposes, many of which are peaceful. They are engaged in ordinary activities of human existence, including family life. As Walzer says

> [C]ivilians have many different purposes; they have been trained in many different pursuits and professions; they participate in a highly differentiated set of organizations and associations, whose internal discipline, compared to that of any army, is commonly very loose. They don't live in barracks but in their own houses and apartments; they don't live with other soldiers but with parents, spouses, and children; they are not all of an age but include the very old and the very young; they are not provided for by the government but provide for themselves and one another. As citizens, they belong to different political parties; they have different views on public issues; many of them take no part at all in political life; and, again, some of them are children. Even a *levée en masse* cannot transform this group of people into anything like an organized military collective.[40]

Second, civilians differ from soldiers in that they, together with the members of their military, form a distinctive political community.

Organized political societies have unique identities, cultures, and institutions. These are the groups who go to war.

> [Civilians] are, together with their sons and daughters in the army, a people. Whether their peoplehood is ethnic or national in character or wholly political, constituted only by their citizenship, doesn't matter here. They identify themselves as French, or Irish, or Bulgarian; they commonly share a language and a history and, in some prosaic sense of the term, a destiny. Their individual futures are closely linked, and this linkage is especially tight when their country is at war.[41]

Corresponding to the above two features separating civilians from soldiers, Walzer distinguishes two relevant types of attacks on civilians. Murder is the name for deliberately attacking civilians individually. To kill specific civilians such as political leaders, collaborators, or symbols of power is to kill the innocent. Unlike soldiers, they have done nothing to make themselves legitimate targets. In contrast with simple murder, terrorism is the name for indiscriminate attacks against the civilian population as such. To do this is to treat an entire political community as expendable. One can permissibly go to war with a political community but one cannot make the annihilation of that community a goal of war. To take the entirety of the enemy community as a legitimate target would be to devalue them as a people. Terrorists devalue both communities and individuals.

> Terrorists attack both these immunities [individual and collective]. They devalue not only the individuals they kill but also the group to which the individuals belong. They signal a political intention to destroy or remove or radically subordinate these people individually and this "people" collectively. That is the long-term purpose of the fear they inspire. Hence, while all terrorists are murderers, all murderers are not terrorists. Most murderers intend to kill specific people; terrorists kill at random within a specific group of people. The message they deliver is directed at the group: *we don't want you here.* We will not accept you or make our peace with you as fellow-citizens or partners in any political project. You are not candidates for equality or even co-existence. [emphasis in original][42]

In this way, terrorism and murder are both wrong, but for different reasons. Terrorism is unlimited war; murder is not. With terrorism "identity is liability," but not necessarily with murder.

But isn't there a tactic of targeting civilians in war that falls between what Walzer describes as simple murder on one hand and terrorism on the other? Suppose a group targets, randomly, some subgroup within the larger enemy community, say women or the industrial working class or intellectuals, but respects the immunity of the other members of the community. Perhaps the Katyn Massacre is a case in point: The Soviet Union executed some 22,000 officers, police, and intellectuals in an effort to solidify its control over Poland in 1940. This was apparently an attempt to incapacitate Polish resistance, not simply to assassinate specific individuals. The individual targets were irrelevant; it was the social position they occupied that mattered. If the individual victims had different roles, they presumably would not have been targeted. Still, the attack was not random in the sense that it did not treat any Polish person as a legitimate target. Is this an act of simple (mass) murder or terrorism as Walzer understands them?

It seems Walzer wants to call this terrorism rather than murder because it rests on an arbitrary line and thereby makes all members of the community vulnerable. According to his position, there is no moral reason for limiting attacks to one specific group. Hence, anyone who would go this far in war would also go further if necessary. Targeting civilians in this way is a totalizing practice and puts the entirety of the community in danger. This is Walzer's view of the Atomic bombing of Japan in World War Two. While the Allies did not aim to destroy Japan itself and would cease fighting as soon as Japan surrendered, their willingness to use nuclear weapons against Japanese cities to attain this showed that their war was unlimited morally. As he says, "There can't be any doubt that the destruction of Hiroshima and Nagasaki implied, at the moment the bombs were dropped, a radical devaluation of Japanese lives and a generalized threat to the Japanese people."[43]

But if targeting, at random, a subgroup of civilians within a community is terrorism, why isn't targeting soldiers at random terrorism too? What is the difference between randomly attacking intellectuals, say, and randomly attacking military servicemembers? The answer must be that there is a morally significant difference between soldiers and civilians whereas there is no morally significant difference between other subgroups within a community. Soldiers, unlike civilians, are liable to attack because they are members of a highly organized, threatening military. In other words, soldiers are materially non-innocent whereas civilians are materially innocent. Randomly attacking only combatants is not to draw an arbitrary line and does not devalue the enemy people as such.

However, this attempt to draw a line between attacking soldiers and attacking civilians randomly won't do because it relies on this appeal to the argument from material non-innocence. As we've seen, it is highly questionable that material threats are liable to attack. Moreover, in as much as we are committed to the theory of public war, the liability of soldiers precedes their engagement in combat. Without this appeal to material non-innocence, the argument cannot distinguish between attacking soldiers as a class and attacking civilians. Therefore, we are still lacking a reason for allowing indiscriminate attacks on combatants. This being said, it would be uncharitable to dismiss Walzer's argument here altogether. There is another argument for combatant non-immunity that could be implied by the above passages. Perhaps what Walzer is doing is appealing to the principle of necessity to distinguish combatants from noncombatants.

The Argument from Necessity

The principle of necessity says that states are permitted to do what is necessary to achieve their just cause for war and nothing more. A just cause for war permits violence but only the violence that is necessary to achieve that cause. Any violence that is unnecessary is simply wanton cruelty. Moreover, to carry out attacks that are unnecessary to achieve a just cause would seem to indicate that one's aims go beyond the defensive. Why else would one do something that is unnecessary to defensive war? It must be because one has aims (expansion, conquest, and extermination?) that make such acts necessary.

According to the conventional principle of just cause, the only justifiable reason for war is defense against aggression. A just war seeks to thwart an unjust attack on another community. This view is based on a collectivist conception of war in that the participants are understood as organized political communities with communal rights. A just war is, in part, an act by or on behalf of an innocent political community against another community that is currently attacking it.

According to Walzer's discussion in "Terrorism and Just War," political communities have militaries which sequester their members from the broader society in times of war. These militaries train for fighting exclusively and in war constitute a singular, unified threat to their enemies.

In the case of a community committing aggression, their military will be the unique source of the threat to their victims. To thwart aggression one need simply stop and roll back an attack. To do that would seem to require only targeting the armed forces of the aggressor.

Perhaps this is what Walzer is suggesting in this essay. This argument would provide a good reason for concluding, as Walzer does, that targeting noncombatants indiscriminately indicates unjust war aims. If it is true that in a defensive war it is only necessary to target combatants to thwart the threat and never necessary to target noncombatants, then targeting noncombatants would suggest that one is not fighting a defensive war. Targeting noncombatants would indicate that one aims to subjugate or destroy the enemy community. It sends the message that "*we don't want you here.*" Why else would noncombatants be under attack?

Traditionally, the principle of discrimination is thought to be a side-constraint on the conduct of war independent of the cause of the war and the necessary means to that end. In other words, one cannot violate the principle of discrimination even if it is necessary to achieve a just cause. But, according to the argument from necessity, the principle of discrimination is not independent of necessity. Rather, discrimination is derived from necessity. This argument holds that targeting noncombatants is never, or very rarely, necessary to achieve a just cause; only targeting combatants could be necessary.

As a case against targeting noncombatants, I happen to think this argument has promise. But as a defense of unrestricted attacks on combatants, the argument does not fare well. While the argument does render a justification for attacks on certain combatants in certain circumstances, it generates tight restrictions on attacks against combatants generally.

On its face, the argument only permits attacks on combatants that are necessary to achieve the just cause of the war. Surely, not all attacks on combatants are necessary to win every war. One needn't kill all combatants to get to the goal. The principle of necessity requires adopting strategies and tactics that minimize the harm to the enemy community. Even if it is true that attacking noncombatants always or usually fails to minimize the destructiveness of one's war, it does not follow that one cannot minimize the destructiveness further. We can look for and adopt methods of war that are strategically effective but more or less destructive to combatants. The argument from necessity requires that we find and adopt the least harmful of the methods at our disposal. It does not permit indiscriminate attacks on combatants.[44]

Walzer's argument also makes claims about the nature of military ser-vicemembers and the military-civilian distinction that, if true, minimize the destructiveness of attacks on combatants. According to Walzer, civilians are a highly differentiated set of people who occupy many distinct roles and relationships. Civilians are in close relation to intimate others including parents, spouses, and children. They come in all possible ages and could accept any possible political perspective. In general, they are highly integrated into the broader civil society. If this description is true, and I do not doubt that it is, then attacking civilians runs the risk of significant harm to the community affected. Not only will civilians be difficult to isolate from others physically, but their integration into the broader community means that many people and institutions are dependent on them. Hurting civilians will hurt all those in physical and social proximity to them.

Walzer argues that soldiers, on the other hand, are isolated from the broader community. Not only do they live sequestered from civilians but they also do not occupy the various roles and responsibilities that civilians do. They have "a singular purpose," as Walzer says. If this is true, then it would seem that attacking soldiers risks significantly less harm to the community than attacking civilians. There will not be the same dreadful indirect effects of such attacks on the broader community. Hence, while the argument from necessity may not permit indiscriminate attacks against combatants, it would treat taking the life of a combatant as significantly less injurious than taking the life of a noncombatant.

However, it only takes a moment's reflection to determine that this description of soldiers is false. This account of soldiers and the military-civilian distinction rests on an extraordinary presumption—the individuals who are military servicemembers are reducible to their office. Only if we do not distinguish the individual soldier from their office could Walzer's description be true. But, obviously, we can distinguish the individual from the office. Just like civilians, soldiers are a diverse set who occupy just as many roles and relationships. They too are our parents, spouses, children, and friends. And not only nominally. They are actively engaged in intimate, caring work with loved ones. They too have all types of polit-ical perspectives. Many people and civilian institutions are dependent on them materially and morally. There is no reason to assume that attacking them is less destructive than attacking civilians. In general, soldiers are no more disposable than civilians. For this reason, the argument from necessity should permit attacks on combatants in much more restricted circumstances than Walzer's discussion would seem to suggest.

The clear connection between Walzer's reduction of the individual soldier to their office and the traditional gender-based defense of military service must be pointed out. First, note that his discussion in "Terrorism and Just War" treats "combatant" as synonymous with "soldier" and "noncombatant" as synonymous with "civilian." There are numerous background assumptions that motivate this move. To treat combatants as soldiers and noncombatants as civilians is to presume the framework of public war and its supposedly neat separation of the civilian and the military realms. As we have seen, the traditional defense of military service grounded the office of the soldier in the nature of the individual who was to occupy the office. Men were held to have the natural duty to serve in war upon command. This is their primary social purpose and it springs from their nature, not from any particular contract they have elected to sign. Walzer's presumption of the identity of individual soldiers and their office appears to be a vestige of this traditional view of gender.

The Rights of Combatants

Perhaps, then, the intuition that something is wrong with the indiscriminate killing of unarmed soldiers adrift in the open ocean is telling. We have found that the false assumption that it is naturally virtuous for men to risk their lives in war has played an important role in arguments defending combatant non-immunity in war. Traditional just war theorists made the assumption explicit. Walzer, while attempting to defend the theory of public war and the traditional principle of discrimination in a gender-neutral way, nevertheless struggles to do so. His arguments either assume methods that are too accommodating to gender discrimination, do not adequately eschew gendered positions, or fail to validly defend combatant non-immunity. For this reason, it might be best to think not only of the treatment of Japanese soldiers in the Battle of the Bismarck Sea but of any act of war that treats combatants merely as "fair game" as unjust, gender-based violence. Throughout modern history combatants have been treated as disposable instruments of war because of the gendered character of their work. I think we owe more to soldiers, our own as well as our enemy's.

NOTES

1. Quoted in Arthur Herman, *Douglas MacArthur: American Warrior* (New York: Random House, 2016), 469.
2. Ibid.
3. *Just and Unjust Wars*, 5th ed. (New York: Basic Books, 2015 [1977]), 138.
4. "The Dispensable Lives of Soldiers," *Journal of Legal Analysis* 2, no. 1 (Spring 2010): 72.
5. See Blum, "The Dispensable Lives of Soldiers." For similar readings of the law see Larry May, "Humanity, Necessity, and the Rights of Soldiers," in *Weighing Lives in War*, eds. Jens David Ohlin, Larry May, and Claire Finkelstein (New York: Oxford University Press, 2017), 77–110; Adil Haque, *Law and Morality at War* (New York: Oxford University Press, 2017), 84–105.
6. Joshua Goldstein, *War and Gender* (New York: Cambridge University Press, 2001), 10–22.
7. Jean Bethke Elshtain, *Women and War* (Chicago: University of Chicago Press, 1995), 174–75.
8. See Tom Digby, *Love and War: How Militarism Shapes Sexuality and Romance* (New York: Columbia University Press, 2014); Goldstein, *War and Gender*; and Elshtain, *Women and War*.
9. *Women and War*, 205.
10. Quoted in Stanley Hirshson, *General Patton: A Soldier's Life* (New York: HarperCollins, 2002), 474.
11. *War and Gender*, 287–88.
12. A large school in moral philosophy has even concluded that justice itself is based on the assumption of masculine individuals. For one representative statement, see Virginia Held, *The Ethics of Care: Personal, Political, and Global* (New York: Oxford University Press, 2006).
13. *Elements of the Philosophy of Right*, ed. Allen Wood (New York: Cambridge University Press, 1991 [1821]), §324, 361.
14. For more detailed readings of Grotius, Pufendorf, and Hobbes on these issues see my "Contract, Gender, and the Emergence of the Civil-Military Distinction," forthcoming in *The Review of Politics*.
15. *Rights of War and Peace*, ed. Richard Tuck (Indianapolis: Liberty Fund Inc., 2005 [1625]), I.IV.VII, 357.
16. Ibid., II.XXV.VII, 1158.
17. *Commentary on the Law of Prize and Booty*, ed. Martine Julia van Ittersum (Indianapolis: Liberty Fund, Inc., 2006), 440.
18. Ibid., 441.
19. *Leviathan*, ed. Edwin Curley (Indianapolis: Hackett Publishing Co., 1994 [1651]), XXI.16, 142.

20. Ibid., XIX.22, 126.
21. *The Law of Nature and Nations*, trans. Basil Kennett (New Jersey: The Lawbook Exchange, Ltd., 2005 [1672]), VIII.II.IV, 759.
22. *The Law of Nations*, eds. Béla Kapossy and Richard Whatmore (Indianapolis: Liberty Fund, Inc., 2008 [1758]), III.II.10, 474.
23. *Just and Unjust Wars*, 135–36.
24. Ibid., 136.
25. Ibid., 146.
26. For more sophisticated articulations of this objection see Jeff McMahan, "Innocence, Self-Defense, and Killing in War," *Journal of Political Philosophy* 2, no. 3 (September 1994): 193–221; David Rodin, *War and Self-Defense* (New York: Oxford University Press, 2002).
27. Many commentators miss Walzer's conviction about this. For substantiation of this reading of him see my "The Incoherence of Walzer's Just War Theory," *Social Theory and Practice* 38, no. 4 (October 2012): 663–88.
28. *Just and Unjust Wars*, 53.
29. See Will Kymlicka, "Community and Multiculturalism," in *A Companion to Contemporary Political Philosophy*, 2nd ed., eds. Robert E. Goodin, Philip Pettit, and Thomas Pogge, vol. 2 (New York: Blackwell, 2007), 463–77.
30. See *Spheres of Justice: A Defense of Pluralism and Equality* (New York: Basic Books, 1983), 312–13.
31. "The Obligation to Die for the State," in *Obligations: Essays on Disobedience, War, and Citizenship* (Cambridge: Harvard University Press, 1970), 92. See also "Involuntary Association," in *Freedom of Association*, ed. Amy Gutmann (Princeton: Princeton University Press, 1998), 64–74.
32. *Spheres of Justice*, 169.
33. Ibid., 180.
34. Ibid., 169.
35. See Susan Moller Okin, *Justice, Gender, and the Family* (New York: Basic Books, 1989); Elizabeth Fraser and Nicola Lacey, *The Politics of Community: A Feminist Critique of the Liberal-Communitarian Debate* (Toronto: University of Toronto, 1993).
36. *Spheres of Justice*, 168–69.
37. In *Thinking Politically: Essays in Political Theory*, ed. David Miller (New Haven: Yale University Press, 2007), 264–77.
38. Ibid., 264–65.
39. Ibid., 265.
40. Ibid., 265–66.
41. Ibid., 266.
42. Ibid., 266–67.
43. Ibid., 267.

44. This seems to cohere with Jeff McMahan's distinction between narrow and wide proportionality. See his "Proportionate Defense," in *Weighing Lives in War*, eds. Claire Finkelstein, Jens David Ohlin, and Larry May (New York: Oxford University Press, 2017), 131–54.

BIBLIOGRAPHY

Blum, Gabriella. "The Dispensable Lives of Soldiers." *Journal of Legal Analysis* 2, no. 1 (Spring 2010): 69–124.

Digby, Tom. *Love and War: How Militarism Shapes Sexuality and Romance*. New York: Columbia University Press, 2014.

Elshtain, Jean Bethke. *Women and War*. Chicago: University of Chicago Press, 1995.

Fraser, Elizabeth, and Nicola Lacey. *The Politics of Community: A Feminist Critique of the Liberal-Communitarian Debate*. Toronto: University of Toronto Press, 1993.

Goldstein, Joshua. *War and Gender*. New York: Cambridge University Press, 2001.

Grotius, Hugo. *Commentary on the Law of Prize and Booty*. Edited by Martine Julia van Ittersum. Indianapolis: Liberty Fund, Inc., 2006.

———. *Rights of War and Peace*. Edited by Richard Tuck. Indianapolis: Liberty Fund Inc., 2005 [1625].

Haque, Adil. *Law and Morality at War*. New York: Oxford University Press, 2017.

Hegel, G. W. F. *Elements of the Philosophy of Right*. Edited by Allen Wood. New York: Cambridge University Press, 1991 [1821].

Held, Virginia. *The Ethics of Care: Personal, Political, and Global*. New York: Oxford University Press, 2006.

Herman, Arthur. *Douglas MacArthur: American Warrior*. New York: Random House, 2016.

Hirshson, Stanley. *General Patton: A Soldier's Life*. New York: HarperCollins, 2002.

Hobbes, Thomas. *Leviathan*. Edited by Edwin Curley. Indianapolis: Hackett Publishing Co., 1994 [1651].

Kymlicka, Will. "Community and Multiculturalism." In *A Companion to Contemporary Political Philosophy*. 2nd ed., edited by Robert E. Goodin, Philip Pettit, and Thomas Pogge, vol. 2, 463–77. New York: Blackwell, 2007.

May, Larry. "Humanity, Necessity, and the Rights of Soldiers." In *Weighing Lives in War*, edited by Jens David Ohlin, Larry May, and Claire Finkelstein, 77–110. New York: Oxford University Press, 2017.

McMahan, Jeff. "Innocence, Self-Defense, and Killing in War." *Journal of Political Philosophy* 2, no. 3 (September 1994): 193–221.

————. "Proportionate Defense." In *Weighing Lives in War*, edited by Claire Finkelstein, Jens David Ohlin, and Larry May, 131–54. New York: Oxford University Press, 2017.

Okin, Susan Moller. *Justice, Gender, and the Family*. New York: Basic Books, 1989.

Parsons, Graham. "The Incoherence of Walzer's Just War Theory." *Social Theory and Practice* 38, no. 4 (October 2012): 663–88.

————. "Contract, Gender, and the Emergence of the Civil-Military Distinction." Forthcoming *The Review of Politics*.

Pufendorf, Samuel von. *The Law of Nature and Nations*. Translated by Basil Kennett. New Jersey: The Lawbook Exchange, Ltd., 2005 [1672].

Rodin, David. *War and Self-Defense*. New York: Oxford University Press, 2002.

Vattel, Emer. *The Law of Nations*. Edited by Béla Kapossy and Richard Whatmore. Indianapolis: Liberty Fund, Inc., 2008 [1758].

Walzer, Michael. "The Obligation to Die for the State." In *Obligations: Essays on Disobedience, War, and Citizenship*. Cambridge: Harvard University Press, 1970.

————. *Just and Unjust Wars*. 5th ed. New York: Basic Books, 2015 [1977].

————. *Spheres of Justice: A Defense of Pluralism and Equality*. New York: Basic Books, 1983.

————. "Involuntary Association." In *Freedom of Association*, edited by Amy Gutmann, 64–74. Princeton: Princeton University Press, 1998.

————. "Terrorism and Just War." In *Thinking Politically: Essays in Political Theory*, edited by David Miller, 264–77. New Haven: Yale University Press, 2007.

CHAPTER 12

Postscript

Michael Walzer

I chose to address three of the topics discussed by the contributors to the present volume—three that seem to me critically important when we think about the future of just war theory or, better, when we imagine the arguments that we will continue to have about war and morality. I don't doubt the importance of the many other issues raised in the chapters above, but I thought that my concluding remarks would be better if they were more focused. The three topics are self-determination as a reason for political struggle and, sometimes, war; the liability of soldiers and civilians (often represented as men [soldiers] and women and children [civilians]) in war; and "supreme emergency" as the ultimate dilemma.

SELF-DETERMINATION AND "THE PEOPLE"

The key idea of Margaret Moore's chapter is that the collective agent for self-determination and for territorial claims is "the People" understood "without appealing to any kind of cultural community or to an inherited culture shared among the group" (40).[1] I am inclined to think that any group of men and women capable of exercising, and wanting to

M. Walzer (✉)
Institute for Advanced Study, Princeton, NJ, USA
e-mail: walzer@ias.edu

© The Author(s) 2020
G. Parsons and M. A. Wilson (eds.), *Walzer and War*,
https://doi.org/10.1007/978-3-030-41657-7_12

exercise, self-determination in a particular place will themselves make this communitarian appeal. They will refer to their shared culture as a reason for their political ambition. Moore comes very close to accepting this position when she says that place-rights don't attach to individuals alone "since individuals are not isolated and atomistic but operate within a structure of relationships that give meaning to their life and have collective identities that are integral to their sense of who they are..." (42). Yes, the People could not act as a collective agent without that structure of relationships and that shared sense of who they are.

In any case, I agree that the People, however this entity is constituted, have a right to self-determination in a particular place. But Moore's very strong account of this right brings us to some hard questions that she doesn't address—perhaps because she is reluctant to acknowledge or to focus on the cultural and religious differences that divide actual Peoples. That is my only argument with her chapter, and it leads me to suggest some difficulties that arise, as it were, after we recognize the rights she writes about.

What if two Peoples inhabit the same territory, politically defined: "the domain of a state"? Or more than two, ruled by a tyrant from one of the Peoples? Consider the case of Iraq in 2003. I thought that the American invasion that year was an unjust war, first, because it was unnecessary (there was good reason to think that Saddam Hussein did not possess weapons of mass destruction) and, second, because regime change is not a just cause of war—even if the regime we aim to change is not the result of democratic self-determination (Moore explains why her argument extends to undemocratic regimes). But the invasion, though not the occupation later on, was welcomed by some 80% of the Iraqi people, the Shi'ites and the Kurds, who believed that it opened the way for their self-determination. So how were we to understand the injustice of the war? Whose right of self-determination was being violated?

I would have to argue that there are forms of unjust war that are not violations of a People's right to self-determination on a particular piece of territory—though these may not be easy to describe or recognize. Here was a terrible regime in a multi-ethnic or multi-religious country. The United States attacked: which People had a right to self-defense? The Kurds and the Shi'ites had neither a right nor a desire; their self-determination was not under attack; it wasn't yet operational. The Sunnis, in power at that time, were certainly under attack, but they didn't have a legitimate claim to the territorial domain, or not to the entire domain, that they were defending. How can there be an unjust war that no one has a right to oppose? And yet I thought, and continue to think, the war was wrong. The occupation and the war-after-the-war made these questions even harder. Only the Kurds were making claims to a place and to self-determination in that place. Sunnis and Shi'ites were seeking domination, each over the other. Too many Peoples, and the United States in the middle.

Here is another issue that figures in contemporary politics and may figure more largely in the future: Is there a right of secession for one of the Peoples in a multi-ethnic country—a right to establish a separate territorial domain? Moore raises this issue at the end of her chapter, but does not take it up. Her argument would seem to favor secession, at least initially, and I think that is right. But further consideration might lead us to reject particular secessionist claims. For self-determination doesn't always or necessarily require sovereignty. Moore's description of the People as a collective agent seems to point to sovereignty since that is the standard form of collective agency: the People's state ruling over its domain. But maybe the other Peoples in the already existing domain have competing rights—if, for example, economic cooperation and exchange have been going on for a long time and secession would leave the others less well off (as in the case of Katanga and maybe Catalonia). Doesn't justice come into the argument along with self-determination? Maybe something like autonomy within a federal system would be better than sovereignty for all the Peoples taken together. Or, if self-determination requires it, asymmetrical federalism as in the case of Quebec in Canada. These are issues that we will have to address if we agree with Moore that self-determination is the right of a People, and if we recognize that there is often a plurality of Peoples in a given domain.

Gendered Soldiers and Civilians

Graham Parsons's chapter is engaging and provocative on many fronts. I am going to concede the historical argument, but before that let me offer a brief objection to what Parsons says about the liability of soldiers, which is not quite as radical as he suggests. Consider, for example, the question of killing sailors in the water after their warship sinks. Their liability is certainly disputed. In Nuremberg in 1945, Admiral Doenitz was charged with ordering the killing of sailors in the water (the Laconia order). But "the charges were not assessed," presumably because Allied officers had issued similar orders. Still, the lawyers who brought the charges clearly believed that the killings were criminal, and that belief is widely shared by people who, in 1945 and after, probably also shared the old gendered view of manly, self-sacrificing warriors. Most just war theorists would probably say that the charges should have been assessed.

Another example, which I think is not disputed: soldiers on leave, back home with their families, are not liable to attack. They are like workers in a tank factory, who can be attacked in the factory but not when they return to the residential neighborhoods around the factory. We might think of this as the domestic exemption, and domesticity is mostly identified with women and children. But men in fact are there (as they should be).

Parsons' historical argument is persuasive: yes, warriors were taken to be men with the manly virtues, and that may account for our original conception that they are uniformly, all of them, all the time, subject to attack. And civilians were historically feminized—women and children—and therefore declared to be uniformly immune from attack. They were shielded from the cruelties of war, which male warriors were expected to endure. One might even say that engaging warriors in warfare is a way of recognizing and respecting their manliness. But I don't think that Parsons is right to say that this engagement turns the warriors into mere "instruments" of the state. For manliness, as anciently conceived, includes the virtue of self-restraint. The warriors are still moral agents, subject, say, to the code of chivalry and, later on, to the rules of engagement. But I agree that as warriors, they are at war and can be killed at (almost) any time. That's the history, which Parsons amply illustrates.

Now consider the state of affairs today: once women refuse to accept the idea that the warrior virtues are exclusively male, our "shared understandings" about manliness are no longer shared. We are on our way to a new set of understandings. We recognize (or more and more of us do) that the manly virtues are actually human virtues, possessed by some men and some women. But what follows from this recognition? Our warriors, now men and women, are still "virtuous" in the same way—so why should we think of a mixed-gender band of warriors any differently than a single-gender band? Why should we treat them differently? "Add women and stir" seems a sensible position. Women who are warriors have the same rights, the same obligations, and the same liabilities as men who are warriors. And men who are civilians have the same immunities as women and children.

The line between soldiers and civilians is still central to the very idea of fighting justly. As Henry Shue argues in his contribution to this volume, the line cannot be drawn differently without endangering the lives of innocent civilians—nor would a different line make soldiers any safer. Consider an example that I used in *Just and Unjust Wars*: George Orwell's refusal to shoot a young soldier running along a fascist army trench with a message in his hand, struggling to hold up his pants as he ran. A man holding up his pants, Orwell decided, isn't a fascist. But maybe he was carrying a message whose receipt was crucial to the coming attack? More generally, soldiers behind the lines may be doing many things necessary to the next military engagement. We can argue about cases like these, but I don't see why we would need to take into account the gender of the vulnerable soldiers.

SUPREME EMERGENCY

Jeremy Waldron expected, he says in his contribution to this volume, to write a critical account of my chapter on supreme emergency, and I expected him to do that. Instead, he has written an extraordinarily generous account of what I am doing in that chapter. He insists that it isn't "doctrine" that I am offering (though there may be some sentences that suggest a doctrinal argument) but rather a meditation on the hardest questions in just war theory. I would only say that I have never worried so much over anything that I've written—and worrying is probably my way of meditating.

Let me focus on one of Waldron's sentences: he is writing about my "dirty hands" article,[2] which underlies the argument in *Just and Unjust Wars*, and which says that sometimes, rarely, but sometimes, the right thing to do is something that it is unequivocally wrong to do. And Waldron says: "When you explore the limits of what is possible in the normative regulation of human extremity, this is the sort of mess you come up with" (166). That may not sound like a generous sentence, but it is, and I am grateful for it. My "dirty hands" article, I'm told, is sometimes taught in first-year philosophy courses as an example of philosophical incoherence. Waldron is saying that when the bottom falls out of the moral universe, incoherence may be an understandable, even a good faith response. In any case, I am sure that the belief of many philosophers that there is a single right thing to do, and we can always do it without anxiety or regret—I am sure that can't be right.

I will comment briefly on two issues that Waldron raises, neutrality and community (the two go together), though without pretending to resolve them. When I talk about a threat to the common life of a people—the accumulating memories and traditions, the sense of connection and responsibility to ancestors and descendants, "the Burkean stuff"—I have in mind a murderous threat. That's usually what extremity means to me (this may come from growing up during the Second World War). Think of the Khmer Rouge in Cambodia, who acted as if they were a force external to Cambodian history and society and who set out to kill every educated person, every professional man and woman, every religious leader or scribe. That constitutes a supreme emergency for the Cambodians, and in resisting the communist cadres, it might be defensible, if it were really necessary, to break the moral rules. But I hope that soldiers fighting a just war would never attempt a murderous campaign like that of the Khmer Rouge. So my argument, such as it is, is neutral only in the sense that if they did, and even if we didn't value the community whose educated members were being murdered, this would be a supreme emergency for the intended victims.

As for lesser threats, like Morgenthau's suggestion that Germany be de-industrialized after the War, I doubt that the doctrine of supreme emergency applies. But I should also note that it would be extremely difficult for any Western democracy to carry out a program of that sort. And if such a program involved not only destroying industrial plants but killing or systematically starving industrial workers and their families, yes, that sounds to me like a supreme emergency for the German people—but not like the work of men and women who have just fought a just war. So supreme emergency is indeed a neutral concept, but we have reason to believe, well, reason to hope, that it will never have to be applied neutrally in defense, as it were, of countries with Nazi-like regimes.

Thanks to Jeremy Waldron, I don't have to deliver a definitive judgment about such cases, and I am grateful, again, for that exemption from what moral philosophers generally try to do, but shouldn't always insist on doing.

JUST WAR'S FUTURE

What are the arguments to come? Or, better, what are the old arguments that won't go away? I will follow the order of the three issues I've just discussed.

(1) There will be more groups of men and women, culturally coherent and territorially-based groups, looking to separate from the political domain in which they find themselves, aiming at sovereignty or, maybe, at autonomy. We can hope that these claims won't produce wars like those of the former Yugoslavia, but avoiding wars of that kind will require some sensible adjudication of the claims. Whose wars would be just in disputes over secession? I would like to say: no-one's. And that seems to be the view of both sides in the arguments, for example, about Scottish and Catalan separation. Only in cases of unrelenting oppression would a war of national liberation be justified. But there may be oppressed Peoples for whom liberation is not an option. They cannot make secessionist claims because they are territorially dispersed, or there are other groups inside what might be their territory, or they are a small and powerless minority. These Peoples, helpless, let's say, in the face of political or religious persecution, can rightly look for external help, which need not always, but may sometimes, take military forms.

(2) In the contemporary annals of humanity at risk, oppressed Peoples are closely followed by vulnerable and sometimes targeted civilians. These are mostly women and children, but the category isn't gendered and there isn't much chivalry left in the attention these people get. The key arguments are about the moral obligations of soldiers confronting enemies who hide among civilians who may or may not themselves be enemies. What risks should soldiers take to minimize the risks they impose upon these civilians? I think that many of the soldiers who take risks of this kind, beyond the risks of the military mission itself, would say that they are motivated by a sense of honor. Historically, soldierly honor was a male virtue, but I assume that contemporary military training aims to teach it to men and women alike. Indeed, armies have a moral obligation to do just that.

Still, civilians are vulnerable in new ways in contemporary warfare. In the past, they were killed not only in the course of the fighting but also routinely looted, raped, and massacred afterwards. That sort of thing is less routine today (except in genocidal warfare), but civilians are more than ever implicated in the fighting itself: closely involved, often indistinguishable from the fighters, and sometimes deliberately exposed to enemy fire because their deaths are politically useful. It is harder and harder to maintain the distinction between combatants and noncombatants—and at the same time it's never been so important to do just that. Indeed, writers in the just war tradition should work hard to figure out how to assign responsibility for civilian death and injury in asymmetric warfare between high-tech armies and low-tech insurgents. The insurgents using civilians and the soldiers killing civilians (taking risks, or not, to minimize the numbers they kill), each bear some degree of responsibility. Getting the degrees right may be crucial in ensuring the victory of the "good guys" in political engagements that could well determine the outcome of the military engagements. Better outcomes in both politics and war will over time mean fewer civilian deaths.

(3) We would all be happy if the category "supreme emergency" were never again invoked. But I suspect that it will be invoked, and there are two possible future moments when it might be invoked justly. The first such moment might come if terrorist organizations were on the verge of acquiring weapons of mass destruction—biological or nuclear—or after the first use of such weapons in a terror attack. It would be hard for any government, even a liberal democratic government, to avoid a radical curtailment of our civil liberties in its effort to avoid an attack or, worse, another attack. Since minimizing the threat of an emergency like that is itself a moral and political obligation, we have every reason to oppose nuclear proliferation and to aim at an international regime capable of controlling the production and distribution of the most dangerous weapons.

The second moment of emergency, all too likely, will come when climate change makes many parts of the globe uninhabitable and tens of millions of refugees appear at the borders of the best-off countries. No one at that moment, except perhaps for our most saintly fellow-citizens, will argue for open borders. I find it hard to believe that any kind of liberal humanitarianism will survive that moment of global crisis. I don't mean that there won't be acts of generosity, philanthropic organization, efforts to reduce the suffering of some of the refugees. But millions of people will simply have no place to go.

In 2018 and 2019, the President of the United States sent American soldiers to guard the southern border against what were relatively small numbers of bedraggled refugees struggling northwards from Honduras and Guatemala. That was, in my view, a misuse of our armed forces. But when the flood comes, borders will certainly be closed, and soldiers will be used to defend the common life. And, assuming that large numbers of climate refugees have already been taken in, that use will be both morally justifiable and morally disastrous.

That may seem an implausible combination. It can fit only a very bad time, which our political leaders will rightly call a supreme emergency. We are bound to do everything we can to avoid that bad time.

While describing these arguments that we will have or may have in the future, I have assumed that we will deal with them in the language of just war theory. So, finally, I need to respond to David Luban's suggestion that in the age of authoritarian populism, theories that start from the human right to life and liberty may have lost their grip. In the old days, Luban writes, political leaders would deny their human rights violations. "Today they feel no need" (26). That last sentence may be true of rulers in places like Myanmar, the Philippines, Syria, and Turkey (Luban's examples), but it isn't true or not yet true for our leaders here in the United States. Consider the 2017 bombing of Mosul in the course of the war against ISIS. An Associated Press investigative team, working the morgues, reported some 9000 civilian deaths caused by the bombing. The US government admitted to 326.

So we are still in the denial business, which means that the theory still has some grip, and reporting like that of the Associated Press still has some value. Just war theory, though it justifies some wars, is and has always been a critical theory. Ideological and religious arguments about demonized enemies who must be destroyed at any cost are very old. Think of the Crusades, which provided some of the earliest occasions for just war critique. If Luban is right, we will have to be critics in the years to come. Having grown up politically during the Vietnam years, I never thought we could be anything else.

NOTES

1. The issues of collectivity, self-determination, and state rights are also discussed, though to lesser extents, in the chapters by David Luban, Sally Scholz, Jeremy Waldron, and Graham Parsons in the present volume.
2. Michael Walzer, "Political Action: The Problem of Dirty Hands," *Philosophy and Public Affairs* 2, no. 2 (Winter 1973): 160–80.

BIBLIOGRAPHY

Walzer, Michael. "Political Action: The Problem of Dirty Hands." *Philosophy and Public Affairs* 2, no. 2 (Winter 1973): 160–80.

INDEX

© The Editor(s) (if applicable) and The Author(s), under exclusive license to Springer Nature Switzerland AG 2020
G. Parsons and M. A. Wilson (eds.), *Walzer and War*,
https://doi.org/10.1007/978-3-030-41657-7

Printed by Printforce, the Netherlands